# Looking Back

## AND

# Thinking Forward

## REEXAMINATIONS

### of

### Teaching and Schooling

Lillian Weber at the City College Workshop Center, mid-1970s.     Photo: Stan Chu.

# *Looking Back*
## AND
# *Thinking Forward*

### *REEXAMINATIONS*
### *of*
### *Teaching and Schooling*

## LILLIAN WEBER
### Edited by Beth Alberty

Teachers College, Columbia University
New York and London

Published by Teachers College Press, 1234 Amsterdam Avenue, New York, NY 10027

Copyright © 1997 by Teachers College, Columbia University

*Library of Congress Cataloging-in-Publication Data*

Weber, Lillian.
   Looking back and thinking forward : reexaminations of teaching and
schooling / Lillian Weber ; edited by Beth Alberty ; foreword by
Patricia F. Carini.
      p.    cm.
   Includes bibliographical references and index.
   ISBN 0-8077-3674-0 (cloth), — ISBN 0-8077-3673-2 (pbk.)
   1. Weber, Lillian.  2. Teaching—Philosophy.  3. Education—
Philosophy.  I. Alberty, Beth.  II. Title.
   LB885.W33W33  1997
370'.1—dc21                               97-20829
   ISBN 0-8077-3673-2 (paper)
   ISBN 0-8077-3674-0 (cloth)

Printed on acid-free paper

Manufactured in the United States of America

04  03  02  01  00  99  98  97    8  7  6  5  4  3  2  1

40.00

# Contents

# Foreword

Lillian Weber was my cherished friend and invaluable colleague for over 20 years. When she died, my experience of loss was immediate and visceral: I was in Phoenix, working with a teacher study group, and thought of cancelling. Then I thought of Lillian, and what a *not* good idea she would think that was. I told the study group of her death and read some passages from Lillian's work. Then, as I made my way through the teaching day, I became aware that I was being inwardly companioned by a persistent undersong, a line from a Richard Wilbur poem: "Love calls us to the things of this world." In the days that followed, that line became a repeating refrain, a comfort and a buffer against the stark reality of loss. And then, rather suddenly, I awoke to it as both code and key to that loss — and to Lillian.

Lillian and I had always done a lot of our talking together over the telephone, she located in New York and me in Vermont. In the months preceding her death, those conversations intensified. She was doing what she called "brain cracking" work on the paper that concludes this volume, "Reexaminations: What Is the Teacher and What Is Teaching?" Interwoven in these conversations was the upcoming North Dakota Study Group meeting, and her decision to make the "positive uses of discomfort" the focus of what she would say to the group. Following on several years of racial tension and unease in the group, she was urgent to continue to speak at the meetings about the value that very discomfort could and would yield — if, and about this she was adamant, we white folks didn't pull away, self-protectively, from the painfulness of struggling with our own unease.

The third piece we were talking about was Prospect's fall conference, in which I was heavily involved. I wanted her to speak and had sent her an outline which focused on teachers and teaching. She called me and promptly took me to task: "Teachers and teaching, yes! But the center has to be the child — the context that will support the child. Restructuring misses that point. De-schooling the schools — that's the point." Straight to the heart of it. Clear-eyed. Uncompromising. With her permission, we centered the conference around that exactly right phrase and idea: "To de-school the schools."

Because these conversations were the last Lillian and I were to have, they are etched in my mind. But they weren't different really from many others — or the conversations Lillian characteristically had with colleagues and friends. An active, extended present — a "very now" — was Lillian's milieu: a current school situation that must be responsibly addressed; a group of loved people who are veering off the track and require some redirection; the surfacing in whatever circle of issues of equity and justice and the requirement to be unflagging in making clear, uncompromising response each and every time.

Lillian took the world unvarnished and planted herself squarely and actively within it. Nothing was too small or insignificant for her to give it close attention. She believed in the human capacity to make a difference and it was, she observed, often by changing small things that the difference could be made. For Lillian, that attentiveness to making a difference was at the very heart of teaching. As she said, we must in every circumstance do "that which can be done to support what is possible for the child in that situation." To be vigilant in our attention to "the things of this world," to make those things a little better, a shade kinder, a bit more bearable, a degree freer, an iota richer, this much Lillian knew we could do and insisted we must do. For Lillian, that vigilance is a moral imperative. She referred to it famously as "looking for the cracks" — cracks that you could push on and widen, all the while looking for bigger cracks and opportunities to make changes on a larger scale.

Complicating and expanding that present was what Lillian characteristically referred to as an "inextricable mesh" of ideas and values. It is that mesh, that integrity of idea and value that lends to all Lillian's work — written, spoken, enacted in the schools — an extraordinary generative power philosophically, morally, and intellectually. Lillian could be trusted to have the value weight of any issue squarely centered, as she was herself, where it — and she — belonged. This dialectic of embracing world view and immediacy of response in relating to important issues is majorly a reason that the papers that compose this book are as compelling for today's readers as they were when even the earliest of them were published.

I return to Wilbur's lovely poetic line. In that line, I have been emphasizing "the things of this world" both small and large to which Lillian was called. But "love" is, of course, the operative word. It is love that called Lillian to her task. Love isn't an easy word. Lillian had no stomach for sentiment — or trivialization. In Lillian, love wasn't a throbbing heart or a soulful imploring—love was, as the poetic line suggests, a call to action. It was doing the work that needs doing and doing it now. It was doing that work in the conviction that the value and possibleness of human life exists everywhere and is inclusive of all. It was doing that work in the world without flinching from the realities and circumstances, some of them devastating, in which children and families and schools find themselves in a society that overvalues and inequitably distributes material resources—and has lost sight of human "goods."

That is the weighty legacy Lillian leaves us in these papers—a legacy of struggle and love enacted daily and without faltering. I conclude where I began: "Love calls us to the things of this world."

Patricia F. Carini
Prospect Center
North Bennington, VT
March, 1997

# Acknowledgments

I undertook to realize this book in a spirit of gratitude to Lillian Weber for her many gifts to me of learning and love, and because we had planned to work on it together. She is first among those whom I am happy to acknowledge. It has been a privilege to work on her papers, hearing her voice continually in my ear, being reminded of the possibility of high intellectual and moral standards joined with effective, nuanced activism and wise friendship.

Lillian's sons, William P. Weber and John P. Weber, have been enormously generous, patient, and facilitating at every step. I offer heartfelt thanks to them, their wives Heather Weber and Elsa Weber, and their families. I am grateful to Lillian's older brother, John Dropkin, for his help as executor, and to his wife, Ruth Dropkin, long-time editor at the Workshop Center, who graciously contributed the biography, and read and commented helpfully. It was through Elizabeth Starčević, Lillian's niece and my cherished friend for over 30 years, that I met Lillian in the early 1960s. This is but one of countless ways in which Elizabeth has enriched my life. It is a deep pleasure to acknowledge her contribution to my thinking. Her daughter, Maia Starčević, has put me in touch with the fresh energy and passion for teaching of a new generation of teachers, among them Lillian's eldest grandsons, Ted and Daniel.

As this project was forming, Lillian expressed to me her gratitude to William Ayers for his enthusiasm and help. Bill stimulated the interest of Teachers College Press in the idea of her book and proposed to Lillian that she apply for a Spencer Foundation grant. He also invited her to write "Reexaminations," which became her final, summative essay, and was also the first step in this project. I am deeply appreciative of his efforts on Lillian's behalf and for extending his help to me after her death.

My thanks to the Spencer Foundation. Its grant enabled me to establish the texts and write the introductions, as well as to prepare two talks on Lillian's work. Teachers College Press has likewise been a supportive and unintrusive help; thanks especially to Susan Liddicoat, Lori Tate, and Dave Strauss. At Teachers College, I have also enjoyed the help of David Ment of Special Collections, Milbank Memorial Library, who facilitated the deposit there of Lillian's papers and assisted in other ways.

Hubert Dyasi, director of the City College Workshop Center, has provided invaluable help. He brought "The Teacher's Own Resources" to my attention as an important statement, helped with matters of interpretation, and identified references. Not least, he prodded me to pull together my thoughts on Lillian's work by inviting me to give the 1995 Catherine Molony Lecture at the Workshop Center. He also administered the Spencer grant at City College. As always, I am indebted to the staff of the Workshop Center as well for their ready responses and cheer. I thank Yolanda Moses, President of City College, who sponsored the grant, and Ethel Brehenny, Office of Research Administration, for smoothing its bureaucratic path.

Participants in Prospect Center's experienced professionals Summer Institutes in 1994 and 1995 joined me in work sessions focused on specific papers and ideas in Weber's writings, and gave me new perspectives. The planning committee for the 1995 North Dakota Study Group on Evaluation meeting, by asking me to speak, provided another opportunity to think through what I was learning about Lillian's work. To both groups, I offer thanks.

Vicki Reed Hurko made an observation that helped crystallize the book's structure, for which, in addition to her sensitivity to Lillian's ideas, I am very grateful. Stan Chu responded efficiently and with good humor to my several requests for photos and information. Thanks also to Arthur Tobier who, as editor of *The Urban Review,* initiated and produced "Comments on Language by a Silent Child," and gave his permission to reprint. Countless other colleagues and friends of Lillian's wished and helped, knowingly or not, this project along, and I am grateful for the sense of momentum they created, although I cannot name them all.

I acknowledge with special pleasure and gratitude Patricia F. Carini, who has sustained me throughout the project. The book has been advanced and deepened by our many conversations about Lillian and her work and by her ever thoughtful comments on drafts and problems. She and Louis Carini have also generously offered Vermont respite and stimulating companionship at opportune moments.

# Editor's Introduction

Lillian Weber had been preparing to do a book of her writings for some years before she died in 1994. She culled her massive files, setting aside three drawers of papers going back to her graduate school days at the University of Virginia. In 1988 she drafted an introduction, parts of which are included in this volume as "Planning a Book Upon Retirement: A Reflection." Probably around the same time, she sketched a table of contents with the title "Schooling and Teaching — Where Are We Now?" followed by several pages of topic headings with short notes, in the form of cryptic phrases, under them.[1] In conversation with me and others, she announced her intent to dictate an introduction to each paper (or perhaps to each group of papers around an issue) that would indicate how her thinking about the theme of the paper had evolved since the paper was written.

I have tried to be faithful to Weber's intent as far as I have understood it from these scant indications and without, of course, being able to supply the commentary she would have. Certain features of her title, contents, and introduction came across to me as particularly important. The book was to be forward-looking, as her title and her intent to update her thinking indicated, rather than being a retrospective of her work. It was to be organized around educational issues, elements of schooling, and some of her persisting concerns and ideas. She identified some papers by title in the table of contents.

I have retained these features as much as possible. But her outline was too sketchy for me to follow, and regrettably, her ambition to include her work from about 1967 on could not be realized in one volume. After reading all of the material she had culled, I settled on her work after 1980. This was when she increasingly addressed principles, ideas, and policies of education in writing rather than through practice. A number of significant and relatively self-contained statements dated from these later years. Being so focused and more recent, this work lent itself more easily to a forward-looking emphasis. Although many of Weber's earlier papers also met these criteria, some that she particularly valued were contained in memos and reports that were highly specific to a situation and an audience. For an audience at a remove, they would have required a great deal of context.

The change in chronological scope entailed losses that continue to pain me. Communication through practice rather than words was one of Weber's great strengths. The nature of that communication is perhaps most vividly conveyed through those early daily and weekly memos describing, for example, her meetings with the corridor teachers or an interaction with a principal. They also suggest the context in which she was trying to start a change in the public elementary schools, when hope (and federal funding) was focused largely on preschool education, and the idea of alternatives within the public sector did not exist. The risk, the courage, the sense of growing energy as people joined, as obstacles were faced and overcome, are perhaps less apparent in the later papers. Nevertheless, in the later works she continued to speak with the voice and eyes and detail of someone immersed in practice, who connected directly with children, teachers, and parents, and her ideas and style in them depend, of course, on all of her experience.

To counter a bit of the loss, I have incorporated some references to and quotations from earlier works in the introductions to the parts of this book. Also, readers should be aware that she did publish extensively in the earlier period. Among the more significant of published pieces were her book, *The English Infant School and Informal Education* (1971; now out of print); and statements on curriculum, inclusion, testing, public policy, and other issues in the occasional monographs and the quarterly journal *Notes from Workshop Center for Open Education,* published by the Workshop Center throughout the 1970s.[2]

Weber's proposed table of contents was the source of most of the selection of individual papers. "Inquiry, Noticing, Joining-With, and Following-After" was cited as the "MIT paper." Other phrases Weber used in the outline — "the morality of the classroom," "black curriculum," "the teacher as professional authority," and "democratic community" — represent ideas that she discussed many times but they do not necessarily identify specific papers and, in cases like "black curriculum," the corresponding paper postdates the proposed contents. On these subjects, however, I have included her papers "Moral Issues for Teachers," "Black or Multicultural Curriculum: Of Course — But What More?," "The Status of the Vision of a Democratic Community in Education Today," and "The Authority of the Teacher." I was unable to attach existing papers to notes such as "'self-development' elitism and alternative schools" or "running counter community," although these ideas are discussed in several of the papers.

Not mentioned in Weber's table of contents is "Comments on Language by a Silent Child," which I nevertheless included. It was a major statement, but is available only in specialized libraries. Its scope and synthesizing grasp seem to me to have established the tone and style that she continued to employ in her later work. I chose several other papers, "On Parents," for example, because their subject matter was important to Weber, even if they were incomplete and in some ways unsatisfactory statements.

About half of the papers in this volume are being published here for the first time. Of the five previously published, three appeared in publications no longer readily available. "Reexaminations" (Part IV), though recently published (Ayers, 1995), was too importantly linked to Weber's project for this book to be left out.

Some of the previously unpublished papers included here have been adapted directly from raw transcripts of Weber's public talks; others are based on transcripts previously edited by her and others, but never published. The origin of all these papers in extemporaneous oral language, whether to a public audience or to an individual listener and a tape recorder, deserves special note. For her, talk was packed with significance. It was a valued family heritage: Her mother, Celia Dropkin, and her sister, Esther Unger, were poets; and her father, brothers, sons, and many nieces and nephews, and, increasingly, her grown grandchildren, grandnieces and grandnephews, were and are professional talkers of various kinds — teachers, professors, labor organizers. Talk was a medium of lively relationship for her, enabling observation and response to listeners. These papers, narratives of her thought, were spun from the material of the relationships that she created by talking. For this reason, perhaps, her work has an immediacy, an earthiness, and a feeling of common humanity unwonted in academic circles. Her vocabulary and syntax were sometimes idiosyncratic or awkward, a tendency accentuated by the translation from oral to written form and by her efforts to loosen the grip of educational jargon on our thinking. But her writing also flashes with apt and pointed phrases and, if we attend, reinvigorates and gives new subtleties of meaning to ordinary words and familiar truths.

As far as editing is concerned: Previously published papers have not been reedited, although in the case of talks I have deleted introductory remarks specific to the occasion. Headings in all but "Silent Child" are my additions. Papers left as raw transcripts only have obviously been the most heavily edited. In the absence of Weber's final authorial approval, I have exercised some simple guidelines for myself, keeping in mind what I know of her approach to this process from our years of working together. My goal has been to smooth the reader's task, not to polish or even to achieve an evenness of finish among them. With the raw transcripts in particular, I know that Weber herself would have made, or accepted from an editor, drastic cuts, but that she would have been largely indifferent to copy editing. What she would have bridled at were changes in particular words and phrasings that seemed to her important to her meaning. I know also that she would not be enthusiastic about, but would accept, some restructuring to eliminate the repetitions that resulted from her way of building a talk or paper, since with each return to a point she brought a new meaning or nuance to it. Hence, I have sometimes done substantial cutting, reconnected the narrative flow, made sentences of incomplete phrases, clarified frequently vague pronouns, untangled convoluted run-on passages, and eliminated rhetorical flourishes that, on paper, appeared repetitious. With exceptions, however, I have not moved paragraphs or sections around, changed vocabulary, rewritten passages, or sought to transform all traces of spoken language into conventional written style. The exception is "Reexaminations." We worked on this paper together right before her death, and she knew it had repetitions and needed editing. I did this while the memory of our conversations about it was fresh.

The papers, once selected, seemed to group naturally around four of Weber's enduring concerns or principles—the topics around which she might frame an answer to her proposed title's question, "Where are we now?" These topics are the themes of the parts of the book. By the sequence of the topics I intend to suggest the way in which Weber's thought typically organized itself, that is, the relationships and priorities among its various overarching themes. The rest of my comments recapitulate and explicate the connections among the four parts and some of the underlying ideas that link the papers across the parts.

Weber's thought begins with the particular, and the interpenetration of the particular with a context that extends and enriches it. Action and interaction within this complex of particularity and context arise from and are animated by commitment and intent, which are the basis of professionalism. The commitment is informed throughout by unshakable belief in human capacity for making meaning, that is, for being what she called "educable." Another way of saying this would be to point to the strong dialectic between action and philosophic thought that characterized her work.

The belief in human capacity was Weber's interpretation into education terms of the political proposition that all people are created equal. Together, context and commitment, but particularly belief in capacity, form the outline of a strategy for and vision of educational change. Two of the important aspects of the strategy were, in Weber's shorthand terms, *reassessment* and *small changes*. These and related terms (such as a wide assortment of "re" words) appear throughout the papers. The place she gives to reassessment is perhaps summed up in a sentence whose stepped infinitives culminate in the child, and which conveys the foundation of all her work in grappling (a favorite word) for understanding:

> The school exists and so one continues the effort to make it better. The first principle of making it better must be to do no harm.... Second, continue your efforts *to understand* the thing enough *to make* it possible *to continue* trying *to better* the impact of one's effort and *to release* the efforts of the child. ("Reexaminations," Part IV; emphasis added)

From reassessment came revision, which often took the form of *small changes*. This strategy evolved from her nursery school experiences of adjusting the environment and activities to accommodate the interests and proclivities of particular children or groups of children (Weber, 1959). It became a mode and strategy for initiating program and institutional change in classrooms, schools, and at the City College School of Education Workshop Center. Most of her reports on the first two years of work with Open Corridor groups at P. S. 123 and P. S. 84 include the words "Small Things" or "Small Changes" in their titles: for example, "Comments from teachers on all the small things that contributed to the function or dysfunction of the corridor and whether they feel that in so far as it functions, it was a success" (Weber, 1968).

This ground-up way of working did not preclude ambition to have a big impact. She connected small changes, considered as partial solutions, to a vision:

> I think we limit ourselves if we say "well that's how the school is" and then work out little frameworks of adjustment that will only make the situation a *little* bit better. We have to do that anyway, of course ... *but* we have to also have a vision of where it *should* be, of where we can go forward, of where it *might* go. ("Black Curriculum," Part III; emphasis in original)

*Vision, revision, visionary,* are words and ideas that occur frequently in the papers of Weber's later years as she herself described in "Planning a Book Upon Retirement: A Reflection": "The papers I wrote in the 80s comment . . . on the deeper issues of vision." In a time of hostility to progressive ideas and when people's energy for change was at a low ebb, she wanted to hold out a vision to which people could return:

> The biggest thing I want to say, that you want to help teachers visualize, is possibility.... We have a depression in our visualization of possibility right now and I'm saying that it's both the task and the challenge to keep alive the visions that do exist, even if you can't use them right away. (Weber, 1994)

## NOTES

1.  Weber's book outline, circa 1988:

Introduction
- review of papers, retirement, etc.
- possibilities and visibilities
- critique of limitations

Definitions and First Purposes
- humanism, relationship to *all,* to compulsory education
- letter to Scribner
- intent & reality
- confidence in children

Space
- changing structure of elementary classrooms
- corridor as community, an interactive community, reinforcing continuities, the creativity of the teacher released
- what new organization made possible, access, breakthrough of isolation of child, visibility, maximization of use of language
- "small things"
- respect and interest

The Persistence of Privacy
- the teacher's *own* classroom
- running counter community

The Creativity of the Teacher
- "self-development" elitism and alternative schools

Curriculum
- language, science, social studies
- but is it science
- MIT paper
- testing

Parents
- a changing relationship
- language

Teacher Education
• Summer Institute, workshops, the *teacher's* autonomy vs. advising

Education
• testing answers vs. ongoing engagement and extension of engagements

The Workshop Center
• grappling, on and off self-initiated reengagements, variety, density, multiplicity, diversity, firsthand experiences at books that tell about grappling

Small Beginnings
• even just noticing

Interest Problems
• teaching and control vs. joining-with and following-after. The adult *as* adult

Work and Contribution
• value, a black curriculum, care and compassion, the morality of the classroom

Schoolwork, Engaging of Kids as Responsible Parties in Maintenance of Life Space
• the teacher as professional authority, a continuing vision of a democratic community

Inherent Limitations of Schooling
• community, continuity

2. Workshop Center publications are available from the Center, Attn: Henny Wong, Room 4/220, North Academic Center, City College School of Education, 138th and Convent Avenue, New York, NY 10031. Unpublished works can be consulted in the Milbank Memorial Library, Special Collections, Teachers College, Columbia University, New York.

# Planning a Book Upon Retirement:
## A Reflection

*1988*

In my last term of teaching, I formed a plan for sharing with the students an overview of the development of my ideas. I selected 10 of my papers[1] that were written at points of change in my thought and shared at the time as something different from what I had said before. In my lectures accompanying the students' reading of the papers, I explained what the change was and why something that was basically in continuity neverthe-less had new elements, expansions into additional areas of concerns, at certain points. How did that reflect pressures from the external world on our work and pressures of my own evaluation of our work? How did it reflect my thinking through of what had been left out in the previous statement? Of what needed sharpening or additional focus? How did it reflect my thinking through, indeed, of what needed restatement because the first statement didn't take into account the essential thing that I was seeking — the real, essential thing presumably staying as the continuous thread?

When I retired, the idea was to go over the lectures and papers to see whether they gave a good picture of the development in my thought, and to plan a book. I faced the need to unpackage from the accumulation of 20 years of papers at the Workshop Center the things that were statements of my own thought. Twenty years of papers is an enormous amount of paper. The Open Corridor, the Advisory Service, the Workshop Center — it was a very active organization. And everything had been kept in a copy; it was also a history of the copy machine. What I thought would take me just a few months has taken me a year and a half.

The year and a half has been not just a disentangling but a rereading, a rethinking, and a reconfirmation for me: "I was right to make that change," or "I made that statement better the year before and should have pulled that one out as the public formulation." This process linked the last 20 years of work with my work in the 20 years before, when I was a nursery school teacher and director, which was also included in the papers I asked the students to read.

The tangling and untangling of thought has been a discovery for me. At the end, I faced the need for revision in my first idea of what I needed to share about my thought. The 10 papers I had originally selected for the students were from a more recent period; I had forgotten the earlier contribution. My outline for the book worked out in a different way. My new list came to about 80 different papers — not fully worked out papers, but fairly well worked out papers, some complete. There were memos or transcriptions of speeches made at meetings that were special points that I thought it was necessary to emphasize, for example, the parent role or access. These points were not included in the original statement around children and the nature of the whole process of relationships and environment in children's learning. Although the background of this statement was awareness of the need to find responses to issues raised in the civil rights struggle and even before that, it did not include specific engagement with this struggle.

Before I came to City College in 1967, my work involved working out for myself the nature of teaching: an unintrusive, bypassing engagement with the child, taking the child's own statement, the child's own way as a pattern or mode, as important. The adult's role, then, was to bring resources to support the child's way, rather than to have an abstract or *generalized* mode that was imposed. It was a period of becoming deeply aware of myself as person, as parent, as someone struggling to do the best I could and to be supportive of parents in general as being equally engaged in this: I, not unique, but a human process. It was a period of working out a deep conviction about possibilities. It was a period where these things were part of my own survival as well as, I think, a continuous expansion of sensitivity to the context, the child, the possibilities, the nature of very small changes.

I went to England, and I took in things that I could recognize because I had already done them or seen them in the process of my own work and struggles. When I came back from England and joined the faculty at City College, there was a period of implementation, from 1967 to about 1972. All along, I felt my contribution was to actualize, to make real in action, so that what I had learned about children and teaching could be seen, so it wasn't a theoretical discussion but something that actually happened in school, with children, with teachers. Writing had to be put aside.

From this period I find a collection of letters that can be considered a conversation, with Harvey Scribner, with Ewald Nyquist, with Edythe Gaines.[2] I was asked by them such questions as what did I think was the most important thing about teacher training. These letters are basic statements on humanism. The rest of the documentation of this early period of implementation includes hundreds of memos and notes, many that were put directly into teachers' hands. They constitute a manual, not prescriptive but descriptive, of what the implementation was. They are a detailed look at how each element of implementation was working or not working—the small revisions, tightenings or expansions, or help to teachers to go a little further, the first steps that needed to be taken, the first overtures to administration. They were specific about difficulties and what was needed in response: "This is something that should bother us about the corridor or is developing in a way that isn't what we were talking about. Were we really talking about an extra room staffed by a teacher or were we talking about a community and is that really happening? Is the community fading away while people grab the chance to be tremendously creative in their own, single room, which is precisely what we were trying to get past?" But they always came back to the big point, the central core of creating an environment in which teachers, children, and parents could live, that would recognize their capacity. I consider this an important period of my work.

Next—picking from 1975 but appearing in 1974 and even in 1973—I found a series of papers on what the curriculum is, what interest is, what the social context is. These papers look at pieces of the curriculum more deeply than happened in the first building and provisioning of a good environment. In this period the Workshop Center was developing as a support system for teachers who wanted to be engaged with our way of working but did not have an enclave that supported engagement, in the fashion of an Open Corridor, with an advisor. They included students at City College, who went one or two to a school and had to feel there were at least ways of beginning, whether or not they had this enclave.

Then, in 1975, with the great crisis [of New York City bankruptcy and deep cuts in the school budget], in which 18,000 teachers were fired and many others moved around the school system, the baby Open Corridor communities, which had begun to breathe, were seriously disrupted. People were moved from places where they had begun to feel a sense of community, where they had begun to know each other and could begin to make decisions as a group, into other schools. Tremendously important public issues faced these teachers, issues that were not part of the specifics of implementation in the classroom and on which there had to be a stance. This was a period of papers, such as "Education for ALL the Children" (Weber, 1974), on public issues.

The support for intelligence that we at the Workshop Center asserted as a public issue in the mid and late 1970s in the face of this crisis was also raised about the Workshop Center itself, especially when external funding for it ended in 1979. The Workshop Center had to approach access in terms of the acceptance of every teacher's capacity and tremendous acceptance of diversity. What it was supporting — teachers as inquiring minds being the backdrop for children's inquiring minds — had to be stated clearly. This came down to restating the Workshop Center as a center of support for inquiry, inquiry very broadly interpreted as active learning from the realities of the world as well as from the bedrock shared personal realities of being part of the world.

On a public level this was a period of discarding almost everything we had done in our programs. It was a schizophrenic discard in that, if you looked at pictures of a gifted class or a good program, you saw things such as children directly using materials, just like you saw in the pictures of our big changes of 1968–1970. What was supposed to be different was that the new programs were "serious" and the previous ones had been "fun." In all my work that I have gone over, no paper said that the essential aim was that kids should have fun. I don't think fun is something to be discarded, but the notion that people feel better about themselves and the world when they are seriously engaged in it and see where it's all going seems to me a sufficient statement of fun, just so. In spite of the obvious fact that what was done by serious teachers in the 1970s continues and can be found in many of the schools, the word that describes that history ["open" or "progressive"] is wiped out. Instead you have either a new kind of thing that has the same elements but has them "seriously" or you have an approach of total prescription.

I see a danger in losing the account of how our work in the public schools, based on active engagement, evolved to start with and why, a danger in losing the fact that it exists now, and that, like any complex change, it will need many revisions and restatements but not discard. Progressive education conferences are held today to defend against the threat of extreme prescription and testing that now impinges even on private, middle-class schools. But what is raised in these forums is not the possibilities this kind of schooling opened up, that more is needed, and where it fell short, but a disconnected discussion about bettering the atmosphere within a single school. It is certainly not about the obligations for *all* children or the capacity of *all* children — which were the subject of earlier discussions of public issues raised by Vito Perrone, Patricia Carini, Kenneth Haskins, and myself. The papers I wrote in the period of the 1980s comment on these deeper issues of vision: Is the present discussion of progressive education sufficient? How does this relate to the first, essential kind of search? What more is needed?

The period of the 1980s brings a return to the questions of access and all the children and where the roots are to find this. It brings connection with the world view, a connection emerging from the directions and problems of the late 1960s and 1970s shared worldwide. My examination of letters and visits to our programs from practically every country in the world shows how much these questions concerned my correspondents, as they and we faced questions of diversity of population, access, capacity, of how you relate to the universe of discourse about education, and of how you relate to the people you are serving. We were not solely concerned with a narrow way of seeing how this particular process went better in this small thing or with some teachers who were specially gifted, disregarding the broad mass of teachers and children.

As I finished rereading, questions came to me on the schools overall. What are the elements of the vision that perhaps can't be encompassed in school and therefore engage with society as a whole? What, in all my work, had drawn on a serious look at the home, at the street, at external-to-school learning, at processes of learning about which I asked: Could they happen in school? Are these processes so important that whether they can be in school or not, we have to be aware of them and support them wherever they occur?

I'm preparing this book as a public statement that transcends my earlier work with a staff that could understand the problems and think with me and argue with me to help me develop my own mind. The statement is no longer on that level of specific struggle. The work we did exists in the schools; it was not wasted. But where were we with it and where are we with it now? People think of retirement as an end, that you're finished with work, but it's different when it's work that you're shaping rather than having imposed on you. This work is my lifeblood, so does one welcome retirement? Writing without the impetus of concrete involvement is very different, your whole thought cast is different. The contrast is between memos on what is happening that day and a broader view of what's been missing altogether, even after all kinds of wonderful implementations.

In retirement, I set myself this task of disentangling my papers. It was like a year of research into my own developing thought, allowing me to regain it, to rehold it, and through this to discover forgotten pieces, threads lost and important to regain. Not because they were my personal possession; they were not thoughts just for myself, yet my self was very important in it. Your head can't stop until it stops. At the same time, you're never dealing just with your own sense of who are you. You're also dealing with how this is read back to you from others. When you retire, people think of you as having ended your work. In a sense they have to, because they have to start taking on responsibility and use what's been built in their own way, as though you weren't there. Nevertheless, I've come to feel this review of my own thought is an important contribution to their thinking.

Ideas are in the framework of an argument with one's own ideas, with implementation, with other people's comments on it, with things that block implementation, with things in the world that reflect on it. And ideas are contentious. They exist in this world of struggle. That is true of everything in education. There will always be some people who think children learn actively and can engage with things, and there will be others who think you have to give information to them right off. Given that, it's important to see how a leader of a program maintained her direction. Every one of my papers shares the struggle of my mind, my engagement, and of the people who worked with me. The process of one's own thought is interesting, and you share it with others partly because this is a state-ment of your belief that everyone's process is interesting: This is how my mind works. How does yours work?

Beyond this, there is an unevenness in history: You can predict that almost as a movement reaches a peak there'll be a countermove to devalue. The question is what the thread is that, no matter what, can't get devalued because it exists. For me, individual difference and active learning can't be taken away. Over and over again there are attempts to establish a frame of expanding possibility, and then you get this return to "basics." At a given point, one frame is more predominant than the other. If our frame be-comes a dogma, then the unevenness, where the complexities of the world don't fit the box, will result in the box being broken. That doesn't mean the thread disappears entirely. In the enormous complexity of the world and of phenomena, some aspect of truth was in that thing as well.

It's not a case of all ideas being the same; you can't deny an idea's history. Everyone's idea counts in the progress of your thought. Your idea is not some pristine piece of crystal that's all shaped and never, never will it grow or perhaps be smashed because another crystal will be a better shape for your idea. If you consider it pristine, then you're fixing yourself in your so-called relativism into a static thing instead of into something that looks at things in the process of growth. That you've had an idea, fine, but you're going to have to stick with that idea, consider it further, and see how it relates to other ideas.

## NOTES

1. The 10 papers were: "Development in Open Corridor Organization: Intent and Reality" (Weber & Dropkin, 1972); "But Is It Science?" (1973c); "Education for ALL the Children" (1974); "Moral Issues for Teachers" (published in Part III; 1982);

"Comments on Language by a Silent Child" (published in Part I; 1976); "Issues in Parent Participation" (1977); *Continuity and Connection: Curriculum in Five Open Classrooms* (cited under Alberty & Weber, 1979); "Toward the Finer Specificity" (1973b); *Use and Setting: Development in a Teachers' Center* (cited under Alberty, Weber, & Neujahr, 1981); "On Teacher Education" (1972–1985). Three additional manuscripts — identified only as "Bank Street, North Dakota Study Group, Berlin" — were cited under the course subtopic "On the Community and Collaboration." The three are probably referring to "The Status of the Vision of a Democratic Community in Education Today," published in Part IV, 1986; *Reflections,* a talk to the North Dakota Study Group in 1986, published in 1994; and an unidentified talk from her visit to Berlin in 1986.

2. Letter to Harvey Scribner, Chancellor of the New York City Schools (1971), and subsequently expanded; letter to Ewald B. Nyquist, Commissioner of the New York State Department of Education, October 12, 1972; notes of meeting with Dr. Edythe Gaines and Mr. Rubin of the New York City Learning Cooperative, 1971, and memo to Gaines, June 25, 1975.

# PART I

# The Context of Learning

Context is the horizon, both bounding and expanding, for all of Weber's practice and thought. It was a word with layered meanings for her, and generally interpenetrated with other matters; some reference to context in one or more of the meanings she ascribed to it occurs in almost every paper in this volume. The papers in this section provide a chronologically evolving overview of her ideas on it.

First among its meanings was the physical and relational *surround,* as Weber called it, of the classroom and of the child's immediate environment. She believed children learned by having real experiences, and this required that classrooms provide real, preferably open-ended materials, books, equipment, and work space, and time to actually work with them. Over 20 years of nursery school experience she had cultivated her skill, which she enjoyed practicing, in working out the organization of materials and spaces to foster easy, productive use of them by groups and individuals. Both the Open Corridor and the Workshop Center embodied her belief in an enriched material context that invited use; they afforded new challenges to her experience in organizing them. (In a journal entry from Africa, 9/14/87, she notes a conversation at Kenyatta University about what work she would like to undertake there: "... asked ... I said I saw myself as lots of things—a resource on interpretation of issues, but that really I was especially resourceful on context, on use of local resources" [Weber, 1987b].) She was clear, however, that an enriched material context was insufficient. Educating teachers to understand how the children were making use of what the context offered and how to respond to their use was one of the purposes of the Summer Institutes and of the Workshop Center.

The *surround* also meant the human relationships and interactions around children and learning. This context should also be dense, with multiple generations, cultures, languages, and roles (parent as well as teacher) interacting. The nursery school, a parent co-op, had here, too, provided the ground for many years of experimentation, which she was able to take to another level in the Open Corridor and Workshop Center settings. Classrooms in the Open Corridor were mixed-age, and they were grouped on a corridor across a range of grades. The Workshop Center encouraged simultaneous uses, in different ways, by various groups. In a larger sense, cultural inheritance, family, extended cultural community, and neighborhood were part of context, and she thought they should be present in schools in various forms.

In Weber's view the prototypical educative context was real life, of which teaching and schools were, so to speak, a smaller, professionalized area. She articulated this with increasing clarity in her later work. A discussion of the "conditions accompanying growth" in her last paper, "Reexaminations" (Part IV), is an illustration in which she synthesizes all the meanings of context mentioned so far. Among the conditions were the presence of people of different ages and backgrounds; school structures that more closely emulated the pace and relationships familiar to children from their lives outside school; and classroom arrangements that allowed children to exercise multiple modes of learning. Children's external-to-school context was a reference and measure for enhancing in-school opportunities and support for children's learning.

In Weber's usage, context also referred to the social and political structures, events, and policies that affected children, families, and schools. For example, although she welcomed the mainstreaming law in the 1970s as an endorsement of diversity in the classroom and a definition of ordinary functioning that was broadly inclusive, she was critical of the narrowness in how it came to be interpreted and implemented. Awareness of the impact of historical and political context at various levels of immediacy and analysis was braided into her work. The 1975 conference she organized on the roots of open education in America offered, at a moment of school crisis, an alternative vision of the context for progressive education (Dropkin and Tobier, 1976). On another level are her comments in "Inquiry" (in Part I) on the impact of large political agendas in different countries on national stances toward the education of ordinary citizens. She observes sharply that when a nation needs its people to function well—for example, in times of war (in the United States during World War II) or of newly acquired independence and self-definition (in postcolonial nations)—its educational apparatus proceeds as though the people can do so. It assumes widespread intelligence and capacity to learn. Conversely, when many are ill-served and diminished by educational institutions, the implication is that national priorities are creating a context in which developed capacities among the citizenry are neither required nor, shamefully, desired.

All of these meanings of context are present in the three papers in this section, but a sequence, a development, is also visible. "Comments on Language by a Silent Child" written in 1976, which is about language learning, concentrates on the child's (the person's) search for meaning or understanding in the midst of experience, in contrast to educators' emphasis on directing the child's learning and understanding. What the school offers, Weber says, and what the school structure recognizes of the child's language, is minimal. She argues for broadening the school context by likening it to life, by making it *real*. In "Language Development and Observation of the Local Environment: First Steps in Providing Primary-School Science Education for Non-Dominant Groups," written in 1985, she reiterates and expands on this argument, introducing the investigative modes of science as an analogy for as well as means of children's development of language. Primary science, as Weber conceives it, represents real experience. When it is organized around ordinary materials and phenomena with which children are familiar, it offers them opportunity to "know more, to shape and to contribute, and could be the basis for a curriculum of real power."

The child's search for meaning that was the theme of "Silent Child" becomes the point of departure in "Inquiry, Noticing, Joining With, and Following After," composed in 1986–1991. Here, Weber develops her ideas about learning in an intergenerational and real-world context of adult work and child living. She analyzes the mingling and overlapping of modes of teaching in the institutions of school and family considered as contexts of learning. She integrates ideas developed in her early practice and articulated in *Use and Setting* (Alberty, Weber, & Neujahr, 1981) about the way in which activity that is allowed to impact on a setting enriches further uses— that is, how a thick setting invites extended, complex learning, not just programmed learning. Thus, she circles back, at the end of the article, to the emphasis on enhancing classroom context that was the starting point of her work in the schools, but with the added weight and complexity of intervening thought.

Other differences between the three papers stem from their differences in date and audience. "Silent Child" was written at a time of flourishing research and policy discussions on language, especially on bilingualism, the language of so-called disadvantaged children, and concern about "comprehension." Like many of Weber's statements, it was prompted by the work of an admired colleague, in this case Courtney Cazden (1976), in an article on the usefulness of having a researcher's knowledge about language development when one was actually teaching children. Cazden's and Weber's articles were published in successive issues of *The Urban Review*. Credit for this important piece in Weber's work goes to Arthur Tobier, who initiated, taped, and edited the conversation that became "Comments on Language by a Silent Child." This was one of a series of such oral history narratives he collaborated on with educators in the early 1970s, while editor of the journal.

In "Language Development and Observation of the Local Environment: First Steps in Providing Primary-School Science Education for Non-Dominant Groups," Weber responds to discussions about children's "needs" and, concomitantly, their rights. Inspired by her collaboration with science educator Hubert Dyasi, it represented virtually a position paper on the direction the Workshop Center would emphasize under his leadership. "Language Development" was published in UNESCO's periodical, *Prospects*. The first half of the paper, published here, is by Weber, the second half by Dyasi, who graciously consented to republishing only the first half, in the interests of space. The international audience accounts in part for Weber's emphasis in the beginning on the Workshop Center's relationship to overseas visitors and efforts.

In this article, Weber explores the connections she finds between the Center's (and her own) earlier preoccupation with language and its more recent and future focus on primary science, the area of Dyasi's experience and interest. These connections are in the realm of context. The authors emphasize the role of real experience, particularly with ordinary materials, in stimulating children's language and thus how primary science is integral to language development. Such experience with real materials they term "inquiry."

"Inquiry" was given first as a talk in honor of physicist Philip Morrison on the occasion of his retirement from MIT in 1986, and published with editorial revision in 1991 by the Workshop Center. In this period, Weber found the schools again stripped of context, this time on the theory that anything other than what the teacher is talking about distracts children from learning. She returns to the defense of context, pointing to the usefulness of being able to notice things in passing over a period of time and of being reminded by materials and evidence of past experiences of a point learned earlier, now connecting with a new point being offered. She describes context as supporting learning by holding for children the *history* of their learning as well as being a source of new learning. She formalizes and expands her ideas about different modes of learning along a continuum from "being told" to "noticing, joining with, and following after." She talks about the mix of these different modes in both formal (school) and informal (home) contexts. She observes that schools do not offer an effective context for the full range of modes that children employ and relates this in some ways to the larger social and political context.

Not surprisingly, context was the locus of Weber's continuing critique of educational inadequacy and her efforts for change. Her question was always how to change the context so that it would "release" the active process of all learners. In both "Silent Child" and "Language Development," for example, she points out how confusions in *adult* definitions (of comprehension, of children's educational needs) have led, wrongly, to diminished views of children and have created obstacles to helpful understanding. It was a given that the children were capable of learning. Therefore, if there were problems, they lay elsewhere, in the context of educational provision, assumption, definition, structure, policy, and of adult understanding.

In a late letter to her friends Anne and Dale Bussis (July 26, 1989), she pulls together her early and late concerns with context and the process of learning:

> I continue to be absolutely gripped by a need to explore the context of schooling and whether (or not!!!) this context and its relationships provide for educational processes like "joining-with" and "following-after"—essential additions in my view to the of course inherent core of all learning—that is *active.*

The three papers in this section are as much statements about language and science, which were enduring concerns for Weber, as they are about context. Indeed, they are important statements on these topics, although I have not treated this aspect of their content here. Reading them together from a curriculum perspective, however, one senses the encompassing nature of these realms for Weber: language extending to reading and writing as well as to issues of bilingualism; science involving all the activities of finding out about the physical world and its phenomena. In sequence they reveal how, in her later work, the "search for meaning" flowed into the investigative approach to primary science, termed inquiry, which came to serve for her as the prototype of all investigation and knowledge-building, that is, of learning. Behind this evolution were 30-plus years of practice, study, and thought about language and science expressed in scores of writings. Although outside the scope of this volume, these earlier writings claim attention for insights that are not summarized in the papers here.[1]

## NOTE

1. In her nursery school years, for example, Weber wrote "Study on Maureen" (1949), about a child who came to the nursery at age 4 with a three-word vocabulary, the three words "used indiscriminately"; made notes about use of light and shadow, air and wind, hot and cold as natural phenomena available to all children, no matter what their circumstances; and published an article on nature curriculum, "It Is Winter" (1960). The nature program at the nursery school also inspired a book by Weber's colleague Ruth Rea Howell and photographer Arline Strong, a parent (1968, with photographs of Weber with the children dating as far back as the early 1950s). Weber's book The English Infant School and Informal Education (1971) contains analyses of past and present thinking about language (e.g., "The Adult Role in Language Growth," pp. 222–224). Between 1967 and the late 1970s, Weber issued many memos to advisors and teachers in the Open Corridor on language and reading, among other things; organized teacher and advisor discussion groups, including seminars with Courtney Cazden, Vera John-Steiner, and others; instigated workshop series based on Peter S. Stevens's Patterns in Nature (1974) and the work of Constance Kamii as represented, for example, in Physical knowledge in preschool education: implications of Piaget's theory (Kamii & DeVries, 1993); and published in Workshop Center publications articles by others as well as by herself about language, reading, and science (e.g., in Notes from Workshop Center for Open Education, 1973d; Science in the Open Classroom, 1973c).

# CHAPTER 1

## Comments on Language by a Silent Child

*1976*

My commitment to the study of language has a long, natural history—personal and professional. First, in all the work I have done with small children since 1946, I have always had some who were what you'd call slow to talk and some, even, who were extremely slow, or what you would call language-disabled. What I did from the start was respond to any bits of language they offered, and through one form of stimulation or another tried to create in them a need, a desire, to communicate. I have never wavered from that general approach.

When the Open Corridor Advisory Service was set up to work with teachers in the New York City public schools, the schools were preoccupied with issues of language and reading—remedial and compensatory issues. I knew from the start of that work, as I had known for a long time before then, that any involvement in school change would involve us in language development, but language development considered from the stance we had taken in the whole of our work: namely, that we would deal with the language of all the children, without exclusion, just as we'd accepted responsibility for doing something so schools could support children in *all* of their potentiality. The task we set for ourselves was to try to understand what was characteristic of children's language in general and in particular, and to do what we could so that children could use their language in the school by working at different things, explaining their work, being listened to.

In reorganizing the classrooms and schools in which we worked, we were afforded new opportunities to observe language use. We also studied what was being written about language acquisition. It became clear that a better understanding of children's language would lead to a better understanding of children and, as we understood the parents' role in how their children acquired language, to a better respect for parents.

So my focus on what would support the emergence of stronger language in children has been a sharp and continuous one, in that each thing that was learned supported a deeper exploration, and it has left me more than dubious about easy formulations.

Similarly, my own language experience, which goes back further than my professional work, leaves me — as I reflect on some of what I read about language — more than a bit doubtful about some of the stereotypes and generalizations that people pose. The fact is that *I* had been called a "dumb doll" when I was a child. And they didn't mean that I was dumb as in "mute"; they meant that I didn't answer questions and that I was not quick to talk and that I was going to be silent. Of course, we know tons of children who were described this way in the past and not much was made of it, one way or another. It was not a terrible handicap to be this way, provided you *did* speak and *could* answer, because, after all, the school structure didn't really expect an enormous amount of performance. The teacher did most of the talking. The teacher asked the questions and you answered to the point of the information. You certainly weren't expected to have every range of function or to speculate or to be imaginative in your language.

It had not been a handicap to me in school to be a rather silent child, which was natural for my placement as a middle child in a large family, because I was the kind of child who was constantly stretching to catch on to what was going on, to comprehend. And there was an awful lot going on, because it was a home with a lot of "language surround." My mother was a poet and my father was a kind of political arguer. There were always people there, at home, where big issues and things were being argued; there was immigrant talk and angry talk and all kinds of talk. It isn't that the talk came from us necessarily. You listened to it and you appreciated it.

On the other hand, if the talk puzzled you or was too much for you, you ran away or you did something else. You did not necessarily feel a burden of participation or expectation of performance. It's funny to me, because I'm perfectly at ease with language now (and I don't mean ease in the sense of being a marvel of literateness like some of my English friends, who don't make grammatical mistakes; I make a million, but I don't tremble with what I want to say), but indeed I remember that when I began to say anything it would come out like an explosion, because it was fueled by an enormous internal pressure to say something about a topic that I had given thought to and that didn't sit right with me. And it would embarrass me a certain amount. I would tremble inside. But children always trembled. You'd fear that you would forget. It had nothing to do with dysfunction. It had to do with memory. You'd memorize these things — other people's words, not your own — for a school assembly, and then when the time came, you'd have to go to the john, so extreme was your anxiety sitting on the platform. And you'd get sweaty hands and shake. I know that other people have suffered from this too.

I met up with many silent children, even more silent than I in my family, who were my classmates in the South. That silence was typical of my peers. There's a whole history of the two- or three-word speech of the Vermont farmer or small shopkeeper. When I was in Norway, I again heard that the rural children hardly speak, and this was a widespread cultural phenomenon for children from working-class families on school entrance. The academic descriptions of disadvantaged children have never rung a bell in my head. These descriptions go on as if the limited answer on a test or in an interview is a strange new phenomenon. Both Courtney Cazden and William Labov have described the dynamics of these situations. Both have pointed out that children, to each other, speak a whole lot more than to adults asking them questions. I contend, though, that there's something more in it. Vera John-Steiner (John-Steiner & Osterreich, 1975) wrote recently about how Pueblo children grow up in a culture that treats the development of language as something that is wisdom. In the Pueblo culture, language is wise words and one doesn't use it profusely and fluently and a whole lot or easily; it develops very slowly.

Professor John-Steiner's description evoked memories of language in my own home, evoked all the cultural experiences with language I have had — of being the "dumb doll" and the silent "stone face," always listening and holding myself impassive while I sought comprehension, but not yet ready to take a chance on speaking. It set my focus somewhat differently on a question that I want to raise as I discuss how the study of language acquisition *is* important.

## LANGUAGE DEVELOPS OVER TIME

The discussion that has emerged has centered on the tremendous responsibility of the adult for bringing out language in children, on a one-to-one basis, even when it is acknowledged that children's language is freer child-to-child. Such a focus disregards almost completely the cultural and historical influences on development in a single life, in a family, in a time period. In other words, it disregards the continuities and transformations that people embody, like the eloquence that can come to women in their late thirties or forties, which is stronger in the paraprofessional who has worked in community control and has struggled politically for her rights, or in the undergraduate black who has fought, and continues to fight, in the civil rights movement. Language development is part of the whole cultural setting in which a person grows up. It is influenced by what is expected in the family, and a child's or adolescent's "silence" or shyness does not mean an incapacity for further development later. This is part of what I knew had to be communicated in the understanding of language acquisition — not only how children as infants develop language, but how they do it as part of a whole time sweep and a cultural sweep. In understanding how children, and indeed people, have developed language over time, you begin to understand the dynamics of some of the supportive processes that are involved — what parents are and what they do. Questions about shared experience and language surround become central for you. You become capable of understanding the current controversies in education about learning theory because the understanding of language is, I think, central to these controversies.

We must always remember that the functions of language are just that — functions. There has to be a need for that function, there has to *be* that function for its development. In other words, you're not going to get much "governmental" talk or "judgmental" talk if there's no need to make a judgment or there's no power in your judgment. These kinds of talk are comments on life. Basil Bernstein (1972) observed that the struggle for civil rights was a greater asset to the development of functional power in many blacks than anything a school could do.

It is from this perspective that it worries me that Joan Tough's (1976) excellent description of how to assess 5-year-olds in five different parameters of function will be taken too literally, not as a useful way of sensitizing teachers to what is happening in their classes but as though it were really essential that 5-year-old children *have* a developed range of language function. We are putting a tremendous stress on "performance" at this point and this has to be questioned.

As Cazden (1968) has written, summing up a broad range of research, there is no need for the testing of language acquisition. Language acquisition, short of major troubles in a child, occurs. It occurs if there's someone around who talks better than the child, if the child has a chance to speak, and if the child has something to talk about. There are teachers, nevertheless, who say, "Oh, but you don't know these children. They have very limited vocabularies." You meet this barrier of perception about children's speech in student teachers and working teachers over and over again. Recognizing that teachers are enormously busy, I thought that one way to deal with this "blindness" was to ask them to spend exactly five minutes in a different area of the classroom every day, and to jot down the words that they heard there, whether of a particular child or of a group. The result was that it became entirely evident that a child does not simply have *a* vocabulary; each has vocabularies. It became evident that when a child, or anyone else for that matter, is working with clay, he has a vocabulary, and when he's building blocks he has another vocabulary and talks to the blocks with 100 words that are related to what that's about, and when he's doing something else, he uses 100 other words, and so on endlessly.

This is a terribly important and very simple thing to build upon. If you want to go into language lessons after that, if this is the requirement within which a teacher functions, then at least the teacher can say, "Do you know what I heard this morning?" and play back a tape 5 minutes after it's been recorded and bring out those words that were spoken, and say "You know, those were the words that you were using as a block builder," so that the children can immediately correct and add additional words. This is far more productive than a stance of seeing a child as an empty pot whom you fill with words. This is the acceptance of the child's own agenda; it's what his parents have been doing for him naturally. It also helps the teacher understand what is so clear in the child's acquisition of speech, that out of this big buzzing swarm of speech going on around the child, speech clots out like cream in clumps around a context.

When I said "camping" to my grandson, Teddy, who was 2 at the time and interested in camping, he said—and he had used few of the words before—"Ah, camping! Fifty dollars! Get the gas! Where's the sleeping bag?" The point is, his image of camping brought out a lot of unused words. If you were to question him directly—"Teddy, tell me three words about camping"—you would get nothing, unless your question tipped his magic point of interest, of context. Then all the words that are appropriate are expressed. Appropriate is the correct word: That's how speech clots out. The child doesn't suddenly say "raining chocolate pudding." He says "chocolate pudding" when he's talking about chocolate pudding, and "raining" when he's looking at the rain. The mother understands this. She assumes intelligence and intent and understands it. When a kid looks out the window and it's raining and the kid says "eh eh," the mother says, "Yes, it's raining." The mother responds to all the gestural language that the child has, his eyes looking, his nose pointing, everything pointing, and helps the child "clot out" by accepting his or her agenda, intent, and purpose.

Language acquisition isn't a vocabulary list, a disconnected thing. It occurs around an object. When I said something about a baby to 2-year-old Teddy, whose mother had just had a baby, his immediate response was, "Oh, the baby! The baby crying! Change the baby!" The baby was 4 days old, but it didn't matter. He had already heard those words about changing diapers. And as a very enterprising, working child, he pulled up his shirt to demonstrate himself and said, "I feed him. Baby crying. I feed him." It is not only the words that he has learned but the intonation, the expression. Talking about the baby, his voice in mellifluous; talking about playing ball, it's big-boy talk. The child clots out the words using all the drama of his existence, and that is exactly what you will hear if you go to where the child is working and listen in on the vocabulary. In school, you will hear it at a slightly older level than what I've described. It is that interchange, bounced back with a child, that helps the language capacity to grow further, because it's confirmed at that point.

It is this same awareness of and concern for context that has to inform the "sharing" session, where the children sit in a circle and each child says what she or he did. This is supposed to encourage language, and I think it does, but only for the couple of children who are already very verbal. After all, why should children who cannot yet conserve in math be expected to recall the details of their experience when the details are no longer in front of them? How well do we recall in this situation the detail of our trips without slides, journals, and the like? In far too many of these children, their recall comes to three words: "I played blocks"; "I did math." Three words, over and over. The point is, if you think about it and you are aware that children do talk in *their* setting and that speech is often contextual, then you support speech by showing slides, by looking at pictures, by the immediate excitement generated when someone else has, say, made the same trip and it's recalled while you piece out each other's experience.

## USING THE CHILD'S PATH OF DEVELOPMENT

In school, the tape recorder is a tool that can help bring back some of this language. In addition, the teacher, having joined the discussion, can help by saying "You know, when I was watching you people I heard somebody say something like this." You will then find a tremendous energizing of the children. We have done this a lot. In one instance, the same thing was played back four times to the children, at their request, because they got so interested in their own words. And they corrected: "Oh no, it was three cups, not two cups." "Oh no, he wasn't doing that, he was doing this." So-called nonverbal children suddenly offered a profusion of words around the reality of the concrete. The "rich life" is fostered in the school by these kinds of things; the rich life is what I'm saying teachers have to be aware of. You need to be aware of the fact not that the child has a limited vocabulary, which you therefore will fill up, but that the child has a richer vocabulary than you knew. Even if it is limited compared to someone else's, it is still richer than when you elicited it just one-to-one, and it can be built on. Nor is it simply a case of syntax development, but of the special nature of the way in which individual children have constructed a language that is common to all of us, and how they use it. If we don't respect this in children, we may actually be *cutting across* the path of their development instead of *using* it.

At City College, all our student teachers are asked, as part of their work, to do a language observation of one child. Since they're for the most part working with older children, only a few of them have come up with anything striking. A meaningful observation requires long records. But one student account that ran 45 pages had at least six instances on every page that bears out what I'm going to say. The child had a small, visual focus in the way in which he used language. Everything was "like a." All children will do some of this, but for this child it was special. That is the way in which he thought and saw. Using a curved block, he would say, "Oh, that's like a snake." "Oh, that's like the letter in your name." Everything was the small thing, not the global, whole thing. I'm talking about a child who is rather bright, who was functioning, listening to stories, and so on. Yet 90% of his remarks on things were made in this way. So you say, "Well, maybe he's going to be an artist." Maybe he is. We don't know that. One thing is for sure—he is not approaching language phonetically, but from the looks of the thing, like an e.e.cummings poem.

Similarly, for the grandchild I mentioned earlier, the way speech clots out in clumps around contexts is more marked than for another child. He is a storyteller. He puts together a whole thing and has from the very beginning. He is interested in how things work and creates folksongs to express his understanding. A year ago Christmas, I had fallen in a bad accident and when I went to see him my face was black and blue and looked quite interesting. He was, at that point, about 3½ years old. He asked me about it and, like all children, he asked again and again and again, and each time I described what had happened. Finally he said, "Would you like a song?" He had put together the whole story in a complete folksong format that he had absorbed from the Mexican household where he stayed while his mother worked. In that household, with a lot of teenagers, he had become very interested in the big boys, whose guitars and folksinging were attractive to him. He ran and got a block to be his guitar and he gave me a block—and when he saw that I didn't hold it correctly, he gave me a short block—so it could be my horn. "Well, it was raining," he sang, "and the wind was blowing cold, and my grandmother had an accident, and there was blood, blood, blood." "Now you make the music, olé, olé," he instructed me, and he went on to the next verse and the next verse, each time stopping for the olé olé part, which was when I "blew" on my block.

I'd say that some of this exists in all children. They make up songs while they're block-building, and so on. My grandson, clearly, is an excessive piece of the continuum. Yet, a few months later, when his nursery school teacher decided that phonics was essential for a 4-year-old, he almost stopped talking. This extremely verbal child almost became handicapped in his speech because, although he is interested in almost anything an adult tells him, the phonics approach cut across the rhythm of how he looked at speech. He began to go "er, er, er, er," and stopped having these big clumps of speech that had rhythm and pattern and held together tightly around a context, where every element was important. On his own, quite probably, he would approach reading having memorized the familiar, like *The Three Little Kittens,* as so many of us did as children. Phonics, which he would teach himself, would come later for him because it segmentalizes the language and, for him right now, confuses and cuts across his perception of it, which isn't in words at all but in whole thoughts, with a rhythm and a pattern.

Another child I know does it still another way, with great succinctness of observation, where the relevant and important words about a process are what he hits on, as well as a few little words around it. There are many ways of putting together language, and the description of syntax is hardly the whole story for us as teachers, working to provide a supportive surround. One child with great deliberation savors the sound, the syllables. Another will chatter part of the time to hear himself. One child is succinct, another speculates, another storytells. And none of this contradicts what has been observed about how children acquire syntax and grammar. Each is working within his or her style. Style is relevant to understanding children's language and how you support children; it must be. I don't know fully in what sense *relevant,* but I am certain that it is deeply important— and remains important. After all, we identify each other in part by the style of our speech, not only by its pace and rhythms but by the characteristic ways we put speech together. This is something that's always been understood by novelists; it's what makes Shakespeare's work so enduring.

## THE QUESTION OF PUBLIC SPEECH

Let's turn to a question that I think has been too little studied, the question of public speech. There are children who are highly socially related, just like one of the children I've been describing, and who are fascinated with the expression of public speech, the manners of speech: "Oh, would you like to stay to dinner?" Even the very young ones will say this: "Oh, how nice. I'd love to have you stay," and so on. Their grasp of what is essential in their environment is total. With the truest kind of touch, the piece of public speech they bring out will be an important one in that household or in the school. I have seen this again and again. When children have a chance to role-play and dramatic-play, they will try out public speech. This also assists their further development and their taking on of other patterns. Children can be in a doll corner and you can hear them doing a take-off on how you yourself speak. You can see this clearly in Kenneth Haskins's (Leitman, 1977) film about the Morgan School, where the children have this "language surround" of a lot of discussion and meetings. In one part of the film, the children are in the cloakroom, and one of them, the bigger girl, is being Kenneth Haskins; she's "chairing" the meeting in the cloakroom. One of the littler kids reports to her: "Well, and he pulled up that girl's dress, and he saw her pussy, and he didn't even say please." And I thought, shades of *High Winds to Jamaica*. I mean it is so beautiful for the way it expresses the child's perception, for the basic sex education that is in it, for the manners that are in it, for the dead seriousness with which the chairman, the older girl, listens and says, "Well, Mr. Haskins says 'please' is a very important word." You can see what supports language development in that school.

You can also see this principle at work in another marvelous film, about the Netsilik Eskimos—from Education Development Center's (1970) *Man: A Course of Study*—where they're building the ice house, on the ice cap, and the older children are playing back and forth with the baby, eliciting language from it. It is very clear that the children are in the midst of language that is about houses and jokes and this and that. It is also clear that there is intergenerational support for language. It is deeply necessary for teachers to understand the significance of this—and to let a great humility enter their souls when they see it. It is incumbent on them to study how parents, and others in the family, support language acquisition in the child. I'm not talking about it as a conscious effort; it is done intuitively, unconsciously. And it is not only the middle-class mother who does this.

There are community studies of rural families in the South, black rural families, and African families that describe mothers doing this. There is one beautiful account of a mother sitting on the floor in a Buddha-position, with the baby nesting in her legs, practically breathing in its breath and talking with it, responding to every sound. Hardly a picture of no-language stimulation from the "disadvantaged." It is true, as is also reported, that when the baby is a knee-baby, it is no longer in this "breathing back and forth" kind of language response and elicitation with the mother. Nevertheless, the children are still on the edge of a great deal of talk, so that it is not that language stimulation has ended, but that *very direct* language stimulation has ended. Language then comes from a larger nexus. The child hears language on the street, in the store, at the washing machine, during the love process, the anger process, the landlord process, from older kids, and so on.

If you are concerned about a child having a range of language function, what kind of language do you suppose results if language is drawn only from the one-to-one contact — the adult talking back to the baby — essential as this may be? How much range is there in the language of the teacher, even when it is more than question and answer and the giving of orders? Function, diversified function, does not develop that way. It develops where the kid hears higher-level language, lower-level language, street language, love language, and so on: contrastive language. At a very early age, children do hear contrastive language and they understand it. "Grandma is coming to dinner. Be sure you talk nicely for Grandma." The contrasts of language have to do with what is proper. The contrasts of language are, "Well, you know you don't talk that way at the table." Just as teachers need to ask themselves constantly whether they have offered enough life in the classroom to bring out any discussion, they must question whether they have provided a "language surround" with sufficient contrastive elements, like the language of those wise experts that John-Steiner (John-Steiner & Osterreich, 1975) has described, or for that matter, the language of the not-so-wise experts, symbolic language, rhetorical language, this language, that language.

I'm not saying that children are expected to use it. I'm saying that that is what they live with, and is around. We provide it, in part, when we read poetry to children, when we read them stories. These activities introduce new language, new pauses, new phrases, new rhythms, extended phrases, all kinds of things that are not in the spoken language. Frederick Erickson (1974), in his paper "Politics of Speaking," discussed these different functions, and described how narrow it is if a child is exposed only to standard Spanish. There's playground speech, for example. If a kid speaks pompously to all the other kids all the time, he doesn't fit.

For teachers, it is a question of looking at the range of possibilities, and what the situation elicits, in order to stretch the situation. Occasionally, poets will come into the classroom and present the image, say, of a perfect Spanish, but that isn't necessarily what the kids have, or could be expected to have. Similarly, if the adults in a child's environment are engaged in decision-making processes, in politics, for example, then the child will hear various linguistic functions. If their own living gives them a chance to hear people using their language to speculate, children will use some of it on their own level, or at least it will be possible for them to do so.

This brings us to another question that Cazden (1976) raised in her paper, about the power that adults wield in the classroom and how it affects the development of a diversity of function. Directiveness on the part of the adult is in the cards. I concur with her on that. The informal educative experiences of the home include the very simple process of telling the child to sit down, to go to bed, to take certain nourishment. That's part of life, but that isn't the whole story. At home, children have ample opportunity to express and define themselves in other than a subordinate relationship. But what happens in the traditional school? Is the "life surround" there strong enough in its elements of "language surround"? For instance, what are the responsibilities that children have in school? Are they part of the building of the school? When playgrounds are filthy, do they get a chance to clean them? It is difficult to answer those questions in the affirmative. The fact is that in most cases children aren't helped to define themselves; no one even thinks of it that way—that we build an atmosphere and environment together. Collaboration like that—construction of a kiln or the care of younger children—would support further functional developments, a further kind of language, a further clotting of contextually generated vocabulary. So my response to the question of directiveness in the classroom is, yes, but toward what end?

## THE SHARED HUMAN CONTEXT

Finally, let me comment on one other problem that Cazden (1976) reflected on—the difficulty she had generating language around a shared experience in her class because she lived in a community that was different physically, culturally, and in social class from the one in which her pupils did. In order to build up a shared experience, she took the children on trips and brought in other adults, all of which are wonderful things. But I would like to suggest that the shared experience really emerges from the human context that we share, and comes from very ordinary things. My experience is that the familiar encourages a tremendous use of language. You don't get a great language extension out of a new experience with, say, magnetism. You get a few additional vocabulary words; you don't get a proliferation of the use of language or a diversification of function. It's too strange to do anything with except name it: "Oh, yes. Magnetism!" But you don't have a whole story about it. What you have a whole story about is your own soap opera and that—the basic human drama—is something we all share. We all know about mothers, fathers, babies, harshness, illness, vomiting, sore throats. Children are not necessarily hypochondriacs, but a great deal of what they talk about is illness. That is not difficult to share. It is not difficult to share tons of things that are just simply part of the human condition. That is the point made by Connie and Harold Rosen (1973) in their book *The Language of Primary School Children*. They describe shared experiences around simple aspects of the human condition and of human commonalities that, whether you have actually experienced them or not, you can empathize with. I suggest that this is very little understood. It is on the basis of this that children should have a continuation of the house corner, the hospital corner — which isn't provided half the time, the classroom store (at the very least, mini-toys with which they can construct their familiar worlds). The Rosens make the wonderful point that, in accepting children, you take as a given that they have language. Then the question is whether they have the opportunity to use that language in increasingly complicated ways — *that* language, not another language that you're going to teach them. They will build the other language with connections to the language they already have. Indeed, there will be contrasts, because children will use language in somewhat different ways. It is this that must be supported.

I am in no way derogating the value of new experiences. I'm simply saying that the basic thing must be the teacher's ability, using the classroom setting — its focus on ordinary natural materials and shared experiences — to evoke in children memories of their earlier experiences. These will clot out language that the teacher can extend. But the extensions have to come out of the "reawakening" instead of from something new, even when this is called "science."

## THE QUESTION OF COMPREHENSION

I've been uneasy about so many aspects of adult focus on children's language development. It is not only the question of stimulating function; there is also the question of comprehension, which seems to be *the* big "worry" currently, fed by all the testing and the emphasis on scores. Actually, there are two sides to this question that trouble me: One is the way we worry about it and the other is what we do about it — how we go about *teaching* comprehension. In our worry, we seem to be afraid comprehension might not *be* there, or not be there unless we teach it. But what does *that* mean? Is our questioning of whether a child comprehends a questioning of fundamental processing, suspecting malfunction or dysfunction? Surely a reference to malfunction must be very, very small — not a basis for a *teaching* approach to comprehension. Surely, if a child's comprehension is found to be faulty, it would be seen not only in an isolated aspect of that child's functioning, namely in "reading" that is tested and scored, but all through the child's function, as inappropriate response.

Clearly such *inappropriate* function needs help, but the reference nationally must be small. So why the pervasive big worry? I cannot be anything but uneasy with the trend of the Arthur Jensen-type analyses of test scores and the consequent focus on *how much* comprehension is being achieved, which constantly seems to be summoning up reference to specific groups.

How can we be so sure of language acquisition and so unsure of comprehension? Surely comprehension is confirmed *by* language acquisition and must be treated similarly. If language acquisition is assumed — a given — so must comprehension be assumed. If the mother's assumption of intelligence and purpose was accepted as central for language acquisition, why shouldn't the same be true for the mother's assumption of comprehension, as her child uses language appropriately and acts appropriately? I end up thinking that we're asking the wrong questions, focusing on the wrong things in our efforts to assume a responsible adult role and to *teach* comprehension. I end up thinking that we draw from unclear and confused meanings of comprehension. I end up thinking that maybe we shouldn't be focusing on the children at all — but on what *we* understand by this term.

Certainly what is seen in low comprehension scores isn't the inappropriate response that implies noncomprehension or nonprocessing. In the first place, the scores are of *reading* comprehension. Children are asked to read something or do something. If they comprehend it and want to do it or are obedient, they do it. If they don't comprehend or won't, they don't do it. Do they comprehend when you tell them what it is about? Well, if they do, then the processing is all there and they *can* comprehend. They may have neglected to read the material. Or they weren't focused on it and failed to get any cues from it. Or they couldn't read it. If they can't read, they need help in reading. In the meantime, they require information. If they can take in the information, they can comprehend. I stick with this argument because, though it is not stated quite that way, I think what is rubbed back and forth underneath the general discussion of lesser, or poor, comprehension is the issue of noncomprehension dealt with as some sort of *thing*, something innate, rather than as instances of poor experience, poor information, elision, getting mixed up, being bewildered, or having a different focus in one's response. Dealt with this way, the issue of comprehension is reduced to what? A matter of I.Q.? I think we should stop a moment to make sure that, in our analysis, we don't confuse the process of reading with the *basic* process of comprehension. To the extent that we have comprehension itself as our central focus, we should be drawing in our work on meanings from the analysis of thinking, and thinking as it relates to language, in Piaget, in Vygotsky and, of course, in the work of the psycholinguists who also draw from these sources. Piaget's discussion of clinical methods applies here. His analysis of the play or random response, the response that "cases" the interviewer's mind — the inevitably less-than-full match of thought with language — may give us some perspective on our attempts to reach out to the child's *total* comprehension and on our expectation of responses that demand from the child generalizations and an understanding of the conceptual drift of the material.

Rather than this emphasis on generalizations and conceptualizing, we might better relate to the child's recall of concrete detail and begin to uncover what we understand about long-term memory links and the single or multiple threads of which they are composed. We might begin to observe more perceptively for the times and situations that stimulate the sharing and organization of comprehension and for the styles of comprehension. By uncovering our confused meanings, we might be able to move toward a closer analysis of what we understand by reading and a better critique of our approaches in reading. Either way, our approaches will be different — whether we concentrate on comprehension itself or, if we come to accept comprehension as a given, we analyze why it is that we get rather poor responses from children.

I want to relate Basil Bernstein's (1970, 1972) analysis of restricted language to this issue. Bernstein analyzed the restricted language he ascribed to poor children as related to poor function in school, and he pointed out that it occurs within a set of common meanings and is, therefore, the language of primary relationships. Implicit meanings, where a gesture or phrase takes you into the heart of the matter, without the need for explication, are common to playgrounds, to mother-child relationships, to fraternities, to wherever the universe of discourse is already understood. I think that much of children's poor response and "comprehension" falls within this analysis of restricted language — the assumption of a common frame in the universe of discourse and the lack of it in the school situation. This common frame allows us, as adult friends, to go to a movie or read a novel and then, discussing our shared experience, bat at each other sometimes totally different responses. But we *recognize* these responses and accept that their differences do not represent brain dysfunction or lack of processing or psychotic behavior or something out of this world. One person says, "Oh, you know I thought this," and the other person looks a little startled and says, "You did? Oh yes, I see that, but. . . ." This is how conversations develop; people who are closely attuned to each other intellectually carry on such discussions for hours, even on a deep level, exactly this way — where they catch the half-phrase that reminds them of something else. That type of brainstorming is enormously exciting.

Such conversations also go on with oneself and, on a higher level, this process is of the essence in the intuitive leap — the associative thinking — of the artist, in his poetry and painting. An analogy comes to the fore, possibly from the deepest recesses of one's being, yet it is recognizable and because we recognize it, we don't exclude it from our universe of discourse. Now, what happens when, in school, you ask children questions to test their comprehension? With all the good will in the world, you are approaching them externally, not from the restricted, in-group context of the common universe of discourse. You are asking them to explicate to you, an outsider, their meaning. If you want to understand and share children's meanings, then there are several ways of doing it. Certainly, what the Rosens (1973) describe — the informally shared experience — is a better way for children to organize their thoughts for you, as a teacher, to know these. The social interaction emphasized by Piaget relates here and, in direct adult–child interaction, a Piagetian interview that accepts the child's meanings, an open-ended Piagetian clinical interview, may be far more appropriate: "That's interesting." "How did you get that?" "What were you thinking of?" If the child does process, and most of humanity does, then you can get pretty far — that is, if the child wants to talk with you and accepts the legitimacy of your interest.

If what you are trying to elicit is not children's meaning but a reproduction of what specifically has been read — and there are times when you want to know whether directions are understood — well then, if they follow the directions, you know they comprehend. If you don't want their action as a demonstration, then if they are able to explain it to someone else, you know they understand. If children can't read, but they understand the information when you give it to them, or read it to them, then of course they can comprehend. They may not have understood what "turn to the left, sit down three times, and exit" really means. Sometimes directions are quite hard to follow because they are so muddy, or simply because you don't quite know what it's about and you tune out. Many of us have had this experience. We force ourselves to look at the directions on a machine, but we tune out. We stand there helpless in front of it, but not because we could not do it. Thus the issue of competence and performance also is raised. If the child really doesn't understand, then that is the relevant issue for the teacher.

I've related my concerns about comprehension to some of Bernstein's (1970, 1972) work. They are also related to the psycholinguistic work on language acquisition and development and to Frank Smith's (1971) discussion, in a Piagetian frame, of how the child is making sense of the world. Now I want to go a step further, to bring a bit of personal history to bear on my perception that what we can get from children's responses about their deep-level comprehension is, inevitably, only the tip of the iceberg. For me, as a middle child in a household with a lot of complicated things going on, the performance of tasks that became the structure of life, whether in school or at home, had nothing to do with my sense of a whole world of meanings around me, which I was thinking about and taking in constantly. In this world, a whole swirling mass — and I can only call it a river — of not-quite-located, ordered, and categorized feelings, intuitions, and understandings exists, of which only a few could possibly surface. As a young "good" reader, I *swallowed* books sometimes almost as if in a dream, unable to verbalize my comprehension even internally, except in the most simple fashion, perhaps not even in any fashion. I can remember reading *Anna Karenina, Les Miserables,* Dickens, all before I was 13. There was skipping, there was search for the conversations, the story line, there was wallowing in the pity of it all, and much of it I couldn't remember even if I turned the page, even though I was reading it. The *feeling* of it, and some of the story, held me. If a thin-enough question was asked me or if I was asked a *little* bit about it, I could say something about it. Certainly I was absolutely devastated when at 30 I reread some of these books. I had missed full essays in Victor Hugo. I had missed the entire political point in Fielding. I had missed the entire argument on the agricultural struggle in *Anna Karenina,* plus tons of other things where the wording was too difficult for me and I just swept on. But that's how I became a good reader, totally unaware of some of the issues that were important to me later — studying philosophy, contemplating the "critical line," discussing the tensions between good and evil and the meaning of the image of the cave. Metaphor didn't exist for me, as a child, because meaning was all on the same level. I hardly caught on that there were other meanings to discern. Ah, but if my sister told me something more, did I take it in? If you *tell* it to a child, does that child take it in? Is it within his universe of discourse? Does he say, "Oh yes, I see what you mean?" If that is the case, again you have an understanding child. If that is not the case, perhaps the idea is too strange, not within the child's experience.

I think our task is to open up for ourselves these quite new questions, to uncover them for examination. We have not done this before. We have not really been aware. There has been a certain arrogance about teaching "open classrooms" or "other" classrooms, and a certain arrogance about the child's learning. We've talked in terms of children working up to capacity, of stimulating children, and so on, without a real awareness of the private spaces, of the river that must exist with much deeper meanings to feed children's further progress, and which are not yet accessible to them. When we talked about comprehension, we actually thought we had something. Well we do have something, but we are only beginning to understand what it is, and it is *our understanding* of this interesting phenomenon that needs to be examined, not the child's comprehension — as if that were an entity.

# CHAPTER 2

# Language Development and Observation of the Local Environment: First Steps in Providing Primary-School Science Education for Non-Dominant Groups

*with Hubert M. Dyasi, 1985*

We welcome the opportunity to analyze the reasons as we see them for the wide-ranging interest expressed by groups from many parts of the world in what we do at the City College Workshop Center. The interest is not centered solely on some specific aspect of our work or on its immediate or current focus. It seems rather to search out our underlying presumptions and to seek to understand the relationship we make between these and our present work focus.

Our present focus seems more than anything else to be in the area of primary-school science. But of course the Center is not a science institution. Some years ago, at the inception of our work, we could have described ourselves as working to further develop children's language by maximizing language use, though at no time did we consider ourselves a language-development center. At that time we were also described as focusing on classroom organization, as assisting teachers on-site with classroom changes. We continue to relate to how teachers can make their classrooms better contexts for active learning and to respond to teachers' questions on fitting science into their classrooms. Our help with classroom organization is now in the service of primary-school science, but most of the work we do with teachers is at the Workshop Center rather than in classrooms, and centers on how the teachers themselves understand the common everyday phenomena that engage children.

What is implied by this changing focus? It has certainly not been the result of any retreat from our earlier critique of schooling or from our sense of needed change. Rather the underlying presumptions that motivated our early efforts to reorganize classrooms in ways that would encourage more use of language seem to have remained essentially constant, though more clearly defined as we understood them better. What happened was that we did not restrict ourselves to discussions about our presumptions. We actually made changes, and these changes, which often seemed insignificant in the total structure of the schooling we were confronting — full of insufficiencies and limitations though they always were — could be examined and reflected on. Through this process we gained a better understanding of what we had to do to increase language use and why, and readjusted what seemed too limited or inadequate.

## MOVING FROM LANGUAGE DIFFICULTIES TO EXPERIENCE

As we look back, it seems to us that within our present focus — which subsumes all prior elements of analysis under the rubric of inquiry — our previous directions continue to exist with even stronger impact and expansion. It is this process in our own development and the presumptions guiding our development that we share, responding to the expressed interest of other groups ranging far beyond our own community. Visitors come from all over the United States and from many countries in Western Europe, Africa, Central America, and the Caribbean. Usually what are represented are small-group efforts to relate to nondominant elements within a country. Always they represent a search for change from the established, a search for something better, for more inclusive relationships, and they relate to the Workshop Center in that context. In turn, the authors have been invited to see their work: with Turkish immigrants in West Berlin, with Yugoslavs and Lebanese in Australia, with Sephardic Jews in Israel, Hopi or Zuni in Arizona or New Mexico, Pakistanis and Bangladeshis in Birmingham or London. Although it is they who are active in research and in invitation, of course there is gainful reciprocity in these visits. We have found that, as a result of our efforts to reply to their questions about what we do as clearly as possible, we realized more fully the implications of our work for our own people and why what we do in New York has interest and relevance for these visitors.

We mention these visits because they have been instrumental in arriving at the core meaning of our work. Certainly these visitors know perfectly well that the Workshop Center is not a great language or science institution. Rather they come to us because what we do is in Harlem, in New York City, and because the children we work with and those our visitors work with have been analyzed as lacking understanding, even sometimes as lacking the capability of developing understanding. They come to us because we refuse to accept this analysis and assert the capacity for active and further development in all children.

They come to us also because both the people with whom they work and those with whom we work often speak and use language in ways different from the ways used by the politically, socially, and economically dominant group, whose use of language defines the "standard." This situation pulls nondominant language users in at least two directions: They struggle for the inclusion necessary for survival, making the dominant language their own as much as they can, and/or they struggle to maintain the link with their own language, which they feel is a necessary part of their identity. The struggle is a difficult one, because even though the dominant group acknowledges that differences do not preclude communication and comprehension, judgments continue to be made by the dominant group's "standard" measure: that the nondominant use is of lesser value. Measured by this standard, large numbers of nondominant language users are pronounced failures. The difficulties we have described appear to be worldwide and spreading, as uneven distribution of the world's economic resources compels large numbers of people to move to where life is supposed to offer better opportunities. For many, however, the heavy price of narrow concentration on language is not only failure but also reduced access to information, skill, and sources of knowledge, and exclusion from further self-development. Whatever small opportunities have been made available to them are almost obliterated. The failures mount and this finally causes concern even among dominant sections of society.

The issues are obviously complex, monumental in scale, yet our small story of struggle to reverse the mounting tide of language failure is not unrelated. Certainly, our visitors recognize in our populations the whole range of difficulties related to language and to the failure they face in their own situations, and express a profound interest in the methods we used to break out of these difficulties. They are aware that we refuse to accept the notion of "lesser value" and assert that all languages have the capability of expressing meaning and understanding. This assertion we draw from what we know from the real-life history of almost all children who acquired their first language, their mother tongue, in interaction concerning meaning in their home life, and in interaction with the life experiences in the surrounding community environment. Language was developed through use in a recognized context in the effort to communicate meaning; it then expanded as one meaning was attached in analogy or in contrast to another meaning and always modified in social interaction, first intergenerationally and then in the interaction and exchange of experiences with different persons to whom these experiences also had meaning. From the assertion of the central importance of meaning and experience for language development, it was inevitable that we would move from focusing on language difficulties to focusing on experience and meaning, indeed focusing on primary-school science.

Beyond sharing our educational thought and practice to empower nondominant language groups, our visitors wish to know what we actually did to back up our nonacceptance of the inability of some children to learn, our nonacceptance of any view that separates language from its context of experience and meaning. They ask how we have managed to relate to the potentialities and the capacities of those who use nondominant forms within a structure that accepts only dominant forms, how we went about asserting their ability and potential.

What we do is apparent and can be witnessed, and has a history of progressive efforts that we can and do share. It is a story of overcoming difficulties, of dislodging a way of thinking in teachers that may once have been imposed on them—as they themselves were treated as of lesser value—but it is now a long-established and automatic acceptance of practices based on dominant-language judgments. It is a story of building the teachers' understanding of the context in which language is acquired and develops and of their acceptance that differences do not necessarily mean incapacity. In any account, the insufficiencies and limitations of our efforts are plain. We have tried to create an open learning environment so that children of nondominant groups can learn about their environment at their own pace and in terms relevant to their lives—hence, our attention to primary-school science.

## CREATING CONTEXT IN CLASSROOMS

For our first efforts at change the question was simpler. It is true that public confrontation was central to these first efforts, but it was a verbal confrontation, one of analysis rather than of practice. The requirements set by the school, the pressures on the teacher to follow these requirements—not only from the institution but also from parents who saw this as necessary to ensure their children's success—were too strong for any real examination of how language is assimilated in real life, or any real acknowledgement of the tremendous failure rate resulting from the limited and narrowly prescriptive practice in schools. We had no choice but to work around this already existing practice, making only small changes, but changes we hoped would ultimately be significant and set in motion some real change.

Before we could confront the issues of meaning and interest, a climate favorable to beginning growth had first to be established, a climate of simple acceptance of diversity. Our goal was that children's language should at least be accepted, that they should at least be able to use it. Although later we were reinforced by the psycholinguists' analysis of meaning and active inquiry in language acquisition and by those asserting the right to language and cultural identity in bilingual classrooms, our first efforts were not even challenges to existing language-teaching practice. With classrooms almost totally divorced from real-life language-acquisition settings, which we had recognized as the source of children's capacity, our first efforts had to be concentrated on making the classroom at least a little more like this earlier setting.

We organized small groupings in classrooms where it was at least possible for children to talk to each other about what they were doing while they were doing it, where children could use language. Where it was possible, we organized mixed-age groupings as a further stimulation to language use and because we thought interaction with other group members and curriculum exposure extended over a longer time might allow for growth into understanding and might lessen the prospect of failure. To encourage language use further we filled the classrooms with familiar things from home or neighborhood that would be recognizable to the children, objects confirming them in their cultural identity. An environment of recognition and of acceptance was being built. But to support active inquiry required further effort. The child was not yet regarded as one who makes sense, as a child scientist, building on what he or she already knows. The necessary connection of the process of the child making sense of language while making sense of the language of physical reality was not yet established.

Certainly we discussed active learning, but in fact we came up against the emptiness, the barrenness of the classroom, and we were working with teachers who themselves had had little active engagement with materials. We worked directly in their classrooms with them, because they had had little opportunity to see examples confirming our assertions about active learning and capacity. But most often in these first efforts, what we managed to develop with the teachers were practical experiences with what in fact amounted to very few materials in addition to commercial instructional materials. Sometimes there were only enough for use for a short time by a few children. What was previously offered was distant from the ordinary phenomena of the child's real-life experiences; its meaningfulness was tenuous. Some teachers were still preoccupied with the instructions for use, rather than with engaging the child's attention to consequence and comprehension. They were certainly not responsive to the child's own questions or interests.

But even such limited provision was an improvement. It became evident that, as a result of small grouping, at least some decentralization of focus occurred, reducing the total verbalism and refocusing attention on an object. Even in this restricted sense some legitimacy was established for direct practical experience. Prescription was less complete in small groupings and variation in use was unavoidable. In addition, the children's activity was visible, could be reflected on and discussed and become reflectively and actively their own, rather than simply a directed practical experience. Also, even though small, the changes were real, visible to the teachers and recognizable as their own. With this confirmation they could begin to take a few steps toward autonomous decision making.

In this context of increased language use we were now able to discuss with teachers and other school staff the source of language in real-life experience and relationships. We could discuss what the content of a rich environment could be and therefore the content of the child's understanding. We began to understand what was necessary for intelligent, informed responses to children's inquiries. Intelligent replies to children required that the teachers understand, through their own experience, the process of active inquiry and stretch their own understanding of common phenomena. More and more, our efforts were directed toward teachers' understanding rather than to our own impact on classrooms. They were concentrated around three points — language acquisition, active inquiry, and recognition that these two processes relate to all humans, empowering their further development. Our major effort was to reawaken in teachers interest and inquiry about physical phenomena. The Workshop Center offered such opportunities and at least some of the teachers became active and conscious supporters of our growing focus on primary science.

After all, in support of the child's search for knowledge, who was to confirm it? Did the teacher see how one phenomenon linked up with another? Did he or she give space and time for the children's serious engagement, and encouragement to their search? Was the teacher knowledgeable enough to help children link up to past searches and to prepare for future ones? It had become all too obvious that the teacher's support for children's questions was often very weak because their questions were not even recognized as part of the discourse. So it became important to search out the depth of the teacher's recognition of the deeper questions about the very ordinary things that are part of the ordinary environment.

If active inquiry meant more than the physical manipulation of material, if what we meant was ongoing investigation, if the growth of language needed a context for this kind of work, then we had to involve teachers and assert, as we did in regard to children, that they had potential and capacity. We had to assert that those who teach are capable of understanding more, are able to see complexity in what has been accepted on a surface level, are able to join children as thinkers and support their process.

Of course, at all points it has been correctly stated that the possibility of teachers' proceeding on their understanding is a question of power. Certainly teacher functions occur mostly within the constraints of the institution, which, usually, assumes teacher incapacity. And, for the most part, the response of the teacher is one of acceptance, and constraints are absorbed without resistance. Just as in the child, such assumptions are reflected back to the adult, the external categorization itself creating the reality of incapacity. Cracks in the wall of constraint sometimes allow seepage of more autonomous decision making; they are quite wide where the intermediate institutional power is sympathetic, but some are very narrow indeed. But what we perceived was that where a clear internalization of the presumptions of human capacity and of right have been absorbed, the struggle for these presumptions is possible and is in itself useful. The struggle becomes liberating to the intelligence of the teacher, the parent, and, in turn, the child, and more avenues of actualization are found, more paths to the exercise of intelligence. As a further gain, in the course of struggle the locus impeding further development may be revealed and thus make possible another level of struggle, which can be joined to other societal struggles for further development.

## ORDINARY OBSERVABLE PHENOMENA AS A STARTING POINT

In this progression of efforts, as the teacher developed understanding and as we ourselves better understood the constraints that prevented us from breaking out of our previous failures, now, and only now, has it become possible to examine how we might possibly give some advantage, a head start, to nondominant children. It is in relationship to this question that the focus on primary-school science is writ large. What can offer such an advantage? It had become clear that acceptance was insufficient to offer any advantage, that bilingualism became equalized only where the dominant and nondominant both struggled to communicate with each other, thereby learning from each other. Even with bilingualism the advantage most often remained with the dominant group because it was their terrain and they built on what they already knew. These conclusions of insufficiency did not lead us to discard our insistence on acceptance or our support for bilingualism. Certainly, in some situations bilingual provision at least protected the language of the nondominant or oppressed group long enough to maintain the connectedness of the child's thinking. But it did lead us to some hard thinking about what we meant by primary science and what it was we saw as the additional impact, differentiated from mere acceptance, on the children of nondominant groups of their engagement with what we called primary science.

The primary science that elicits thinking about ordinary observable phenomena familiar to the nondominant group can give at least an advantageous starting point. This orientation was proposed to the group working with Turkish children in West Berlin. Turkish teachers (who were denied full teacher status and therefore were acting as assistants to German teachers) helped identify phenomena that the Turkish children knew better than the German children knew them. To the German teachers, the idea that the Turkish children were better informed seemed to contradict their views of underdevelopment. But they came to realize that, though some of the Turks in their midst may have come from mountain villages, they had heard about economic opportunities in West Berlin through modern sources, such as radio or newspapers; had traveled through Anatolia and negotiated their travel arrangements in a large airport. Some had held jobs in small industry in their country, much like those they held in Germany. And so we started with the things familiar to the Turkish children: travel, changes of climate, changes in time zones, details of negotiating the time and space of their current situation, recognition of the jobs necessary for such negotiation.

Study of these phenomena could reach toward geographical understanding; time-space studies (and travel paths as part of these studies); contrasts in soil, geological formation, plant growth; differences in ordinary kinds of technology; and water-conservation studies. Opportunities for use of language abounded. And then together — German and Turkish — the children concentrated on what was wondrous and inexhaustible to both — a drop of water. For children in other parts of the world, familiarity might be with wind patterns, wind erosion, and soil shifts (not just water erosion) or with vistas and speculation about distances where mountains appear quite close and yet experience makes clear that they are far away — in other words, with perceptions of the mountains as two-dimensional or three-dimensional, and the role of shadows in these perceptions. In some local environments earth, clay, and stones, as building materials for both housing and ovens, are closely related. In some activities, the drama of how rainwater is caught or not caught, the lasting or nonlasting dampness of soil, becomes a subject of close attention. In some environments, the activities of herbalists and pharmacists in the gathering, use, and preservation of all kinds of wild and cultivated plants become drama. The use of local materials may dramatize soft material in structures, and contrasting aspects of elasticity and rigidity are more apparent than in our own urban environment. Unimpeded vistas may dramatize air flow as much as water flow, and the sky takes on a more important aspect than in our restricted view in cities. The concurrent existence of many kinds of household technology and water engineering is more obvious and historical explanation is important.

In our own Harlem context, the children who notice the evening aircraft vapor trails, who notice different flying insects at different apartment levels (the first floor versus the thirteenth), who notice and collect the tent caterpillars that ravage, even if only temporarily, the one or two trees in the street—these children could be the scientists of the future, if only the validity of their focus could be acknowledged, if only the knowledge of ordinary things they have picked up is not dismissed, with no allowance made for unpackaging, analogies, differentiations, specificities, but instead is treated as names or categories, if only that knowledge is not bypassed later in favor of names or categories or similar information that is assumed to be more validly scientific. Unconfirmed, with no expansion of interaction or investigation, the knowledge picked up does indeed often remain at the level of just names. Unfortunately, in the effort to "cover," even these supposedly "valid" content areas remain uninvestigated.

We have used a different vocabulary from those whose similar critique of schools and of the lack of success of children from nondominant groups has centered around what they term "needs," a term we find ambiguous. We find that needs tend to be defined as societal or institutional needs, and then further defined as the "need" for children to accomplish these goals, the blame for nonaccomplishment being put on the child and family and on the community of similar children and families. Such failure is of course predominant among those who do not have a family background of achieving school goals.

Most frequently, children were helped to cope with, to accommodate themselves to, the schools as they were, without challenge. This ability to cope was perceived as necessary because that is how the schools were. But what if the child could not cope? What of the evidence of massive failure? What children needed for their development was our kind of focus, and that need was better described as a right, as defined in the United Nations's "Rights of the Child" declaration. Of course, within the intergenerational inherited aspect of human life, culture, and community, both kinds of needs exist. There is the need to adapt, to take in, to inherit, to cope with, and to survive. But there is also the need to participate, to shape, to contribute, to be supported in seeking to know and to understand, and to be supported in developing the potentialities inherent in one's humanity. These are the needs we equate with rights and that have been the touchstone of our efforts. We saw children's already achieved adaptations and asked ourselves: What did the children know when they came to school? What did they recognize? To regard all children as active learners had to be our stand. We asserted that even the institutional contributions are greater when the child enters as thinker instead of failure.

We related to the real-life experiences of the children with respect for what they had already absorbed through informal educative processes in their interegenerational and community context with respect for their inheritance. Our view was that what had already been assimilated contributed to their ability to know more, to shape and to contribute, and could be the basis for a curriculum of real power. Our efforts remain inadequate, cracks in an almost impenetrable wall of difficulties. But we are sure that even cracks cannot be made unless there is clarity about irreducible goals. The emergence of both teacher and child as actively inquiring human beings is, for us, such a goal.

# CHAPTER 3

# *Inquiry, Noticing, Joining With, and Following After*

*1986–1991*

I listened while all of you [scientists] this morning discussed your work in astrophysics, and became increasingly anxious at the prospect of my participation in this event. . . . All I could bring as an early childhood teacher for 20 years and a grandmother several times over was my knowledge of children and my thoughts about the relatedness of the ways of children's thinking to how scientists think.

My view is that the question posed has nothing to do with *whether* children inquire. As I see what is happening, it is that many of us have almost lost the memories that can support us in joining with children in what the children are looking at. Few teachers support children in their trying to find out about physical realities and the greater number of schools *do not* support children in their trying to find out.

I was amazed this morning to see these great scientists do what I only dare to do with my own graduate classes at City College, that is, use visual aids, doodle, do body gestures, make a line here or there, to show what they're thinking about. But most of the visual aids that are used to show things about primary science show beautiful children and beautiful schools, not the stark reality I want to talk about and the imperative to action that I think remains with us regardless. I want to talk about the visions that you mentioned, but I want also to talk about realities.

To begin with, I want to emphasize something that Philip Morrison has talked about — that in examining inquiry and the capacity for inquiry, the only possible stance is an assumption of *universal* human capacity. I went over all that I could find that Philip has written on primary science. In these papers, Philip (1970, 1971; Morrison & Morrison, 1984) writes about the fundamental place that a broad assumption of human capacity has in attempting even to communicate about science. He says over and over that you look from the stance that the world exists and that children are asking about the world and that you have to believe that it is possible for them to get responses to their quest. He is not claiming this possibility just for kids who are born to MIT professors. He is not using the reminiscences of MIT professors about their childhoods as proof of possibility. Of course, these kids inquire. But any notion that the rest of the world doesn't is rejected in Morrison's formulations. Morrison writes in the context of a belief in children being educable, people being able to think, and teachers being educable.

It is that frame I am referring to when I speak of teachers reminiscing, talking about how they were once children and, in so talking, joining themselves with children in an indivisible enterprise. Obviously this is a very different view from the disconnected approach that pervades the current discussion with the purpose of raising standards of children's achievement. How can it be supposed that teachers treated as dummies can better support intelligent development in children? Withdrawing esteem for teachers is accompanied almost always by a matching loss of respect for children and, of course, for the enterprise of primary science, which bases itself on the assumption of intelligence and the stance of inquiry. Just as Morrison (1970, 1971) is talking not only about the children of MIT professors, I am not talking about some special possibility for much-praised "talented" teachers. It is true that in teachers' first freedom to engage in inquiry and to shape curriculum as a result of our efforts to change schools, much self-approbation occurred—understandably, inevitably. It was a concomitant of "falling in love" with the world all over again, with their own newfound or refound capacity. It was, and is, a pleasure to join with that.

But those of us working with teachers at the Workshop Center soon saw the danger of that intoxication if it then limits views of broad potentiality, if it becomes focused on personal uniqueness, if the teacher defines the curriculum as "hers" or in description and reporting as "my curriculum." We feared that teachers' joint enterprise with children's inquiry and interest, and the commitment, the imperative on *all* teachers to focus their intelligence in the service of the development of children's intelligence, could become blurred. Belief in the universality of inquiry about the world, of efforts to make sense of it, could shrink and become narrow.

For these reasons, at the Workshop Center, where teachers pursue and reexperience their own inquiry, the diversity of participants and the interest and interaction of staff and of participants with each other, fed by this diversity, are stressed and are used to prevent closure around self-infatuation, to maintain an investment in the potentiality for *all* to pursue their inquiries.

We thus take our stance broadly, but the reality is that the space and praise given to even these few "talented" teachers in the schools is slight. The stark reality is of the imposition of teacher-proof materials that deny support for inquiry — for teachers and children, and so the struggle must extend far beyond the correction of small narrowings to a broad advocacy for the intellectual space needed for all.

## INQUIRY IN SCIENCE AND LEARNING

I'm going to take a risk for a nonscientist by extrapolating from what I heard today from some of you scientists who, in the enterprise of looking closely and stretching your thoughts, illustrated how at any moment one conceptualizes from what one knows. I'm not talking about the production of new knowledge, but about the dynamic process of inquiry. I want to relate what I heard to what I think of as similar processes in small children as they grapple to conceptualize at any moment from what *they* know.

I heard you use words like *violence, change, activity* — words describing sometimes a small sphere of complication and sometimes a larger sphere of homogeneity. What struck me particularly was that these are words inherent also to the grappling of children as they seek to understand. After all, they live in the midst of change, in a human body that changes and in a world that changes around them as they perceive it differently at each stage of their own change.

People have thought of primary science as being all those little things where children trip you up, for example, by stopping to look at the anthill and finding it wonderful. But let's remember also that, almost from the time they are born, children live in a world with things they *cannot* put in their hands but of which they have firsthand experience. These are things much bigger in scope than anthills, things like atmospheric changes, life and death, night and day, that engage them whether or not they look closely. Certainly they are touched by these experiences. They have personal involvement. Children don't look more closely without the reality of experience, without their own personal involvement with the experience.

I was interested that you spoke today of your work, objectifying the world, your search, as having an emotional quality. Memories from my work with little children came back. The children's involvement with physical phenomena was often analyzed as an aspect of their emotional development rather than as an effort of inquiry, of making sense. But aren't *both* characteristic of children's involvement? I remember this little girl who stamped her foot and said, "*Make* the rabbit come to me," and I said, "Well, rabbits don't understand English; there's no way I can make the rabbit come to you."

The realization that there are some things outside the child's control has enormous significance. It comes at children in many different forms. There are materials children *can* shape, mold, even seem to control, with the result that at times they can even forget that the material is what it is, subject to its own laws, and not identical with their desires for use. Gradually, however, it becomes clear that shaping and molding are part of the process of understanding, of describing, of discovering the history of the material and to what it is related. Gradually, in an ever-widening process of discovery, of asking "What is it?" and "What happens to it under this circumstance or that?", children define the limits of their control.

Far more is this true about that living thing that Morrison (1970, 1971) has recommended over and over as the essential and minimal requirement in any program of primary science. The living thing has its life cycle, its observable changes over time. In order to maintain it in the classroom we are forced to ask how it is maintained in the natural world. The question forces understanding from a stance that stands apart from manipulation and control. "That rabbit doesn't understand what I mean when I tell him to go to you. Pick him up — but I can't make him act as you want. The minute you let him go, he's going to run away — unless he *wants* to stay. Let's talk about what might make him *want* to stay."

The same point is forced on the child who wants the tree to bow down. Just think of those wonderful hymns about how the cherry tree bowed down to Jesus. The miraculous context is clear. But what if a plain ordinary child wants a tree to bow down so the leaf can be picked? It is a fact that the tree is taller than me, this powerful teacher. Even I cannot make this tree bow down for the child.

To read again in Morrison what I had come to from my own experience with children — the enormous significance for them of the real world, emotionally and in making sense of what impacts on them and what changes around them — could only reinforce my already firm conviction that it is absurd to discuss *whether* there should or should not be primary science in the curriculum. As long as children inquire there is no way to *eliminate* primary science. *What* is offered to children to make sense of and *how* it is offered may be limited and represent distortions in our adult understanding of the physical world and in our understanding of their learning process (present distortions, mandated, are almost incredible!), but children continue their making-sense of the world anyway, necessarily and inevitably.

Another piece I pulled from reexamination of Morrison's papers was his propositional frame that inquiry and search about the real world are inherent human qualities and capacities, descriptors of the human, and that the links and interconnection between language and this searching inquiry about the real world are strong. It was wonderful to rediscover Morrison's discussions of the relatedness of language development to inquiry activities in their common modalities of play, risk-taking, learning from error, confirmation, and growing from that into still further and continual risk, error, and reconfirmation. Reconfirmation of what? In the case of language as well as science understanding, that it has meaning, that it is *about* the world, and that the child lives in that world. When we hear teachers explain their neglect of primary science by saying "Well, you know, I have to do language," we ask, "But what are you going to talk about? Will you draw discussion material, that is language, from what you have provided in your classroom for the children to use in their search for sense in the world?" At the Workshop Center, we try to help teachers with what we understand of the links between language development and the capacity to make sense as a human characteristic, and the need for broad access to opportunities for inquiry about the physical world.

To return to the child's experience of change, life cycles, violence, sudden breaks, as well as of smaller and more gradual changes, and of coming and going—words I heard this morning—what is interesting is that some of these same words are also used in discussion of one of the first things a student of child development learns: how children develop understanding of object permanency. Piaget's vocabulary dealing with children's experiences includes some of these terms, as does Freud's. Indeed, experiences coming and going, for example, seem to be central to understanding the continuity and connections of a child's search.

Perhaps I have made a risky analogy between the processes of child thought and what seems to be fundamental to your inquiry as scientists, but I think it is only from these analogies that it is possible to believe that children as they grow can understand what *you* are doing in your enterprises at MIT. In the dynamic of a child's learning, *all* of these things go on. So if you are talking about primary science, you have to be talking about the things that emerge from the nature of this life and that sensitize the child and us to the complexity of change or to the sameness or not-sameness of things.

Discontinuities exist for children even as they search to make sense of the continuities of the phenomena around them, to establish reliable anticipations of "if this, then that." Children are confronted all the time by metamorphosis — for example, the unrecognizability of themselves, or even more of their parents, as they are now compared with pictures of them when they were babies, or even as they are told stories of eggs and fertilization. Yet, incontrovertibly, they were all there — the coherence and the possibilities. Which possibilities are determined, which can they shape, and which are reshaped in interaction with others and with other elements of context that impinge? These questions confront them over and over again and on every level of expertise and sophistication. Curiouser and curiouser, there are periods of speeded-up change, for example, when 7-year-olds lose their teeth and gain new big ones, or during adolescence.

The task of searching for understanding that is imposed on us by the complexities of the changes encountered in the course of living is not only a task for children. It is a task that must be encountered and reencountered by teachers, who must destabilize, unfix, the definitions that were first approximations for them and that, ungrappled with, block their redefinitions and their flexibility of response to the grappling of children seeking to understand the complexities of change.

The Morrisons made a marvelous speech at the Workshop Center (Morrison & Morrison, 1984) about pulling apart generalizations, about widening the experience of observable phenomena. They used as illustration the false correspondence of meaning imposed by the word *liquid* on such totally different things as water and milk, as though the word *liquid* could encompass and bridge these differences. At the Workshop Center we work with water endlessly. It's an easy thing, it's available from the tap, you don't have to buy it. We immerse teachers in experiences of water. At the beginning some say, "Oh, I know all about water." "Well," we respond, "up at MIT they are always pulling apart and discussing experiences with water. It is possible, isn't it, that together we can find out things about water that we may have forgotten or that we haven't even stopped to think about at all?"

Another beginning response is to reach for a "science" halfway remembered: "I know. $H_2O$! There, that's it." Again we respond, "Is everything about water, then, summed up in that $H_2O$?" And then we get down to a less generalized focus: "Just a minute. Does that naming, that identifying water as $H_2O$ help you sufficiently in what you want to do with this water? What else would you need to know to answer a question about purifying water, for example? Don't you need to know how water is different in different circumstances, as *well* as what is the commonality in all its forms? What do you notice contrastively?" So we help teachers experience water from many perspectives, pushing on it, looking through it, watching a drop pulling other drops into its rounded sphere, seeing it as stream, as flow, as skin on snow, as ice crystals, and so forth.

In a workshop, investigating another common material, some early childhood teachers pour sand. They *have* a conceptualization, taken in from Piaget, of the conservation of liquid, and they treat the sand exactly like water. They set up sand boxes and use tall containers, fat containers, and so on. But contrasts, differences in the material in different circumstances, are not explored. If we are to widen their experience, we must ask, "How does sand behave in this circumstance? In that one? What can you remember about the beach sand on a very hot day? On a blowy day? As the ocean waves come in? Have you tried to pour hot water into one end of the sandbox and find the temperature at the other end? Or, tried to pour hot water into some water trays already half-filled with cold water: Is it the same kind of phenomenon or isn't it?" Simple things like that.

Widening the experience of ordinary observable phenomena — not jumping immediately to atoms or molecules, which can mean nothing to small children — is more likely to happen if the teacher's own experience of these phenomena has been stretched. Then some provisioning of the classroom that brings children closer experience of discrepancies from their established expectations in the behavior of phenomena may actually result. Widening experience may involve bringing instances of decomposition already in the classroom into focus — the uncleared bits of leftover lunch or the rotting material in animal cages or terraria.

At the Workshop Center we grapple to conceive phenomena that present themselves differently, though from another perspective they are all classifiable under the same rubric. Another such phenomenon with which children have experience is the filling of space. Though children may seem to start with some small thing like an empty can, how space is filled engaged them before that, indeed continuously; it is a phenomenon for all our lifetime. Within a child's frame of questioning, just think of the differences in how water in its forms as ice cubes, vapor, steam, or snow fills space. If we include our bodies in our considerations of space filling, we are confronted with, for example, the choreographing of any dance. Organizing a classroom so that you cannot walk over me, because not only you but I also take up some space, becomes by only a small extension the moral dimension of space-filling.

Have I allowed my analogy-making too much scope? Think of it a bit. I and thou and how you move around the classroom is a question that has highly emotional implications as well as investigative potential in the search to understand the physical reality of our living. Children are constantly involved in the limits of their movement because of the presence of others, and they are constantly involved with what it means to be filling space. Think further of the involvement of children in their own starting, stopping, going. Isn't the whole history of this experiencing what makes possible their access to the ideas in Newtonian mechanics? Without that life experience shaping their ideas, and confirming and reshaping them as the experiences widen, how could they have that access? That history is certainly what we draw on while working with teachers, juxtaposing elements to bring to the surface new perspectives, widening their experience so that they may widen what is available to the children in their classrooms.

## THE CURRENT CONTEXT FOR INQUIRY IN SCHOOLS

To return to our previous orientation around active learning: At first we thought of children and their close, immediate sphere of reference almost as if they were nearsighted. We thought of how they stretched this small sphere of things that directly impinged on them and made categories and patterns and developed conceptualizations. I remember writing many years ago that the world of the nursery school was the world of Lucretius's *De Rerum Natura* — the naming of things, first descriptions, first categories. But it is, of course, more than that. Contrasts and overlaps between things, raising questions, are part of the child's "nearsighted" life. Then there are the "far sights" that produce wondering and questioning that go on and on, for example, the question of scale. It seems to be true that children do not have access to the idea of scale as adults talk about it. But elements of scale certainly exist in children's constant talk of themselves relative to the much bigger people and the large world that surround them. These elements exist as a thread in children's stories. Big and small are the most common polarities. There are myriad stories of little, big, or even giant in size on all levels of literature. I was astonished at the tiny cowslip I discovered in England; I had not thought of anything *that* small for Shakespeare's Ariel, "Under the cowslip bell I lie." In addition to the generalized categories of elves and fairies, there are stories like *Thumbelina, Jack and the Beanstalk, The Little Engine That Could, Seven at a Blow,* and the whole category of Grimm's "little tailor" stories — all stories of triumphs over odds. Children seem to be embedded in the physical reality of the intergenerational situation, in the drama of growth, and also in social criticism and the drama of struggle. Here again, the social, emotional, and biological realities are linked with a search to know.

Summing up, I think of possibilities for understanding as being drawn from the very nature of the child's life and more likely to be made accessible for closer looking in the classroom, for continued engagement, if teachers have also been helped to experience deeply their own learning and relearning. Through these experiences teachers may become a little more aware of the stretch of time over which any search to understand extends. They may become more aware that, even for them, adult teachers, it was only over an extended period of time (two weeks? three weeks? a term? — all periods of time longer than the time span of a single lesson) that they came to see in a phenomenon small differences not apparent to them in their first observations. These small differences may make them aware of complications and discrepancies in their first conclusions and lead them, at least sometimes, to understand better the rhythm of small forays, return to prior positions, followed by another small foray, that characterizes both their learning and the child's. Whether the investigators are children or teachers, they must be supported in being active with the detail of the phenomenon, in coming back to look again and again. Their activity must not be devalued by any implication that activity is allowable only as the precursor to a "higher" level called conceptualization.

Some people fear active, investigatory approaches in schools as diversions, allowable only as a confirmation or illustration of known conclusions or as a methodological step in understanding conceptualization. Adding to their fears is their concern that, using investigatory approaches, children will not take in sufficient information. They will not be prepared with answers on tests. "Children need *facts*, not disembodied contentless process," say these critics of exploratory investigation.

Disembodied? Contentless? Consider the accumulation of "fact" illustrated by remembering $H_2O$ as an overall explanation of water versus the detail accumulated in an ongoing investigation. Consider the "fact" embodied in the naming of both water and milk *liquids*, compared with the Morrisons' (1984) detail about the complex differences in milk forms. Consider the facts, the data, possible to accumulate in any *single* lesson. Consider how often these are isolated bits — a list, sometimes a naming — without experiences to give meaning to the naming. Accumulated in this way, unrelated to evidence connected by observation from varying perspectives, such facts may well foster little reflection. Compared with this scenario, the detail from any *ongoing* engagement with phenomena tends, at least, to force many reconsiderations and extensions. Further, and even more extreme in much of the present thinking about primary science, the idea seems to be to speed the process of understanding, "to get on with it," by *imparting* information and conceptualizations. The idea seems to be to "waste" as little time as possible on experiencing. The result is that experience components seem to have all but disappeared in some programs, and definitions and spelling — "evaporation," "condensation," in other words, vocabulary — are stressed.

But what of the information about how these conceptualizations were gained? What of the history of past and present grapplings around conceptualizations seen as unfinished? How is a beginning to be made in understanding these? It seems to us that teachers must themselves experience grappling, must, rather than following steps in a predetermined plan for "project" activity, be encouraged to speculate, reflect, and go on with their next insight, their next question. Their efforts will be unfinished. There will be few answers. But teachers should be joined in these unfinished experiences, sharing memories of their understandings at different periods and levels of their own search and, on another level, sharing the stories of scientists' searches. They may become better able to understand the unfinished character of all search and the different levels of the history of search. They may more readily share with children images of grappling and unfinishedness and learn to join the children's similarly groping efforts to understand and make sense.

In most of what exists in primary-science programs there is so little that either allows or encourages children to grapple with what is theirs by birthright—the nature of the very complicated things of the world that surround them and of which they are a part. Not very often is the child joined by the teacher saying, "Oh, great! I see where you are. I never saw it in that particular way. Let's see what we think about it a little later," or "Let's see what someone else has thought about it." These responses are of the essence, I think, but there is so little of such response.

We have to be critical even of the "good" classrooms that represent our efforts to improve classrooms and teaching. Our first effort was to offer an open context. Morrison (1971) described what this might mean, enumerating what should be minimally included, the offering to children of free access to a context rich in materials. But, of course, the reality is that even when there *are* materials in the classroom, the prescriptions for their use may be confining.

Let us suppose there is a very good situation, rich in context. More and more, what is characteristic even of that setting is staying for a limited time with *a* theme. Often teachers press for this because they feel that boundaries allow them to describe and control better both their input and children's participation. We understand the reasons for this focusing and accept it as the teacher's decision. We are well aware, however, that the match is often poor with young children's focus and shifts of focus—sometimes forward, sometimes in return, sometimes momentarily intense, sometimes bypassing. What we have tried to do is to help teachers explore a theme so large that that in itself ensures many perspectives and many levels of participation. At the Workshop Center we explore with teachers broad themes such as "changes over time" and "starting, moving, stopping." The intent is to support the teachers with flexibility that allows focus on problems that surface as a result of the teacher's own explorations, with an expansive view of theme as well as a response to the teacher's specific focus. This is a direction forged in a constant reflective process of collaborative assessment among the center's staff.

The reality is that there is such pressure on teachers now to justify *each* thing they do — "Does this really belong in the curriculum?" "How do you justify having that branch the child brought in?" — that a starkness may come into the classroom, even when the theme is a good one. Of course, some say that minimal provisioning, even though almost stark, is better than nothing and better than most. But at the Workshop Center we have come back, after a long period of being very casual about context and just assuming that of course it will be enriched and added to as needed, to a *defense* of context and a rethinking of what it is justifiable to include in it. Is *everything* in the context to be purposeful and related to a theme? Is there not value in having things for momentary, bypassing noticing?

I raise this question because what may happen as a response to pressure and hysteria about achievement and tests is that teachers may try to do a great deal but, to protect themselves from criticism, they also try to justify and control each aspect so that it stays on the path they have described to the principal as their plan. This may not be inherently a narrow or limited path, but it is nevertheless characterized by overresistance to any diversion. It may not be quite "Do this, so — here, *this* is the answer," but it may come close to that as the teacher, acting defensively, overcontrols and overteaches. It may end up that it is seen to be dangerous for children to go look at this thing or that or to become engaged even for a short time with any "extra" things. Where — and this is really the predominant picture — the teacher works under more restriction than this or has less vision of the broad theme, then far more limitation occurs. What happens then is not limitation around the teacher's plan for an ongoing theme, but that the teacher *follows* the prescribed lesson and *nothing* is added to the context except as illustration.

What I have described is, I think, regression from an early point of development in the schools. Those who create this scenario may say that their prescriptions about what teachers will teach and what children will be tested on are *all* developed in order to add *more* science to the curriculum. To my mind what they do is take the inquiry toward science understandings *out* of what is offered children in the curriculum. They block teachers' care about the children's engagement, about children's involvement in persistent and honest consideration of observed evidence. The teachers' care is turned into concern about lessons and already established answers, into ensuring that their work with children will show up as good results on tests.

Confronting this situation, we have realized that the anxiety produced by these pressures is often too great to ask any particular teacher to ignore. Instead, we are now trying a different approach, in defense of a minimal context for "noticings." We are saying, "Well now, let's see. How many minutes are there between this lesson and the next one? We're not challenging your lesson, but is there anything in your room for children to notice in the interval between lessons? Is there anything that suggests another aspect of content? Is every single thing in the room related *only* to that lesson and removed in preparation for the next one, so as not to distract attention from what you present next? Are there things left from one lesson to another to stir memory, things found en route to a lesson, marginal to any teacher plan or focus?" In one project at the Workshop Center, we have tried to show a group of K–2 teachers that it won't threaten them or take anything from their lessons to provide at least possibilities for noticing and perhaps even to respond to some of these noticings. We have said, "You don't have to make a lesson from it — put a pan of water on a shelf and don't take it away, so that it can be looked at by any child who passes. Put some earth and a rotting log in a pan. What will it hurt you? A mirror to catch the moving patterns of sun and shadow. A prism to cast a ceiling rainbow. An uneaten remnant from a lunch that has begun to evince mold growth. It's all just for noticing. Then take a couple of minutes out morning and afternoon, just for the children to tell you what they've noticed — something in the classroom, on the way to the classroom, in the street, and so forth." We have suggested that in the course of the sharing, memories of other noticings may surface and that the children's language use may swell and that *maybe* a lesson or even an inquiry theme will emerge.

Thus, without any direct challenge to these teachers' conviction that they must justify all they do by showing how they follow prescribed lessons, the tide of context sterilization has been at least somewhat stemmed and minor noticings are again valued. We chose to work in this way with K–2 teachers because we felt that what had been happening had been especially depriving to little children, who need a context rich in possibility for analogy or recall of connections previously or newly observed even more than do children in the older grades.

It is not only for children that we defend context, but also for teachers. They need respect for the continuities, the rich texture of possible connections, the analogies, in what they have offered. If they are to reflect on their work, consider adaptations and extensions of it and better matches for what they have observed of a child's use, if they are to gather additional perspectives illustrating what they now understand of content, they need evidence of what they provided, of what was used, to stir their recall, to feed their reflection. This evidence can be presented as a history of a classroom's involvements, one that can be seen and pointed to. Asked about some aspect of curriculum, one of the teachers said, "Oh well, of course I did that." My response is, "But there isn't the slightest bit of evidence in your classroom that you did it, or that you refer to it or build on it when you speak to the children. Is it possible for one of the children to look around and say, 'Oh, I remember when we did that'? Why *are* you taking the history away? With the visual image gone, isn't the children's further speculative thought about those things made more difficult?"

This work with K–2 teachers in their classrooms is not intended to take the place of the investigative context of the Workshop Center. At the Center's annual Summer Institute, teachers bring their own perspectives to what we offer and their own focus for serious investigation. They extend and complicate that focus as they work at the Center. The Center isn't cleared of all past work or different activity when the current focus is concentrated on a particular area. It is full of possibilities for interpenetration of focus and dense with reference to past investigations (Alberty et al., 1981). It is full of signs left by past visitors from other settings and cultures. Much that is there can be bypassed or given momentary attention while sustained attention is focused on another thing. But the context is not itself built of one-shot, one-lesson possibilities for experience; on the contrary, it is built for ongoing experiences.

An ongoing investigative context includes, of course, living things, so that one can really look at and study the history of their changes and what it takes to maintain their lives. An ongoing investigative context may include some water from any of the nearby parks or from the Hudson River; it may include a shovel or two of woods earth. When Lynn Margulis (1985) came to the Center to talk about evolution, she latched onto a tank in which earth had been sitting for over 3 years and pointed to the green streaks and said, "That's what I'm going to talk about." The tank was just *there*. Small changes in it were noticed from time to time by a participant passing by, and now and then examined carefully. It was part of the history of *our* classroom, the Center, in which the things of the Center are interacted with differently from one time to another. In the case of the contents of that tank, an unfinished history was carried forward and was present, with changes, of course, because living things naturally change over time, but present also as a reference to its difference in the past. In such an instance, a still-present visual history serves to stimulate and redirect attention. Had the tank been studied as a one-time lesson and then removed, its present reference would have been lost. Such removal and loss occurs in one classroom after another: History and present stimulus are both wiped out in overneat, overpurposeful, overdirected classrooms.

I've used the example of the Workshop Center in arguing for a regard for the history of a classroom. The history of *any* classroom cannot be summed up in record books that are read only by the teacher or her supervisor. The classroom's history is one not only of achievement scores reported to parents, but of accumulated content, something like an archaeological dig, stirring recall and thought about possible revision. My argument is intended to help teachers defend, in increasingly static and sterile classrooms, the time and space for at least minimal bypassing notice of things that, although not purposefully part of lessons, do impact on the child as part of the environment and can stimulate the child's speculation and analogy-making. It is intended to defend recollection as a legitimate purpose in building classroom environment. I present these views as sharp criticism of present practices that limit and even exclude children's own impetus to extend their inquiries, that offer no context for ongoing investigative activity.

## THE CONTEXT FOR INQUIRY OUTSIDE OF SCHOOLS

I return now to complexities that I think are inherent in the teacher's role, or indeed in any adult or intergenerational role, and that prevent us from drawing quite such sharp dichotomies between how teachers function in an inquiry context and how they function in a prescribed context. The issue is posed by teachers as though it were a simple one of the child's need for information: "Children don't know. They are ignorant. Don't they need information?" And further they ask, "How do children get information? Is information gained only in direct, self-focused engagement with materials? Is that what is meant by informal?" These questions indicate the confusion many teachers feel about their roles. Are they *never* to *tell*, to impart?

There is an enormous amount that any adult, not only a teacher, *tells* children. I have heard my grandchildren told, for example, about safety, street crossings, light switches, table behavior, and proper kinds of address: "Did you say please?" "Did you ask nicely?" Along with these directions, perhaps most importantly, they have been *told* stories, histories, about how it was when mother or father or grandparents were children. The history I carry — personal and of my time, past and present — is shared with the grandchildren bit by bit as it is appropriate and as it seems to fit with the history the grandchildren are developing around the circumstances of their lives.

Telling is also complicated. It is modified and made specific in reference according to the child. As we focus on the child's active search to make sense, we note that not *all* is taken in by any one child or in the same way. The child exhibits personal characteristics, a certain autonomy in intake, even when told things. The child's search is an individual search and our telling has its impact in that "context." We note also the individual characteristics of much that is adult-selected *for* the child's focus. The things selected may be those judged by many of the older generation to be important for survival but, along with commonalities, the selection also has individual configurations dependent on the selecting adult's personal history. What is clear is that telling is a definite concomitant of our being born into an intergenerational world. It is even more intergenerational in that it occurs in the context of changes produced by the history of still other generations who lived before us. No matter how inevitable telling is, the *result* of the telling is affected by the individual at whom the telling is directed as well as by the individuality of the teller.

Complexity haunts us with each perspective we bring to bear on our understanding of classroom interaction and the role of the teacher. For instance, suppose the teacher considers the children's "need" as the determinant in her selection of information. Does this mean need in order to meet society's expectations? Need for the child's own development? In view of such questions it becomes clear that what must be considered, taken in, is a *whole* comprised of all kinds of things, making the determination complex. In each case the whole seems to be a complicated web of memberships, all part of wholeness, each part participating in time references and historic accumulations. But no one part of even the whole as whole can be assumed, merely by membership, to have absorbed the accumulation.

The complexity I've described defeats all exclusive formulations. It defeats the formulation that everything can be learned through direct engagement with materials. Equally it defeats the counter-formulation that suggests that this complexity, this whole, this context of accumulated knowledge about things—how to do and make, and what we do not know or no longer know how to do—can be transmitted through telling as the major tool of transmission. If either assumption is accepted as exclusive, the result is that what is understood of complexity and interconnection is reduced and contained, and what is understood of the child's capacity for search is similarly reduced and contained. Moreover, a teacher who accepts either assumption exclusively can be seen to be accepting a reduced definition of her role. After all, a full role includes, in addition to *telling,* holding experience, helping to unpackage it, providing, facilitating, joining with, and much more.

I offer the small instance of plumbing as illustrative. A child, age 15 months, takes in plumbing, watching toilets flush. The child flushes the toilet, flushes the toilet, flushes the toilet. The child tests disappearance as a reliable phenomenon in that situation. It is not raw nature that he or she confronts but a modern plumbing system. Using this modern plumbing system, things disappear. But if you throw a doll in the toilet it may get stuck and *not* disappear, and you'll be punished because that plumber charges a lot of money to fix stuck toilets and very few people know how to fix toilets themselves. The child's direct discoveries interact with what, for the adult, contains elements of the known, the loss of what may once have been known, an awareness of consequences because of the loss. All of this affects the adult's response to the child's explorations as the child lives with, uses, observes this small bit of the environment. The older generation is constantly imparting to the younger, very briefly and without attempting to firm up one piece of information at a time in a sequence or to test for achievement. A child asks about or tries out what the child thinks works. The parents say this, the child says that; the parents say this and that and more, if they are knowledgeable. But both parent and child are living in this century and the context is simultaneous, multiple, repetitive, and complex.

When I was in Germany, working in schools with Turkish *gastarbei-ters,* the Germans said, "Well you know, they're just shepherds. They come from the hills. They don't know about things in our city schools." I said, "Isn't that fascinating? They're shepherds who had a short-wave radio and heard about employment opportunities in Berlin and flew from Anatolia to Berlin." The life circumstances of those Turkish kids from Anatolia happened to give them more space–time comparisons than were available to most of the German kids in Berlin, especially since Berlin at that time was still an invaded city and they didn't go much on trips. They probably didn't know things that the Turkish kids knew. The fact is that children inevitably take in a world context and their awareness is differentiated in particulars by the differences in their life histories and circumstances.

My criticism of the static classroom, of the encroaching sterility, was in defense of active learning and inquiry. But questions about the other relationships of teachers, of adults around the children, to learning — apart from provisioning the context for noticing and investigation, apart from facilitating another's search — surface again and again. As I reflect on these, I am struck again by the importance of context, the importance of *how* the adult responds, of what the adult is doing in this context *as* an adult. The contrast is not only between active learning and prescribed intake. What is the child doing in this context? What is the adult doing? I have been struck over and over again in contexts other than classrooms by the observation of the child following after, of the child joining with, the adult's activity. Children's personal trying out of what they have observed often meets with little notice from the adult, little notice of the level or intensity of the children's interest or actions. This may be because it is indeed an adult's world rather than a child's world and the adult is not focused on the child. I am reworking the frame of reference here from teachers to adults and to the intergenerational situation, broadening the frame by drawing it away from the classroom, although returning to explore possibilities from other contexts *for* the classroom.

Observing, following-after, trying-out, autonomously selecting bits or reconstructing what the child thinks will work within his or her frame of concentrated focus are the major processes of learning as I've observed them in children. It is clear that in contexts *away* from the classroom, there are these other modes in addition to the being-told mode. The adults are busy about their own tasks, and the children live in this world of adult work, observe the use of the materials of the world by the adults, and "join with" the adults who, for their own purposes, use these materials. The adults may stop briefly to comment on a child's trials of what works or to tell what is needed to make it work. What is amazing is that, though the brief bits children are told are only minimum details most of the time, without any expectation from those doing the telling of testing or standards, they seem nevertheless to be enough to support children with their own searches for greater detail and understanding.

Like being-told, joining-with is also complex and dependent on context. There is the joining-with a story or movie, and the joining-with a life situation. The joining-with in reading may have less of the autonomously selected reconstruction, but it is still joining-with, and different from "following-after." I'm not describing now reading for information — information can be given and is given all the time in momentary verbal statements *and* in books. I'm describing the joining-with made possible by books with life histories and foreign settings, joining-with stories of the dynamic of changes, such as you scientists were sharing today. These have to be shared for children in ways that retain the whole context of inquiry, the grappling, the complexity, the ongoingness and personal quality of investigation. There are not enough books with stories of how we came to think the way we do about air, water, or anything else. Perhaps we can work on this deficit by telling stories: "Once we thought about it this way. Once we thought about it that way. Then along came this fellow and he saw a problem in that way of thinking and *he* thought about it *this* way. This is where we are now in our thinking, and we're still working on it."

Another kind of joining-with is illustrated by the series of films known collectively as *The Voyage of the Mimi* (Bank Street College of Education, 1985). In what the films illustrate, joining-with is taken a step beyond following-after. Adults who know what they are doing are shown doing their usual work. They are shown trying to fix something, trying to make something straight, trying to use a bit of common technology, and talking aloud about the problem of it. They ask or allow the children to join in their work. They allow them to follow after them. Children do this with their parents all the time. They join with, without having a "lesson" on how the thing works: "This knife doesn't work. It isn't sharp. I'm going to use the sharpener. Can you see why it works this way? Here, use this." In other words, "Join with me or do it for me."

I have described following after the adult at home. Following-after also happens in village situations where activities that are one step beyond home organization are visible. The ploughman, the carpenter, the blacksmith, the miller, the potter, are followed after. In such village following-after, children's efforts to impact on the environment, to investigate their own questions, may go unnoticed, or children may join with other children if not with the adult in these situations. It is obvious that the child's efforts do not get the prolonged, focused attention of the adults because what comes first is the adults' obligation to their adult jobs.

I have described joining-with and following-after at home and in close-to-home, real-life situations. If we now look at the school situation, we find differences not only in the context but also in the relationships, differences that raise perplexities about *any* possibilities for developing experiences in school settings similar to those that naturally occur in out-of-school situations. Such experiences are essential, in my view, for the child's journey toward making sense of the world. But essential or not, the school setting offers no, or almost no, experiences of real-world setting, of whole contexts that include the child in the *present* purposefulness of the adult world, that *include* the child in what the adult does.

The question may be clearer if we ask about teaching: Other than the teacher's direct focus on what the child does, what does the child see the teacher do that the child can interpret as an adult job? Let us take apart such aspects of the teacher's job and ask whether the child is included. Is the child included in the teacher's planning? In the teacher's reporting of attendance in the roll book? In any of the teacher's preparations for creating an environmental setting? In provisioning, arranging, maintaining, repairing, and reconstructing the setting? In the reflective process that precedes evaluation and responsive adaptation? On a smaller scale, is the child included even in the preparing of paint pots for use in the art program?

It may be that no inclusion occurs because the teacher feels or is pressed to feel that no minute of instructional time can be wasted, that all must be in readiness for use as prescribed by the teacher and for the teacher's "telling." This readiness, often considered efficient, allows for no following-after. The teacher is not seen reflecting on or organizing the environment nor is the teacher seen using, as an adult, for his or her own purposes, any part of what is taught—investigating neither a mathematical relationship nor the quality of light nor plant maintenance. Since the teacher is not pursuing such an adult task or interest, there is certainly no joining-with.

There is a real question in my mind as to whether this situation can be remedied. The idea of adult work, visible to children and organized to allow following-after or joining-with, seems to be alien to schools. That it should take precedence over work organized with focus on the child seems absurd to many people. The way classrooms are defined not only in our country but in most others gives very little hope for remedy. But I have read about and seen striving for another vision, one I think should be examined for what we can learn. Real attempts to develop contexts that include the living situations essential for children's understanding and that they *need* to join with are found, at least in beginning formulations, in those countries where such work-valuing and self-strength and image-enhancing developments are seen to be necessary for the country's success in self-determining the uses of its own resources in people, intelligence, and environment.

I return therefore to questions around school access and universal reference in use of resources and in expectations about children's capacity. In the countries I refer to, the effort, the vision, is to shape the school around the relationships that give life and meaning to the individuals in the community. The proper role for school is defined here, too, as work organized with focus on the child, but work is not seen so entirely as preparation for the future. It includes more referents for joining-with an adult world presently engaged with uses that enhance community life. In contrast to the colonial image of the worker as obedient, the present needs of a self-determining community for active, energetic, self-confident workers and for contribution underline and acknowledge the child's active experiencing as prime. Of course, this is in combination with "telling," but a large component of joining-with and following-after is sought out, using the old out-of-school modalities and village opportunities as the underpinning for the child's trials in active experience and making sense. Personal and group inquiry in the service of person and group is what is considered desirable.

For us, in our country, community meanings are more remote. What we consider good, what we aim for, is more individualistically defined.

We may *aim* to acknowledge the child's active experiencing as prime, but the reality is prescribed learning, demonstration, "telling." Maybe a little of the essential joining-with can also be provided in our situations by fostering more interaction, in helping ways at least, between single children or small groups and, for example, the workers who maintain the school, or by making more connections for children with work that can be observed in the street, around construction, transportation, and stores. But these small possibilities do not add up to the vision of those who seek to define themselves using their own power and resources. I continue to seek that vision, the vision that *would* underpin the development of the capacities of all our own people, but we are not now organized around that as a societal goal. The specific suggestions I make are insufficient for that, but they are at least possible to implement and would, I think, somewhat broaden the outreach in schools for supports to the making-sense processes of more children.

To sum up: I am suggesting a combination of learning and teaching practices, including providing possibilities for these various practices. The combination I am describing includes at the least support for a noticing mode of learning, and for the noticing to perhaps grow into an inquiry, with provision of some ongoing investigative context that the child and the teacher can join with. I hope for a context that fosters joining with the workers in the school and after school. I am suggesting that the teacher loosen up a little bit and include the children in the tasks that are the background of her teaching. Using movies such as *The Voyage of the Mimi* may stir some new thoughts about joining-with. I think all these things are essential and in combination are far more effective for acquiring information than the common teacher modes of "telling" that one finds as an exclusive mode in too many classrooms today.

At the Workshop Center, probably mid-1970s.  Photographer unknown.

# Commitment and Profession

If context was the horizon of Weber's work, commitment was its animating movement. Hence this second selection of work focuses on commitment, specifically the commitment of parents and teachers to children.

What is the nature of a parent's commitment to a child? A teacher's? What are the obligations involved in working with children, especially in public institutions? What is the professionalism of the teacher, and what role does commitment play in his or her professionalism? The papers here address these questions from various angles. They are arranged, not chronologically as in Part I, but thematically. Part II begins with a consideration of the nature of the commitments to children inherent in the roles of parents and teachers. It continues through sometimes lyric passages describing parents' unique relationship to the child and analysis of the discrepancies between home and school modes and the role parents can usefully play in reminding the school of this. The sequence intensifies with forceful statements of teachers' rather different expression of commitment in their efforts to respond adaptively to each child. As a coda, there is a conversation about the resources teachers need to draw on to enact their commitment.

The four papers were given as *ex tempore* talks; none was reworked by Weber for publication. The difference in finish both of content and style from most of the other papers in this book is marked. Nevertheless, the papers convey Weber's sense of an important moral dimension of education and some of its practical implications, without which this representation of her thought would be incomplete.

The first paper, "Irrational Commitment," is from a transcript of a talk to the faculty and students of the City College Day Care Program in 1990. In this talk, Weber expounds on commitment as the foundation of teacher professionalism. She gives to the idea of professionalism the opposite of its common meaning these days as a set of specialized learnings and principles applied, ethically perhaps, but impersonally. Professionalism to her is a matter of bending all one's thought and resources to the expression of valuing. It means taking the full measure of what it entails to further the growth of all the children in one's care, and caring, intensely and personally, to act to that measure.

Weber's phrase "irrational commitment" appears to have been adapted from Urie Bronfenbrenner's reference (1979) to "irrational attachment." It conveys her sense of commitment as being the working from passionate conviction that the child cannot fail, that a child's "failure" is actually the failure of the adults and institutions charged with furthering the child. The "irrationality" of the teacher's commitment lies in the unconditionality of the commitment, not in its unreasonableness. The model for unconditionality is the parent's commitment to the child: The parent has the child, willy-nilly, and generally cannot and will not walk away. This commitment is enacted in many aspects of the parental relationship and in the educative nature and structures of the home. Here and elsewhere in Weber's work, parents are an important frame of reference in thinking about teaching and schools. They came to stand for a complex of out-of-school structures and interactions that Weber viewed as fundamentally more supportive of the child's learning than schools tend to be and from which teachers need to learn.

"On Parents" (1991) sounds this same theme, expanding on the parental mode of adaptation, response, and, as Weber calls it, "luring" that constitutes the prior-to-school support for learning. In the paper, she links several themes she identified, in correspondence of the same period, as her current concerns: "a further defining of what I think about context, about the parenting role, and about outside-of-school learning modes and about teaching modes in classroom relationships." The occasion for "On Parents" is undocumented; the date is written on the transcript, which refers toward the end to applause but includes passages that sound more like dictation.

Weber's ideas about parents, like her ideas about language, had personal roots and a professional history. She freely cited family experiences—her own as a child and those of her sons and grandchildren—in talks and writing. These were not simply illustrations of a point; they represented observations that had formed and continued to feed her analysis. There was her experience in an immigrant family, and her experiences of parental intellectual independence of school expectations and of turning for help with them to older siblings, especially because of the dislocations resulting from the family's frequent moves.

Her years teaching nursery school provided another set of experiences with parent–school relationships. Beginning in 1946 the Spuyten-Duyvil nursery made the transition from parent supervision in a home setting to having a professional teacher and a nonhome setting, while remaining a parent cooperative. Issues of difference between home and school, hence the need to help the child make a transition, came to the fore. This led to multilayered thought about "why separation?" and "why nursery school?" over a period of more than 10 years, a process that became the subject of Weber's (1959) extended Bank Street College master's thesis and the film *First Steps* (Weber & Williams, 1959). Echoes of the ideas Weber formulated in the nursery school years occur throughout her later writing on the home–school relationship.

Moving into the elementary schools in the 1960s, Weber saw the ways in which the schools "forgot" the child's earlier and out-of-school experiences, centered on the home. In fact, one of the deep principles that Weber brought from the nursery experience and her Bank Street study was the importance of stylistic continuity with the child's prior-to-school ways of and context for learning, informal learning in the intergenerational and ongoing enterprise of home life. Not surprisingly, this continuity was one of the features that Weber recognized in English informal education, and that compelled her to go abroad to study it. She adapted the idea of creating better learning environments for children by bringing the classroom into greater continuity with the child's prior-to-school ways of learning as a major argument for and goal of the Open Corridor. She analyzed the idea largely through consideration and reconsideration of the role of the parent.

From *The English Infant School and Informal Education* (1971) through "Reexaminations" (1993—see Part IV), Weber referred to the home as a place where informal and more participatory learning occurs. "On Parents," however, is one of her few papers centered on parents. Its predecessor was a full-blown statement on parental role in the Open Corridor published in *Notes* (1973d). Ideas such as the following from that paper are echoed in "On Parents":

> Home and other informal settings have many functions, and a child is "taken along," "included" within their context. His learning is often an incidental, though amazing, aspect of these functions. (p. 6)

Among other ideas that are restated and expanded in "On Parents" are the unconditionality of parental commitment; the parents' longitudinal perspective on the child, which is limited for the teacher; and the educative structures and interactions characteristic of the home that should be studied and incorporated into classrooms because of their efficacy in supporting the child's learning. The first two ideas are stated as assumptions in both articles; discussion is reserved for the third. In Weber's earlier work, this third idea is articulated as finding ways to modify school structures to effect greater continuity between home and school, between school and "prior-to-school" learning. Weber goes further in "On Parents," analyzing how home and school each have elements of formal and informal modes and cannot be contrasted simply.

"On Parents" remains partial and not fully worked out. Telegraphic notes at the end of the draft indicate the content she planned to add:

> Long term relationships—lifetime duration—unique contribution—not a forced engagement—unique role for that child—my own reminiscences of parenthood—of childhood. Parent relationship is in contrast with street and school relationship—shorter duration—can limit—runaway. Parent as citizen—involved with school as institution—parents and language—converging uniqueness—convey that to teacher.

Instead her analysis of the informal educative structures of the home—that is, of what the parent stood for as she conceived it—became conflated with the whole picture of intergenerational social structures outside of school that have an educative impact on children. Developing this picture preoccupied her in papers like "Inquiry" (Part I), "Black or Multicultural Curriculum" (Part III), and "Reexaminations" (Part IV).

"The Authority of the Teacher" was prepared as a short talk for a meeting of the Joseph Priestley Society in October 1990. Its title comes from the meeting topic, "The Authority and Responsibility of the Teacher." Weber reworked and added to the paper somewhat, but it was left unfinished. In it, she contrasts the interpretation of teacher authority as the administrative *right* to make decisions with what she feels is its true basis. She locates it first in teachers' close daily contact with the child, which puts them in the position to adapt school structures to the child's learning. A second basis is the teachers' cultivated capacities to relate interactively to the child's learning, to do self-consciously what is, as it were, inherent in the parent's role. It is the latter kind of authority that teachers "earn" by undertaking the training that will make them competent to adapt and by continuing afterward their efforts to understand the issues of teaching and schooling and to develop their ideas about them. (However, Weber cautions against conflating professional development with development of self, where development takes the teacher into personal interests that lead to withdrawal from the classroom, a phenomenon Weber had begun to observe in Open Corridor teachers and advisors in the mid-1970s.) The paper ends on a point that suggests another aspect of her interest in commitment and professionalism: that the teacher's developed capacity to observe and respond adaptively to the child's learning is the necessary ground of any revision in schooling generally.

"The Teacher's Own Resources" (my title) is a heavily edited version of a transcript, dated July 12, 1989, that incorporates a conversation between Weber and Celia Houghton and a fragment of Weber's annual talk to the Summer Institute. The conversation with Houghton, a friend, formerly director of the Greenwich Teacher Center and later on the faculty of Goddard College, was evidently meant to reconstruct the untaped first portion of the Summer Institute talk. Weber recasts the topic of "Authority," giving an account of the human resources teachers have accumulated in their lives and how they can mobilize these in the service of better understanding children's process. She stresses cultivating the grounds for *recognizing* children's experiences, using her own history as illustration. Among the resources and experiences she describes are reading stories of other people's efforts to learn, whether stories of scientific discovery or historic struggle; participating with others in learning situations like the Summer Institute; and searching one's own memory for formative experiences, including experiences of natural phenomena, and analyzing them for place, time, and circumstances. At the end of the talk, Weber urges these experiences as part of commitment and professionalism, restating the link between them: In her definition, the professional teacher was "somebody who takes seriously her commitment to support and to affirm the grappling with, the making sense of, that the child is doing."

# CHAPTER 4

## *Irrational Commitment*

*1980*

For more than 20 years I worked with very young children, even babies one summer, when I was director of a nursery school on Staten Island, which was part of the Community Service Society. Children over 8 lived there with counselors, and children under 8 with their parents. None of the teachers that summer wanted to relate to the little ones who were there, and the mothers needed a breather — that's what they were there for. So I said, "Well, okay," but also because I was fascinated with babies. I really couldn't quite take in why the teachers were bored. I had heard them saying "I've discovered that I really like the older ones," or "You can do more with them. They think more." But to me the little miracles of the baby were entirely fascinating. When the mother would come to get her baby at the end of the day I'd say, "You know, he really held on to the fence" or whatever else he had done. The other teachers would look at me and say, "Really? Held on to the fence. Big deal." How could I even say that as an objective accomplishment? Because as soon as he held on to the fence, he also fell down.

Now, though I no longer work with little children and my visits a couple of times a week are in classrooms with older ones, I am fortunate to still have refreshment from little children, because I have grandchildren. And even from the 8-1/2-year-old, I still see these little miracles, "little" because what I'm talking about are not the profound somethings that are put into teaching objectives. They are miracles, like when Teddy, the 8-1/2-year-old, calls me up to try out his latest word. He says, "Well, you know, for that party I exchanged with Robbie. I wore his costume and he wore mine. We vice versa-ed." The total purpose of the phone call was to try out his new word, *vice versa-ed*. Well, there is in me, as in any grandmother, this irrational commitment. I find little bits like that lovely.

## MORE THAN REASONABLE CARE IS NEEDED

The terms "irrational commitment" and "unreasonable care" have been used to describe a strength of parents, but I say that a piece of them has to be *our* thing too, as teachers. A piece of them, perhaps not as big as the parents have, is part of what makes it possible for us to work at all. Preparing for this talk, I thought, "How can I even raise this point about irrational commitment and unreasonable care in today's climate of beating up on teachers, on parents, on principals, and on children?" What I am trying to do is to look at the phenomenon of teachers' being berated and to analyze it beyond saying, as I do, "How awful it is that they talk about firing teachers and call the teachers no good and the principals no good and berate the children." I want to look at the context in which this critique is even accepted.

It's difficult to listen to critique endlessly and not begin, at least a bit, to blame yourself. There are those who say, "Face it. Teachers are stupid and what's needed is to get teacher-proof materials." There are more of those who talk about parents this way, adding noncoping parents to noncoping teachers, so that a large segment of the population is drawn into blame. With noncoping parents, the irrationality is stressed, rather than the commitment. Then the words *burnout* and *stress* are added to the description of noncoping. To confuse things further, it's implied that the *good* teachers burn out, that perhaps they shouldn't give so much: "Be more remote; don't give too much, because look at all the stress, and then you burn out."

Whom does that leave off the hook? The institution. The institution doesn't have to improve conditions: It's just that teachers shouldn't burn out. Then there's the lie that teachers are leaving, instead of that they are being fired. There's talk about 7,000 teachers being fired, but at the same time there's going to be a conference on burnout. What's the sense? The teachers are leaving anyway, they burn out, they can't take this kind of stress, so why worry about the firings?

There are other inconsistencies in the way in which the current situation is discussed. There is a tremendous focus on child abuse by parents, and abuse is awful. On the other hand, the Supreme Court approves corporal punishment, and there was child abuse by teachers reported in its hearings. A 10-year-old child was sent out of the room after taking a math test, and in order to motivate him, the child was beaten up. A 7-year-old child, who objected to somebody beating him up, was given something like 40 paddles, till he was bleeding. New York City okays corporal punishment. Los Angeles, where my grandchildren live, so I object, okays corporal punishment. Only a few places in the country do not. This is all in the same breath with deep concern about child abuse.

When we think about these issues, I come back to my title and say, "Is it *reasonable* care that you want for your child?" Many of you, in addition to being teachers, have children in all-day care; my daughters-in-law do, because they work. I don't think any mother wants just *reasonable* care, just safety, just custodial care, or the least common denominator of care, as though the child were not a person — an enormously complex, unique person who cannot be approached except with humility and search. Since one doesn't know that person until he or she is all grown up, it's true that the parent is in a better position to ease things up over a long period of time. That doesn't mean every parent does this, but as a construct that's so. But the minute you talk about all-day care, you wonder whether this separation of school and home commitment is right. From parents, irrational commitment, but from teachers, from the professionals, can it only be *reasonable*? I think teachers disarm themselves, if that is the case.

Where is the source of rationality in care? How do you, as a teacher, select things? A lot of things *seem* to be rational. They have good syntax. Bereiter and Engelman have a subject and a verb; Piaget has a subject and a verb. How do I know — though Piaget offers just one case study — that he's hands down better than Bereiter and Engelman? The safeguard for any parent's children is not just that the teacher has read some books. The safeguard is that you, the teacher, draw from your resources of reminiscence and empathy for what you as a human being, like that parent, like that child, know to be true. Having made, to the extent that you can, an irrational commitment to persons, then of course you seek out as rationally as possible what you can get to support you in what you are doing. So I propose a change in the title to "Irrational Commitment Done as Rationally as Possible."

The essential stance is that just about every human in the whole world is *overendowed*, not underendowed, with possibility. We hardly reach a drop of it, especially when we start from a simplistic analysis that reduces humans to something that can be checked off on a box. In order to actually handle commitment with rationality, you have to discard reductionist views of rationality that distrust the human and its complexity and turn it into a checklist. In order even to have a commitment you have to assert your own ability, because you are a human being, and build from there, to relate to the pains and problems of other humans.

By irrational I mean an over-and-above feeling that says "What else can I do? *This,* in my gut, is where it makes sense to me." Not because somebody wrote a research report about it. Of course, I have to have read all the reports and books in order to fight back, in order to get a clearer statement of what I know to be true, and to get a slight stretch beyond that. But if you start with nothing, you can have nothing. You must start with yourself as person and as intelligent and believe in human intelligence. And that means believing in children as intelligent.

On that basis, I speak against all the testing of children, and against learning disability programs. I speak for the ordinary run-of-the-mill human. You don't have to be gifted, you don't have to be special. It is perfectly true that there may be children who need an enormous amount of help. *Every* child needs our intelligent response. There may indeed be some children who are out-of-space gifted. But at the moment, in our city schools, if you're middle-class, white, and breathe, you're likely to be called gifted. We're not talking about Mozarts. All over the country, there is an overt public reclassification and reorganizing of curriculum around class and deficit.

Day-care people like you have to know this, because even if they're in a more favored setting than exists in public schools, it filters down. When I hear that one has to fight to have any richness of environment even within day care, I think, "My god, where is it that children can learn? How can they be supported?" This trend has to be seen in its roughness and rudeness; it has to be seen as not helpful. People reach out for it because they think it will be helpful. They want something for their children, and if schools are going to test the children at age 7, wouldn't it be better to start earlier?

Each of my five grandchildren is different. Teddy has learned to read in spite of being regressed in his reading because of a very strict phonics approach. In a million years that approach wasn't going to work for him. Two years went by and Teddy learned every one of the sounds, perfectly, never a mistake. But he never looked on to the next word to see what the whole thing was about, because the teacher didn't encourage that kind of thing. His parents are scientists and knew nothing about learning to read. They just love their children with unreasonable care, so they said, "We believe Teddy will land on his feet, but we wish it weren't this way, and we don't know how to help him." He really liked his teacher, so I said, "Teddy, your teacher has taught you very well and you've really learned. You know every one of the sounds. So you know what? I'm your grandmother and I'm not your teacher. Why don't we forget that and I'll read you this story and then we'll do" — he loves big words — "silent sustained reading." He said, "What?" I said, "That's what they do around me. Silent sustained reading. You go off and read it to yourself and then read it to me." Well, I'd given him the pattern, the rhythm, and the sense of the thing, and in two weeks he was reading. I have a younger grandchild who was reading three years before Teddy. He loves phonics. He loves the workbook. He's reading slower than he could if he weren't so fixed on this, but he is reading.

A quality of parents is that they tolerate individual difference better than do most teachers. Each of these grandchildren has some little quirk and some difference. In some recent reading research that we have been part of (Bussis, Chittenden, Amarel, & Klausner, 1985), what came out is that every child learns to read differently. So what do we have in schools? — the retarding of the reading process by organizing it in such a way that you're a failure if you don't fit into the structure. We educators have to learn more about tolerating different ways of going about it, even without the research reports. Parents learn this very early.

My younger son John would fall into bed asleep, but with my older son Bill getting to sleep was endless. Parents do respond three or four times; they know the child is different. They get impatient after a while, and it may very well end with a sock, but they don't anticipate that two children are going to act similarly. The mother says, "Oh, you always have to wait for him, he pokes at dinner." This sort of sitting back and estimating your children went on in my family. "Well, Henry [my brother] asks very interesting questions but, boy, the temper tantrums!" And they'd say about me — I took a while to get it — "Oh, she's very intelligent, but definitely not shrewd." I was one of five and there was a little summary of each one. There was no notion at all that I was going to change. They had to live with me as I was, as well as urging me: "Come on, now, you know."

Teachers aren't in a situation with the child long enough to have an evolutionary negotiation, so we have to make an act of faith. We have to get a longer-range view, so that we don't commit the insult of summing up a child in a test or in any other way, as though that were the whole story of that child. We have to build this view into ourselves by rethinking our own development. Then we can convey to parents a span of time that can join their time. The parent also happens to be worried, because the parent is responsible.

The teacher is being urged today to blame the materials or to use teacher-proof materials. The teacher's span will end in 9 months, so she can give *reasonable* care and then close off. But if that child makes a total mess of life, the parent cannot escape the responsibility. To be safe with children, we have to build in the idea that we can't make any conclusions, even on a long-term study like the 5-year New York State study (Carini, 1982). The mystery of the child is his whole life. . . .

## HUMAN EXPERIENCE COUNTS

When I was a schoolchild, children would come from another country, and they had certainly not had the curriculum here. They didn't faint over it, because in a lot of schools trivial lessons are repeated endlessly. Partly the children don't get them because they're boring. They can be gotten readily if the child is motivated and wants to catch up. At City College I see remarkable testaments to survival. In my classes, I have students in their mid-30s who have 16-year-old children. Things were not easy for them. They survived. And you know what? I think they're going to do great work as graduate students and as intelligent human beings. I've seen survival over and over again, not only here at City College. It confirms my basic feeling about human capacity, which I have as a gut feeling, but which I also support rationally, by thinking and reading. I don't think it's possible, certainly under the stress of the times we're living in, to do anything that counts with other people — not my work, and certainly not work with little children — unless, as underbase to all the rationality that we do need to reinforce us, we have an irrational commitment to the human, with absolutely no proofs whatever.

Linguists have come to the conclusion that one need not test children at all on language acquisition. Short of very severe brain damage, if children are in a situation where other people speak, where they're allowed to speak, and where there's something to speak about, in 99% of instances, all over the world, the children will speak, in a communicative fashion. Somebody asked me, "Is there a research report on that? With a control group?" Think of what a control group for that would mean! Are there any parents so mad that they would allow their child to be part of a test that involved not being near people with speech, not being spoken to, not being allowed to speak, and not having anything to speak about? We have centuries of human experience that constitutes the wisdom with which we come to commitment that is not based on recent research reports. One has to believe that. I find it fantastic that one should be discussing as learning disability whether a child will learn how to blend sounds, when he or she may be part of a people who survived the Middle Passage or the Holocaust. Yet today we worry ourselves and our teachers and our children to death, looking with Diogenes' lantern not for the child's positive strengths but for his deficit.

Research used to be done on something called "hospitalism." When my younger son was very young, he was in the hospital for a month. The hospital rule then was that you could visit your child only once a week, for a few minutes. The idea was to keep the situation easy to manage for the medical staff, which took precedence over the life force of the child.

The children got upset when the mothers left, but the staff's attitude was "Look at those mothers! The child cries when the mother leaves!" Likewise, for the process of day-care separation, a lot of people think it would be better if the mother never came with the child, because it upsets the child. The attitude is "Well, it's true, you can't have the child, it couldn't have been born, without the mother, but nevertheless the mother really is a pain in the neck." And some people have the feeling that "Gee, the kid is marvelous when the mother is not around." But what happened with the hospitalized child who was not visited? He developed "hospitalism"; he no longer expected to be responded to. Interestingly enough, this same phenomenon is what Bettelheim (1979) reported in the concentration camp. Men who had no hope just turned to the wall and died. The ones who could think with rage or anger could hold themselves together. Under stress, it's better to be alive than to be convenient for the management. A similar thing happened in Korea. A tremendous death rate was described among the men who didn't know what they were fighting about. They turned to the wall and gave up. Struggle and fight! In hospitals they say, "Oh, he's such a good patient." Always be suspicious of that. You're supposed to be full of piss and vinegar—how else could you stay alive?

Parents want a child to be good in school, to behave well. But parents bend rules at home. You make deals with your child. My son Bill came to kindergarten in the middle of the year, and he didn't know the Pledge of Allegiance. The teacher picked him up by his hair, dumped him down— this is true—and she said to me when I came, "He's a naughty boy. He didn't say the Pledge of Allegiance." Well, he didn't know it; he'd never heard it. Young mothers have to learn, and it took me a while (as my boy said to me later, "Mother, you're just like ginger ale. It pops when the cork is open"). You think that the teacher is the authority. So I just stared. I hadn't been yelled at by another adult in quite a while. So I said, "I don't think he's naughty." That's all. I went home and I read to him from a book—making it up frankly, which was terrible: "It's the law—you have to go to school. But when you come home there's nothing you can't do, you'll see, if you can stand it for the three hours." Well, he stood it for the three hours, and at home it was the most creative year of his childhood. He did wonderful things, although providing for them almost killed me. We made a deal. Parents face school with enormous anxiety. They know that the child is going to have trouble over this or that, and they make a deal: "If you listen to the teacher, we'll do something nice later. Okay?" Does anybody think that isn't fair, considering the load put on children? Of course, it's fair.

In the parent cooperative nursery I directed, once we took the responsibility for the children, we felt we were not going to fail them; we were going to figure how to live with them. Sometimes that meant making decisions more like a parent has to make, bending the rules for the individual child rather than being a cool professional, observing and understanding but never intervening. If Johnny had pneumonia, the school had to help Johnny's playmate to understand: "Look, Johnny has pneumonia, so you'll have to play by yourself. As soon as he gets better, we'll do something else." We related in that way. Children felt reassured. Similarly, in the summer referral nursery school, where children came with all kinds of problems, you might give one child a quite different attention than you would give another.

Some of the best things that I learned about teaching came from the few children who came to the nursery school having no speech or with other problems. Games that I concocted for a child who took all my thinking because he needed a special kind of focus were interesting to the other children. You did something with one child, and the other children would say, "Oh, gee, could I do that too?" In fact they joined the specialness, though they quite well understood that I was supporting this child. I've never seen any contradiction in that. It's essential or you get down to a drab least common denominator.

I'm using unreasonable care as a suggestive term that needs to be considered according to your circumstances. If a child is with me from 7 in the morning until 5 o'clock, and the parent is away, I can't be just cool and competent, sterilized and professional.

Things happen at home that couldn't possibly happen at school, that teachers hardly even think of unless they're also parents. Teddy knocks at my bedroom door and says, "Daddy said to knock before I come in. I've knocked." That doesn't happen at school. My grandson Robbie says, "Can I come in for a little yuvving?" and falls into bed with me right away. A teacher wouldn't have to cope with that. Teddy slept at the foot of his parents' bed for months when a new baby was born. He'd bring a sleeping blanket with him, and they'd step over him in the middle of the night. Parents can tell you tons of stories like that, which describe a domain quite different from the teacher's.

I haven't said these things in order to diminish the role of the teacher. But I think the teacher's role *is* diminished if the teacher allows herself to be put in a less-than-human, less-than-responsive kind of a role. Barbara Tizard (Tizard & Hughes, 1984) has made some criticisms of day care and nursery practice. She suggests that there *is* a difference, that parents involve the child more because the world of home is a *real world* and the parent is helping the child use it, helping the child go through the routines of physical care — eating and rest, toileting and washing up, and so forth. I think it is very serious that this element is missing in all-day care. At home children join the work of the household. Things have to get done. Suppose a mother works all week, then on Saturday or Sunday things have to get done, so the child is dragged along. But partly he gains from that. There's a certain grown-upness in it.

Children in institutions miss out if they don't have some sense of the work aspect of life. It's been suggested, discussing the implications of the all-day program, that teachers' work be more visible, as the parents' work is visible. In other words, if the teacher is preparing paint, she needs to say to the child, "I've got to get this done, so, you do it with me." Then the child is not living in a prepared child's world all day. Children's socialization in growing up is in joining in an adult world, where they see adults work.

Because school is set up as a child's world, it could actually involve a loss of language rather than a gain. In school, children don't hear adults talking about the adult world, whereas at home, they hear landlord talk, comments on TV programs, anger talk, love talk. When I asked a class of students yesterday, "Where do you think there's more language—in school or at home?" they said, "In school." But there is absolutely no evidence for this in the work I know on parental and school input to children's language, even past the point of acquisition. There's more language at home and more complex language at home. We have things to learn from this. We who claim a rationality of commitment and a professionalism must draw on this, not just perceived as part of our human experience, which I think it is, but on tape recordings done in all kinds of homes, including poor homes, of language that is more complex.

I don't see a preempting of the parent's role. I'm talking about unreasonable care within the role of a teacher. To the extent that we teachers function well, we can't be nice cool potatos. Teachers who feel robbed of their human functions of decision making and response are the ones who burn out, because it's boring, fatiguing, enervating, if you're not fully engaged as a human being in your work.

# CHAPTER 5

# *On Parents*

*1991*

In the current campaign to better the schools, there seems to be an urgency for action that includes *demanding something* of parents that would help. Teachers are asked to feel an obligation to know about parents' concerns, not to know about parents in a more general fashion. This urgency to include parents comes into the discussions on multiculturalism and the relationships of black parents to the schools. Some black educators take the stance of a black parent and critique the schools for their lack of positive role in building children's self-image and identification. The discussion turns to the parent's role in decision making in school government. This is perhaps best illustrated by the recent campaign in Chicago urging that parents should have a major role in the determination of a number of school policies.

What is *not* discussed is how the parent role in school relates to the inextricable relationships of parents with children. Taking account of parents in that way necessitates giving them credit for input to the child that the teacher then builds on. It means demanding a parental role of transmitting to the teacher the contribution to the child's development that is inevitably carried out at home. Instead, what is demanded is not the contribution *to* the school of parental-home modality, but a demand for supporting in the home the *teacher's* program with the child—what the teacher thinks would be helpful to the child. What is demanded is that obligation to support the teacher become a part of the parent's role.

Sometimes, in the teacher's mind, perhaps even in the parent's mind, this addition to the parent's role takes over entirely, and the nature and even significance to the school of the parents' initial input is forgotten. Parental role vis-à-vis the child becomes school-determined. The teacher calls on parent support for *her* goals in the interest of the betterment of the child's school progress. The school is seen to be the center, the arena where the child is to be helped. There's no real examination of all the other arenas in which the child functions or of how the child's functioning in these arenas helps or does not help the child's school functioning. My discussion of parents in my work up to this point has been circling around these dilemmas, adding one piece and then another, but there's still much to pull apart, much to reintegrate, as we understand what is going on in the relationship of home and school.

## PRIOR-TO-SCHOOL WAYS OF LEARNING

When I talked in my earlier work about the continuation in school of the prior-to-school and outside-of-school ways of learning, which were the ways of learning within the home, on the street, and elsewhere, I thought such a continuity was really possible. I thought of the parent's role as *prior to school*, without truly considering continuities. What I considered first was the largely informal way of learning prior to school, not imposed in a sequential fashion onto the child, and considered it in terms of the adult input into the child's ways of learning. But, of course, there is also direct focus on the child in the prior-to-school situation. There is an interplay between the parent having a program — the parent wants to count on the sequence of the day and is looking for what works — with what works. There is direct focus on the infant's feeding, on trying to get the infant to be regular, and in other ways to come into this world. The parent influences this by response or nonresponse, but it is response to a child's response to that situation, the parent catching on to what the child gets interested in for 5 minutes or longer, or smiles at. It is not assumed that there is some perfect model — "Now, do it, and I'll test you on it, and you have to stay within it." Adapting is the parent's end of it — keeping the child fed, getting the child to sleep, getting the child dressed — all around the child's responses. Then the parent responds to the child's sounds and to the child's first smile. The teacher's interaction is so far from this that what could have been meant by "continuity with the child's prior-to-school ways of learning?"

Having lived through this process as a parent, I was taking for granted the strange way in which the parental experience makes one more responsive, more turned inward, reminiscing about how a previous child acted or how you yourself acted. The parent may involve a grandparent, prompting remarks to the parent like "Oh, you used to do just this same thing," or "You used to turn over in this kind of way." Gradually, like a fleeting image (even though no real images may be evoked), memories from childhood of, say, a certain kind of rocking arise in parents. They arise as part of many things the parents see or do or think someone else is doing. What is involved is the parent's being aware of the child's interaction with physical realities, the child's exploration in the presence of a world that was set up not only for the child's use, with the child entering into this world in forays of trying things out and the adult feeding in another thing. This contrasts with formal lessons and with control and supervision all day long.

Although the parent is doing many things directed at the child, except for a relatively short period in the child's infancy (and even then), there is not a total constancy of that kind of interaction. When the parent goes to relieve herself, she doesn't, or very rarely, carry the child with her. She puts the child down. The assumption is that the environment that has been set up, maybe only a cradle or a headboard, can carry some of the supervision. In contrast to this, in schools one sees a total sense of adult responsibility with very small children in an attempt to build responsibility into the children, so that they will respond to words like "When I say this, then I expect everybody to sit tall." Interaction that way is a big thing at school, but it is not what happens in the more ancient interaction of parent and child.

The parent responds to the child with an appreciative reaction, or gives a feeding, and from time to time offers additional responses like, "Oh, look, he's standing now," but all with a momentariness of adult interaction along with the constancy of continuing care. And then, every few weeks or so some adjustment is made based on what the child does, without any big planning and without any of that absolutely required timing or absolute failure if not. There is a sort of *luring* of progression. No one really says, "It is necessary that this child be able to turn over as of January 15th." Overtures and responses are spread out over time. If one sees that the child seems to be struggling to turn over, then the next reaction is, "What do I have to do to make this safe? I can no longer walk away from this child." And mistakes are made; sometimes the child falls. The parent is learning as the child is learning.

Sometimes the parent's modifications take three months, sometimes two weeks. Almost like a miracle, the parent catches the moment when the child is interested. You don't have parents saying to a two-week old baby, "Say please. Grandma likes it when you do that." Mother introduces that at the point where it is likely, not where it is unlikely. The parent may offer direct kinds of expectations but without any idea that they will happen in a minute. Some things are thrown out perhaps a month before they are going to happen. They are talked about aloud in the presence of the child with no idea that the child will respond. No one has told the parent, "Well, talk while you're holding the child," but the parent does. Though the parent knows the child isn't yet talking, the parent says things like, "Ah, my, you really love that, don't you?" Fixing on a specific gain comes considerably later, at the point where a great amount has been accomplished and the parent now concentrates on that particular word. But that doesn't mean the parent hasn't used that word beforehand. "We were so lucky to have you," the parent says, and looks deep into the child's eyes. It may be said to a child who is only 48 hours old, where the word *lucky* has no specific meaning, other than being a pleasant sound and carrying the aura of the emotion. Such things are done many times, with a modification as the parent sees a response that makes the parent think that it's likely the child will respond. Parents don't test children for whether they know about something that is a million miles away from where they are.

## RETHINKING CONTINUITY WITH PRIOR-TO-SCHOOL WAYS OF LEARNING

Continuance of this prior-to-school learning turned out, as I thought about it, to have implicit in it the hope that some of this responsive relationship, this back-and-forth between adult and child, could be carried on in the school situation (how much is another matter). When I started, I had an immediate recognition that something happened for the child outside of school, and that the school wasn't regarding it. The phrase *continuity with prior-to-school learning* recognized the mobility of these small human beings and that the world had come to them, who had just entered the school arena, in their first earth experiences. It recognized that something absolutely amazing had happened with their first mobility, with crawling and walking, that meant the children could go *to* the world and approach things that were extensions of the world of the crib or high chair, playpen or backseat. This new mobility made the child part of the wider world and also gave the adults a new job of watching the child and seeing what was safe.

Then the child goes to school. The child's moving is a problem for the teacher, because the teacher is responsible for the physical intactness of a group. How can the teacher manage it, since there are boundaries to the classroom space and what can be done in the space? There is the group, which could not be denied; there is the custodial responsibility. Still — and this was an important point we made — there has to be some continuity with prior-to-school ways of learning. The differences between the home context and the school became enormously important in my awareness of what could be expected to happen in the classroom. What piece of responsiveness to the child's use could happen? Frankly, since there is such a difference, if any responsiveness to the child's action occurs,

I felt at that time, and still feel, that you have gained an enormous amount.

The parents and the teachers we worked with in the late 1960s assumed that the parent's role was to help with our changes in the school, to make it easier to have a responsive environment so that the child could remain an individual, with movement, longer. The parents joined. They helped this environment by being responsive to a few children, by bringing in richness and context. They helped the school do some adjustment to bring it somewhat into continuity with the prior-to school ways of learning. Actually, in practice, only a bit of this happened. Instead, in the demand for the parents to help the school was implicit the teacher's determination of how. This demand came long before the teacher had quite fathomed what had propelled the child earlier or realized that if she understood some of it, she would have a greater handle on response to the child, a greater impact on the child, and the child on her. So, only a few surface uses of parents occurred, like working with a small group of children on a lesson.

The question of how to maintain prior-to-school ways of learning, how to open the door to it, was clearly more complex than had been assumed earlier. The one in control, since it was in the classroom arena, was the teacher, who was determining lessons. It was not a matter of the child joining the adult, as happened at home, but of the teacher directing: "I'm going to be doing soap sculpture with the children," or "I'm going to be doing number play with the children." And then, immediately, to the parent or other helping adult: "You're going to be setting this lesson up." It was not: "Does the material have inherent in it some of the possibilities of fooling around, and you [the parent] can make some response back to what is done?" or "Are you doing something that you as an adult do and letting a child join?" or "Are you asking the children for their assistance with what you're doing?" There are enormous possibilities within this approach, all of them easier and less totally controlling, less depriving to children of their powers all around, whether powers of mobility or powers to respond to things, to talk and to make analogies about them. Yet, these situations are still quite far from bringing in a larger context.

As varying permutations of that seemingly simple thing, continuity with the child's prior ways of learning, played out in the school arena — or rather as just some of them played out, since the complexity of prior ways and continuity was hardly understood by any of us — the one thing that was clear, and that began to predominate, was the sense that this was the *teacher's* classroom. The presence of the parents was only with the teacher's consent and definitely the parents were not included as partners.

Parents' suggestions, which had been free and ready at the beginning, became fewer and had less impact as teachers became aware of the limitations on their behavior from the district, the supervisors and curriculum coordinators, and outside. The teachers limited their context and became more controlling, which they had begun to see as a good thing.

So one force that began to have great impact on parents' inclusion was the school as an institution that controlled what the teacher did and that did not want the teachers to change from being simply implementers of the school's orders. In addition, the teacher was becoming perhaps more intrigued with the creativity of shaping an environment and therefore becoming more consciously an owner of her classroom. With the invitation to change, the teacher became more passionately involved in the feeling that "This is my curriculum, this is my setting."

The parents, increasingly excluded from the school as real participants, became another force, impacting on the teacher as criticism. The teacher didn't do something well enough or the teacher wasn't in sufficient control. What did the teacher not do well enough? Well, the parent was interested in the child's being approved of and succeeding in the whole school structure. The school structure still remained and continues to remain very much *not* in an image of the prior-to-school ways of learning, but in a pattern of input-output. Parents want their child to succeed in this framework. So the teachers, trying to be creative, experienced criticism of how well or not well they did. They experienced demands that they do the old thing, since that was "sure" — at least it ended up in the child knowing this and that, even if not exploring or expanding. The whole issue of total failure was just put under the rug.

### RETHINKING A ROLE FOR PARENTS

For me, what the parent had done with the child earlier became terribly important to look at again, because that might be the source of reengaging with the child. The teachers did not, and possibly could not and should not, worry about trying to reconstitute the home in the classroom. They had to keep some continuity, but this did not mean that they were reconstituting the home, not if you really looked at what went on in the home.

Looking at prior-to-school ways of learning meant looking at the parent's bypassing, sometimes more concentrated and direct and other times just peripheral, attention to and confirmation of the child, at the medley of parental response and adjustment and introduction of new things. It meant looking at what is *unique* in a parent's role. Unless the child has had destruction of his home or is displaced into an orphanage, somebody, the parent, has known the child from the time he or she was a baby and not yet doing a million things till now, and is going to know the child longer. This is something the teacher doesn't have as a possibility at all. The child has a continuity in him or herself and in the parent. The parent knows a child's past and can go along with at least some of his or her future. This question of continuity is enormously important. Parents have to know that that is what they have.

In addition, parents have the unconditional attachment. The parent is a parent and the child is a child, and it's not a matter of the parent judging the child, weighing it, finding it failing and throwing it to the heap. These are not possibilities for the parent. The parent may not like it, but fate deals out an unconditionality about being a parent. The child is yours. The teacher, once again, is not in this position.

The differences of home from school have to be probed carefully to see what the enormously powerful kernels in the home are that are supportive of the child's development beyond question, such that, if any are taken away, the child comes close to being destroyed and needs to be enormously bulwarked to get past that point. Whether they are done well or ill by parents, what are these kernels? Awareness of them has to be active within the teacher because they are not automatic and natural in school, as they are in the home. In school, they just don't exist and since they don't, yet they are so powerful in the child's learning, they have to be looked at.

In the present discussion of parent involvement, what is being demanded is that there be parental assistance to the teacher and the school, either at home or in school, in carrying out their programs. And what is being demanded by parents is that the teacher do better in a traditional form of teaching, something that succeeds or "Convince me otherwise." The parent becomes the judge of the teacher's ways, not the carrier of the parent's strength.

What parents ought to demand is that the pieces unique to children's prior-to-school ways of learning, their style, be respected and grasped at. Parents are the avenues within the school for urging that the child's existence as somebody who approaches the world be respected and supported. It is important that, if the school has only one kind of continuity, the parents say, "Hey, just a minute, why can't there be something that supports my child in this other way? How are you providing for *this*?"

The parents' role of unconditionality, that the child exists, that he or she is not to be thrown away, is important to bring to the school. Just as it is illegal to murder a child, it is morally illegal not to realize that the child is still there next year. You cannot just destroy a child, making him or her a failure for not meeting your requirements. What are you doing about it? Such failures have to be reconsidered. How *do* children learn? What *is* important to learn, and then how do we implement it so that it's not totally destructive of the child? It seems to me that the demand that the child not be ignored and the concern for the child's further progress is certainly in the parents as well as in the teacher. I am being critical of parents here. They are not demanding the thing that they know about and that they can convey uniquely. They are not demanding some evidence that the child is at least not being destroyed by the school, that no harm has been done.

If the school attempts to engage the parents in that way and learn from them how the child is also trying to be in this world, how does the school rank up with that? What sense is made of this? In what way is the injunction to do no harm being followed? In what way is continuity with the child's prior-to-school nesting of relationships being at least respected and some little time for it found? If we can't answer these questions, it means that we have done little to really engage with parents.

I have come more and more to feel that we ignore the things that happen outside of the school with very damaging consequences. Our job is to study what relationships and what kinds of things are supportive to the child's further growth, and to try to see how to be a little continuous with those outside-school supports, even though the very nature of the school recreates limitations. In reflecting on my work, in learning from my whole circle of relationships, I have found the parent's role and the whole out-of-school arena to be enormously important. Our reflections about how we can draw these in are insufficient. This has become more and more evident to me as I realize what finally impacts and helps the person get through life. It is the outside-school arenas more than the school that help the person to keep alive, if the child is able to stand the school arena and not be crushed. We do not want parents' help just in doing our thing. We want to respect and be interested in what parents are doing, and help parents be interested in doing it, and together figure out the lines between our arenas.

# CHAPTER 6

# *The Authority of the Teacher*

*1990*

The current writing espousing the rights of the teacher as *decision-maker* often slips to a discussion of the teacher as an *authority* or to still another variant, *the authority of the teacher.* But are we talking about one and the same thing when we move from teacher decision making to teacher authority or the authority of the teacher? Linked under a single heading, the issue becomes permission to *be* decision-maker and to assert authority in this realm. Authority considered as the teacher's *permission* to be decision-maker tends to bring out stories of conflict with the hierarchies of the school or with the city or state authority, which may not give permission to the teacher to make decisions. Therefore the issue becomes a political struggle and tends to get resolved into teachers' representation on committees that make decisions about textbooks, curricula format, or schedule, in conflict with those who have not allowed permission.

But what is it that should give the teacher the right to decision making or authority? Why and what kind of decision making *belongs* with the teacher and what is it about the teacher that gives authority? If these questions are asked then the argument is not about the right to decision making or its denial. It is about what is inherent in the teacher's role that *should* give authority around issues that affect children. It's this focus that I want to assume, not the small authority that is related to carrying out the job defined by the city, the state, the board of education, that is, the authority invested in the teacher to keep control. The center of discussion should come back to the classroom and pedagogy, to the education of the teacher, and to the nature of learning and response to learning.

The trouble with outlining decision making and authority in the way that I've described as the current status is that it limits discussion. Suppose permission for decision making is given. How are decisions to be thought about? Are all decisions equal? Is the authority for decision making being exercised in a way that is inherent in the teacher's role and function or is the decision making merely a reiteration of traditional views?

## EARNED AUTHORITY

Let's start to unpack the teacher's role and function. Certainly in the primary schools, the teacher is the adult, other than the parent, who is closest in relationship to children in a continuous, everyday fashion. In that role the teacher, with a current live view of the child's response, sees where the "fit" of the imposed decisions from others really may be inadequate. No matter how nice the plan for curriculum may look on paper, the question remains, "How is the thing being taken in, responded to, interacted with, from the stance of the child's reasoning and perspective?" The teacher may have covered all that is asked for in any curricular scheme, and even per sonally assessed the coverage, but she may have made no major revisions that relate to the plan not having touched this or that child, or maybe *any* child, with real learning. And that lack of interactive engagement, teacher to child and child to teacher, makes *that* decision making inadequate. The decision has to be to revise, to adapt—and, more than that, to even critique the larger schema. This means the teacher has to not only have the authority to make adaptations, she must be *competent* to exercise it. The authority has to have been earned in the educative process of *becoming* a teacher whose role definition includes interactive response and adjustment.

When I say "an authority that has been earned," I am obviously raising issues about professional development and teacher education. How is this authority earned so that it is internalized and seen as an absolute essential for the teacher in relating to the child? If the teacher doesn't have an educated ability to respond to the child's response to whatever is offered, then the authority of the teacher in adapting the curriculum really doesn't exist. Such ability can be developed through practice, through trial and error, through living with and observing children's responses.

But, you may ask still further, on a broader scale, how does the teacher develop the ability to adapt? In our work at the Workshop Center, we have not relied on happenstance, but have centered on sensitizing teachers through reminiscences and through current experiences with their own learning responses to what may seem to be simple questions. No matter what the question is, the variety and multiplicity of responses by teachers engaging together at the Center in their own learning experiences sensitize them to the complexity of the content and of learning.

Just decision making in the limited sense of authority—the control issue — is complicated. We *cannot* assume that all decisions are equal. Why is that much controlling needed? Has the teacher been adequate in preparing an environment that narrows the need for external control? Has the teacher responded to children's interests sufficiently? Has a general sense of respect and decency permeated the classroom through recognition of interests and a basic valuing of the capacity of each child?

Other questions relate to whether issues of coverage or issues of interaction and response have been dominant in the education of the teacher. What has been found that supports a development in the teacher of authority based on sensitivity to the variety of learning styles? To the many points and perspectives from which a particular object or situation can be viewed? We have found that many teachers gain from the opportunity to experience such support for their own learning. An extension of their *hearing* sensitivity occurs that enables them to catch the special perspective of the child's look or comments or focus. Then they are able to confirm the child's experience. Their own experiences of grappling with learning, searching to understand this thing from many angles, have made them able to join the child's grappling and to relate it to other children's perspectives. A further development occurs when the grappling can be connected with stories of historic searchers for knowledge who, through their grappling, have added to the definitions of what an object or phenomenon is supposed to be. (But if the answers given by these other searchers are seen as an endpoint in grappling and as the *only* answer, a child is not given any clue to the nature of searching or how difficult it was.)

This kind of growth in sensitized hearing clearly depends on extending the teachers' experience. Experience of fresh confrontation with content and fresh search to understand seems to liberate joy in others' grappling and reach and search. This combination of sensitivity to other perspectives, experience of their own grapplings and of the variations and complexity of a particular search, and study of past grappling, seems to widen the context in which teachers see content and how they see it. By so doing, it gives a more certain knowing, an authority, to teachers' response.

That authority also grows through an accumulation of observed data about how children, in their search, take in and react from their various perspectives. Teachers grow from observation and listening, and from being easy about joining with the child's search. This results in the child's accepting the authority of a searching kind of knowing and following after and joining with the search. This is quite different from a simple imposed control coming from a vested authority. It is, rather, a growth in inner authority, recognizable by all as merited authority, merited because it's clear that the teacher understands enough to support another's search for and growth in understanding. This process is what I think of as central to teacher education.

Today, professional development is often assumed to rest on the teacher's intake of current research (Holmes Group, 1990). Knowledge about current research, it is thought, will give the teacher greater authority and can be a scaffolding for the teacher's decision making. More to the point, it seems to me, is a deep familiarity, growing all through the teacher's professional career, confirming her practice and stimulating her reconsiderations, with the thought of those who have looked closely at the knowledge and processes that constitute elements of the profession. These elements are the modes of a child's search and of response to the child's search, of creating settings that support further search and that free the teacher to observe and join with the child, rather than solely transmit. I'm also talking about a growing knowledge of and respect for the depth needed in implementation of support for children's search. There must be a commitment to looking closely, thoughtfully, and reflectively at one's own practice, to becoming familiar with the practice of others, and to the accumulation of past reflection on practice.

This is different from relying on university-based research as the thing that will stamp the teacher with authority. I'm suggesting that we give serious thought and reflection to the "messiness," let's call it, of classroom interaction and classroom life, that we touch it and move it around just *as* messiness and see what it involves. Did what that teacher do support the child's search? What ways *could* further the child's search, ways from research or arising from reflection and analysis and pulling apart of one's own practice or of similar practice? There are those who claim as research their observations of a content presented after sterilizing the classroom, because they worry about the child being diverted. But no child growing up in the world, even from his first few hours, lives in such a sterilized way. The home isn't emptied of everything in order to not overstimulate the child. Nor are the streets emptied when the child walks to school. Is none of this supposed to have any impact on perception and on learning? There is little research on peripheral intake, on the stimulation that comes from seeing a feather in one situation and then another, or from one being reminded of a previous learning experience by a record left of it.

I recommend that everybody read "Beyond the Lonely, Choosing Will: Professional Development in Teacher Thinking" by Margaret Buchmann (1990). Professional development is examined here in ways that I found enormously stimulating. The counterpoise in meaning of profession and professional development is one I found admirable. The questions she asks are: What is the profession you want to develop? What and to whom is the commitment? She states clearly that in the caring professions it is not an equal interaction between parties. It is a caring and therefore a giving. Seymour Sarason (1985) raises similar questions and discusses the loss in adequacy of teacher preparation and, for that matter, doctoral preparation, when this issue of caring is partly wiped out in the name of professionalism.

## THE AUTHORITY OF BELIEF IN EDUCABILITY

Let's start with belief in educability. If you're educating anyone, you had better believe in educability. You're not educating chairs and tables. You are educating human beings who seem—and this is, after all, why you are endeavoring to relate to them in an educative way—to have the capacity to be educated, to learn, though each perhaps in a different way. That is the major commitment that you, as teachers, make—to support the child's capacity.

You *know* that capacity is there and so then you have to know how it works. What stimulates it and what doesn't? We do this because we care, and we do it even if some of it is difficult and some of it seems to take longer than we had been prepared to countenance. Our perspectives on how to support learning are *always* limited because we do not have total knowledge of how it should be and can be. The difficulties are still greater because the context is schooling, which is not necessarily adaptive to learning. Part of our growth in ability to respond must invoke compassion for the trials of the learning process in that imperfect context, as we would have wanted compassion for our own learning when we were children. Of course, there is inequality of giving, because, yes, we've lived longer, so that we have a greater range of perspectives. That should give us the ability to pick up the child's small perspective and unite it with another and broaden it to support its fledgling character and help it to go further.

So there it is: What *did* you profess? What is your profession? Is professional development a growth and deepening and spreading of one's commitment to one's profession and one's understanding of it, or is it self-development? Self-development is, indeed, part of what goes along with the process of a deepening understanding of profession, but the processes are not the same.

I remember well that some of the Open Corridor advisors I worked with got so fascinated with the wonderful experiences I put them in the way of—serious observation and reflection on their observations—that *that* is what they wanted to do. They felt the teacher's needs and the teacher's questions were an intrusion on them. But they were *advisors*. Their *profession* was to help the teacher. Yes, of course, observation was an assist to this, but if what they wanted was *solely* to do observation, then they had entered another profession, the professional research profession; they were no longer either the teacher or the advisor. Buchmann (1990) makes it clear that sometimes another profession has been entered, and that that's fine — only you should know it if that has occurred. The idea in professional development, she points out, is *not* to take the teacher out of the classroom, to develop some new hierarchy that removes the teacher from the classroom. The idea is to uncover, unpack, and get thrilled with the depth and seriousness of the work that we, as teachers, do.

This reminder from Buchmann (1990) and Sarason (1985) about the primacy of caring in the caring professions links for me with the points that I made in "Irrational Commitment," about the reasonableness in the parent's irrational commitment, using as catalysts for my thinking Elizabeth Newson's (1978) thoughts on "unreasonable care" and Bronfenbrenner's (1979) on "irrational attachment." I want to add references to Vito Perrone and Eleanor Duckworth. In the first essay in *Working Papers,* Perrone (1989) discusses the issue of vested authority versus inherent authority. And Duckworth discusses issues of perspective and the ongoingness of complexity in various papers (1979, 1987; Duckworth et al., 1990). All these discussions support me, and I draw from them for my own perspectives on deepening my understanding of and commitment to *profession* and to reflection on the involvement with children, classrooms, setting.

In summary, I think that decision making is inherent in the role of the teacher as relating to and caring about children whom the teacher has observed. As a result of caring and observation, the teacher relates to the content handed down to her in a context of willingness to revise; the caring observation guides these revisions. She also has to make decisions around children's interests. But for all revisions in response to children's needs there has to be a wide enough spread of the teacher's own experience so that the revisions can be intertwined, not as contradictions with a schema offered by the state or the city, but as additional complexities of focus and content. These complexities bring the content closer to the grappling of scientists and scholars, who think about the nature of the content and who take the material beyond the transmission of answers to a broader view of making sense of the world. I think that without this kind of spread of capacity for revision there will be very little.

# CHAPTER 7

# *The Teacher's Own Resources*

*1989*

At the Workshop Center's Summer Institute, we are asked over and over again to refer participants, who are seeking answers, to books. They seek in books final, authoritative statements. In place of that I suggest the use of books as sharings of someone's grappling, which reached *this* formulation at the point of writing and which, as the formulation goes further, will result in another book. If the book does not convey that, then actually it is not useful in understanding the process we are talking about. If, instead, it presents a finality, *that* is not descriptive of human relationship to knowledge, which is drawn from physical reality or a reality between persons and is a reality that is never completely summed up by any single person. Even the account of that person's grappling is finite in the sense that the person has a finite lifetime. The infinity of grappling is what characterizes the capacity of the human race.

If books are used in that fashion, they confirm or recall or enlarge a point or represent an interesting grappling that had not been thought of before. Though their account is of somebody else's grappling, it is recognizable to you because it is drawn from a physical reality that you have seen in context, have been exposed to. You, as a human being, have passed near it, and the book offers an interchange that brings you another perspective, very much as if it were with another human being. If the book is a historical account of many grapplings, or a particular story of one person's grappling, that is still more so. If you do not recognize its focus, then it is probably of questionable use. If you are not at a point of recognition, then you certainly are not ready to draw from it or engage with it in any way, and therefore it becomes irrelevant. Either the book is irrelevant or you're not ready for it.

Very few books share that kind of grappling: Most books that are available or that teachers seek out are secondary sources, not primary sources. They sum up, as though things that were conveyed in the primary

96

source as things someone grappled with were veritable and finished truth. What they convey, in a thin fashion, is that this is *it*. But there is a big question whether this is or is not *it*. Someone else will look at that primary source and say, "Oh, yeah, but he really didn't answer this question, and I'm looking at this other aspect." Every first-rate scientist does this constant return to the physical reality itself, to verify and see again the aspect someone raised that they had not seen or because the point makes them want to raise another question.

Using books as illustrations of grappling has brought to the fore the role of any teacher in support of any person's grappling, including his or her own. Those committed to supporting the development and function of the capacity of all the people to whom they relate have to take responsibility for allowing for grappling. They have to put it in the context of the inadequacy of any single answer when confronting the physical reality of the world, which is never adequately or completely stated by any one person's grappling, no matter how big a scientist.

## USING ONE'S LIFETIME OF GRAPPLING AND MEMORIES

I want to share with you my own lifetime of grappling as a way of reintroducing you to the idea of human grappling with yourselves over a lifetime, of making you confident that you indeed did grapple this way and that all humans do, all children do. This idea has been lost in the current format of half-hour lessons with children and the short, predetermined periods of the courses that you take. The Summer Institute is a way of reconnecting you with that.

The excitement of something that we're still struggling to see for ourselves, not just repeating what someone else said, is part of what keeps us alive as teachers. Your talks about your Summer Institute investigations stressed for me this question of teachers' conveying for children a real involvement with the world, which then can be joined with, and themselves *having* this involvement with the world. Well I, too, am part of this intransigent physical reality: "Look, she's seventy-two and she's still interested in that kind of thing" — and I consider therefore that the account of changes over time in my own thinking is a contribution. We have to think of this sharing of our own process and being aware of our own process as part of how we function as teachers.

We often think that if a teacher knows her subject, she knows everything about it. Is that what is really meant by the professionalism of the teacher? In some current discussions, teacher professionalism is considered totally without reference to the teacher's commitment to support human functioning, human questioning as an active, never-finished kind of thing. But the professionalism of the teacher *has* to be considered in terms of that commitment, and of your own seriousness and purposefulness of constant thinking about "How is my own functioning as a human going on, so that I am part of what draws children further?"

We cannot be interested in geography, say, or be a geographer, except through the nature of being human — that we move through space and time. The same process of moving through space and time, grappling with all the changing perspectives that this means, is precisely what the child has done. You take some of the fright away from the child's experience of this by sharing what you know about this particular human function. Everyone grapples with these experiences: "It's interesting that you say you didn't realize how it was at night. When I was small I didn't see it quite the way you're seeing it. But that's a problem all of us, as human beings, go through."

Part of our resources, which enable me, as a human being, to recognize your experience, is our own fund of memories about our place in physical reality. I think of that meadow with flowers at the level of my head when I was a child, of the flowers brushing my nose. What does it mean about my height if meadow flowers, Queen Anne's lace and the like, brushed my nose? I remember that as a vivid, vivid thing. And I remember black-eyed susans in that meadow. I remember low moss roses down to the ground. I was bigger than they. Or the little dew berries or huckleberries that were right to the ground. Or, waking up very early in the morning when my father would choose one of us to join him, and seeing the very early morning dew. Or going under a waterfall and what going behind it feels like. I could recognize this later because I had seen such things. Snow is soft and made of little white dots, but it is also impenetrable. You cannot see through it. Also it can be picked up, almost as a sheet, in some variation of its form. These things you learn without focus, not as an investigation but just as part of walking through the physical reality of your own place. Not everything is inquiry in the sense of *an* inquiry. Your whole life is a kind of making sense of the setting, with a noticing. It is a welcome, this ability we have to notice something and to place it somewhere that gives us a chance to examine it in a closer focus at another time, or to understand someone else's focus. Think how much richer this is than a small bit where one has to know *a* before *b*.

Often teachers think it is a handicap to have a whole group because they think that then all the children have to handle things the same way. They don't see the group as something that adds to the density of one's perception and as a way things can surface. But I think of my childhood advantage in being a member of a big family, or the advantage you have in being part of a fairly dense social group at the Summer Institute, where everyone is approaching the experience at once. In families, even when an experience is not your own, you have been touched by other family members' experience in some way. It's not just a fact that we've had a mother who sang in the church choir; there was talk about somebody in the choir who had to gargle in order to sing, and so on. This welcome, this touching, brings more of the complexity to us, which sometimes we pull apart with great seriousness and other times look right through.

Another point from my own changes over time, a rock that enabled me to cut through the overlay of books and the traditional way of teaching we all experienced, was the fact that my family had to move a great deal. Contending with the distancing taught me, because I could not treat myself like I was *all* alone in the midst of strangeness. I had to find commonalities that made me see that, yes, these new people are recognizably human, even when they are very strange and even hostile.

The fact that my father did not revere our teachers, that he had respect for his own thought, was a weapon that we must all have and that I offer especially to minorities who meet up with a strangeness that rejects their experience. My father could say, "What does the teacher know? What does the book know? Is it really all in the book?" And if I said, "But the teacher only wants this," he did not buy that. He wanted me to be empowered with my human capacity and therefore not be robbed of the fact that I might learn more about rain by looking at it than just by finding three sentences in the book to solve the assignment. These are the resources that enabled me to question the given conceptualization.

Those of us who teach, who have children, have the gift of seeing again, through our child's unfolding, our own earlier unfolding, and have that resource from which we can confirm, and make acceptable through our affirmation, something that is so easily pulled apart. A framework is being pushed on teachers now as though there's a final theoretical formulation that makes for the professional. The other view is that this formulation is coming out of the data, but the data are always more than the formulation and therefore have the corrective to the formulation and are constantly interacting with theory. Only in the framework of commitment, with seriousness and purposefulness, to thinking of oneself as active — and as active in relation with children as well — can one use the concept of theory and practice in a way that doesn't freeze into being what the book says and nothing else.

Everything that you, as a human being, have taken in and reacted with, aside from the thing called science, gives you a resource with which you can react, if you allow yourself to open up to it. Part of what helps you is the reactions you begin to see in the children. If you have opened yourself up to your own memories, your own pool of resources, then you recognize the thing the child brings up as damned interesting, and it becomes part of the data you will allow and affirm. The child has reminded you.

## BUILDING ON THESE HUMAN RESOURCES

When things stay in the classroom over time, one child recognizes a change and some other child will come to a conclusion: "Oh, look, it's not in the ground any more. It came to the top. Now it's turning green." They have seen this happen over and over again. You cannot have just one experience of planting beans. You have to go over and over it again. It's a continuous kind of activity. If you have one plant in the room, it's hard to draw any conclusions. The plant becomes part of the wallpaper and not part of an obvious changing over time. On the other hand, sometimes people have gotten the sense, even from the Workshop Center itself, that profusion is necessary in a classroom in order for children to experience these things. No. The phenomena are in the world in all kinds of ways. If you're convinced of this, then you're open to the child's seeing it and you, too, will share your noticing: "Goodness, I thought we'd be able to work this afternoon, and it wouldn't be so hot. You know the way it changes in the afternoon." And then one of the children will add, "The sun isn't there in the afternoon." Even without all kinds of fancy equipment, the bits are there.

This pool of noticing was part of the structure I erected around the small child in my earlier work, but it goes on all through life. The child gets to school through space. He doesn't get to school in a sterilized path, where everything has been taken out except what would lead him to that classroom. Inevitably, there are things to notice, things that can be shared by everybody, providing that one is permissive about the noticing and welcomes the noticing and that one is interested and conveys the sense that one is also continuing to notice, that one has not yet noticed all the things in the whole world. I noticed, when I was a small child, the greenish, dark gray light that came just before an eclipse, when the sun is covered; it was an amazing thing and I remember it. So of course I can recognize it in literature and when I live through another eclipse, though it isn't a full-bodied thing anymore.

Children's learning is not dependent just on whether we provide or teach every moment, but on whether we respect it and allow them to verbalize it and make possible moments of noticing. It depends on our confidence that children are active. Even in the most informal educational situation, at home, children are simply *told* things: "Sit down." "Did you say please?" "Did you say goodbye to Grandma?" The question is whether that noticing piece of their lives is allowed in school. But whether you tell them something or they are inquiring actively themselves, whether they are initiating or receiving—we should stop talking about whether it is active learning or not. There is no other way to learn except actively. Even when children immobilize themselves to resist your inquisitorial way of questioning, to protect themselves against your encroachment, and they freeze and say, "Oh, yeah? So what? Make me," children *are* active; resistance also takes a great deal of energy and is an active thing. Children who allow themselves to be swamped by someone else's domination are going to land in a mental home; children who resist may be killed because theirs is a form of activity that is self-destructive, perhaps. You have to realize what you are saying when you say that you are teaching children how to learn actively. You are not. You cannot.

Learning happens anyway. You need not worry to death whether it happens every single moment. Young teachers say, "What can I do to bring this approach all the time?" You have to have enough confidence in the child and in yourself to know that, if some of it is welcomed and shared, and you allow a joining-with and a following-after, then active learning happens. It's not all or nothing. It's not that this teacher can do it and this other one cannot. It's: How else? You keep trying to expand the area of your receptivity and your sharing of active engagement and grappling with how we understand and make sense of the world. You don't think, "I can't be an informal teacher; I can't go the whole hog. So I'll be a formal teacher, I'll do something else." It isn't that way. Whether the formal teacher is affirming it or not, the child keeps on doing some of it.

When you become aware of your own stretching further, when you reflect on it and see it as part of the human process, it will be a "How else?" and "How can I do some of it?" You will stretch your awareness of the pool of physical data and therefore recognize more of it. And you will be acting as professional teachers, as people who take seriously their commitment to support and to affirm the grappling with, the making sense of, that the child is doing anyway.

Lillian Weber in an Open Corridor classroom, late 1960s.        Photo: F. Maresca.

In England, around 1974.        Photo: Leicester Mercury.

# PART III

# Valuing Human Intelligence and Capacity for Meaning

Throughout her writing and her practice, Weber oriented herself by reference to the idea that all human beings are intelligent and capable of making sense of the world, of making meaning. These capacities constituted what she often called "educability." The intelligence and capacity of human beings was a deeply rooted belief:

> My father and his generation in the late 19th century were steeped in a rationalism and a belief in progress and democracy that was based on the assertion of human potential, of human understanding. In my home it was assumed that people were intelligent, that they were strong and capable, and that all were entitled to the dignity of man. (1976b, p. 3)

It was also an operating hypothesis, both on a generalized level and as a posture toward the individual child.

> The essence of this experience as a direct personal kind of relating to the child as a whole child, allowing for and not excluding her differences, but also assuming (certainly in a purely exploratory and "faith" kind of way at first) that she could go along with life in the nursery school, and that we could help her in this direct personal way of relating to her as though of course she could. (1959, p. 60)

Beyond assertion and assumption, the idea of human intelligence and capacity was also a moral imperative, and it carried obligations and required commitment. "What other assumption could justify our presence in the classroom?" she had asked in an article dating from a period of intense activity (1974).

Intelligence and capacity are particularly the themes of the three works in this section. All three are informed by an acute sense of the institutional and societal pressures to devalue children and teachers.

"Education for Young Children in the 80s" is excerpted from the transcript of an invited talk given at the 31st annual conference of the Southern Association on Children Under Six in Roanoke, Virginia, March 26–29, 1980. (Some introductory reminiscences of her days at the University of Virginia were cut; a reference to

Hampton Institute remains.) "Moral Issues for Teachers" was an invited address to the World Congress in Education held at the Université de Québec à Trois-Rivières, July 6–10, 1981. The topic was inspired by the theme of the Congress, *Values and the School.* Both "Education for the 80s" and "Moral Issues for Teachers" were delivered *ex tempore,* although evidently with different degrees of preparation. The transcript of "Education for the 80s" is quite choppy; short quotes only were used by conference organizers in the ring-bound proceedings, *Young Children: Issues for the '80s* (Dickerson, et al., 1980). Weber seems not to have worked on it further. In contrast, she polished the transcript of "Moral Issues" for publication in the conference proceedings the following year.

"Black or Multicultural Curriculum: Of Course—But What More?" was not a public address; rather it was drafted at home in 1990–1991. It was prompted by Weber's concerns about New York City high schools, much in the news at the time, and as a contribution to discussions at the 1990 annual meeting of the North Dakota Study Group on Evaluation, where there had been some tense debate on racial issues at the group's preceding annual meeting. She circulated versions to individual members of the group and to others, and intended to include it in the book she was planning. Of the seven versions that were found at her death, what appears to be the first was attached to a covering letter to the group's convenor, Vito Perrone, dated October 22, 1990. Weber revised the paper fitfully over several years and a number of these revisions have been incorporated here; hence the span of dates indicated.

Looking forward at the turn of the decade, in "Education for Young Children in the 80s," Weber brushes aside the anxious talk of stringent budgets, mainstreaming, and diversity that were the gist of others' predictions. For her, the core issue was the continuing, and increasing, threat to confidence and belief in human capacity and educability as the foundation for the work of education. She cites flourishing manifestations of this threat. Lessons learned in progressive efforts of the immediate past were being forgotten. Individuals were not drawing on their own growth to bolster their belief in change and complexity in children. Difference was becoming ipso facto a "deficit" rather than a survival strength and resource of the human species. People who might formerly have been somewhere along a "broad continuum of the norm" were being parcelled instead into exclusive little categories like "gifted" or "special." A law meant to bring people into the mainstream had become a means to find ever more differences between them rather than to reassert commonality. Nowhere were people valuing the "species-characteristic capabilities," the fact that we humans are more alike than different and that our alikeness, in educational terms, lies in our capacity to learn.

Alikeness at the level of intelligence and human capability is reasserted as a fundamental of teaching in "Moral Issues." "Much has been made of our stress on human uniqueness and difference," she says (the "our/we" referring to her collegial style of work in the 1960s and 1970s), "but it is important to know that we placed even more stress on commonalities, intelligence, inquiry, interaction, and communication as givens." Here she writes that moral issues for teachers inhere in the relationships of respect and belief in the capacity of students, teachers, and parents and not, as the call then was, in discipline, drill, and back to basics. Because her own work had focused on context, most concretely in the form of school structures, people following her ideas sometimes imagined that the outward organizational forms and practices were what mattered. Instead, she says, she had proposed them as supports for and expressions of the relationships that were at the heart of education and its morality.

One structure embodying a principle was, however, essential and that was heterogeneous grouping of children in classes—creating classrooms to accommodate diversity of age, culture, race, language, temperament, need, and ability. "Without this we could not even attempt to give new meaning to compulsory education, to define it as the support structure for the developmental potential in each child" (Weber, 1974). Classification of children was, in Weber's view, one of the major obstacles to implementing diversity because, no matter how well-intended, it resulted in separating and isolating them into groups based on a classificatory sameness. But the commonality Weber recognized was educability, not sameness, and educability cut across all classificatory lines. The "path of educability" would differ for each child, so the classroom and the teacher had to be able to adapt. This was the heart of the moral issue for teachers, as she elaborated it in "Moral Issues for Teachers."

In the face of the dilemmas posed by contemporary institutionalized education, as analyzed in these two papers, Weber identifies continued effort based on belief in human capability as the moral bottom line for all educators. Continued effort must be on the order of "irrational commitment, unreasonable care." Perfection is not an automatic consequence of moral commitment but, she asserts: "The moral statement that releases courage is 'I'll try. I'll try.'" How passionately she held this position is suggested in a response to the New York City funding crises of the mid-1970s. To those who said there was no alternative but to cut staff and programs, to restrict teachers to specified curriculum materials, to rely more heavily on evaluation, she replied:

> What is implied in this no-alternative argument is clearly a distrust of the intelligence of teachers, of administrators, of parents—but mostly of children. Why should more difficult conditions lessen the demand for teacher intelligence and substitute a demand for a robot-like performance on the part of teachers? Why should it be supposed that diminishing the sense of living community in a school will result in less need for discipline, and why are parents expected to assent to a highly passive response from their children? ... Why not, we ask, take another tack? A tack based on trust and human intelligence as the basic presumption of our compulsory educational system.... The children in our schools will not shed their characteristics as humans to accommodate to budget cuts.

In fact, if they are not able to bring these characteristics to bear on their learning, they will lose immeasurably in ways that will not be compensated for later on by simply focusing on their learning disability. (1976a, pp. 2–3)

The points made in "Education for ALL the children" (1974), "Education for the 80s," and "Moral Issues" come back in "Black or Multicultural Curriculum" with fierceness and a more visionary casting. Weber applies again her perception that the relationships in schools are the grounding for education. And what she finds is that often "there is nothing about the presence of black youth (particularly males) in schools that is valued." Using corrosive language to convey this desperate situation— words like *garbage, lethal, encumbrance, stab,* and *eliminate* abound in the paper— she makes it clear that, for example, offering students images of African-American heros, though worthy, is a band-aid. Instead one must ask, "Is any good meaning given to the membership of that participant in the school?" The situation extends to all young people for whom no productive role in society is being provided or planned. If we cannot provide for their meaningful contribution, then we do not in fact value their intelligence and capacity to add meaning to the world.

Faced with such a situation, "what *is* the role of the school and even *is* there any?" The proposals she sets forth involve both school and extraschool institutions and attitudes. Everywhere she seeks hints of what can be tried. The range is testimony to the desperateness of the situation, the paucity of obvious paths to solution, and the intensity of effort that is needed. It also reaffirms Weber's belief, which she reiterates in "Black or Multicultural Curriculum," in the value of small changes, that is, the value of every effort, no matter how small. Her approach is not to say that the situation is so bad that small efforts are wasted, but that the situation is so bad that any effort is worthwhile. This characteristic affirmation—not optimistic, perhaps, but concrete and grounded—creates openings for individual teachers and others to find strength to continue.

Two additional aspects of "Black or Multicultural Curriculum" deserve highlighting in relationship to the theme of this section. One is Weber's focus on work; another is the special place of the so-called minority child, particularly the black child, in her energy and analysis for reform. Opening up opportunities for children to engage in active work meaningful to them, rather than simply to go along with imposed rote tasks, had been a goal of open education. Instilling in teachers a sense of the nature of their work had long been a focus of Weber's efforts. But "work" as a central human activity, uninflected by particular role, came to the forefront of Weber's interest in the early 1990s.

In "Black or Multicultural Curriculum," she proposes that young people be offered work—apprenticeships, assistanceships, and mentoring opportunities for older youth, in and out of school, and for younger children, inclusion in the real work of schools—that contributes to the human surrounding and thereby recognizes and affirms their value and human capability. The notion of work as an educative experience is not new, but Weber energized the idea by the character of the relationships and context she proposed around it: Adults must recognize that young people are a "necessary part of [the adult's] own existence, of their own identification as an adult." The obvious dependency of children on adults must be countered with an appreciation of the dependence of adults on the young.

Work for youth, to be meaningful, would have to be work that evidently needed doing and that contributed to the immediate community. It would have to be paid. The youth would have to be mentored by adults who also worked in the situation. The work also would have to be an entry to other learning experiences—starting perhaps with the history of the kind of work the young people were doing. Work for older youth would sometimes have to involve risk and concrete learning to be real. The work should become a means for reevaluating the heroism of ordinary work, for teaching about other people's efforts to survive and to make things better. The work experiences Weber envisioned extended her lifelong ideas about the necessary intergenerational and heterogeneous context of learning. In "Black or Multicultural Curriculum," they played out on a wider social stage and with insight into the contribution that young people make to adult life.

"Black or Multicultural Curriculum" represents an intensification of Weber's earlier work on how schools can allow children to be responsible and on what in their surroundings can give them a sense of what it means to contribute. In "Silent Child" (1976; see Part I) she had questioned, "What are the responsibilities children have in school? Are children part of the building of the school?" In "Education in the 80s" (1980), she talked about how children learn from being part of an ongoing adult enterprise, the maintenance of a home. By the time of "Moral Issues" (1982), the theme emerges in her comments on the community of the Open Corridor, where obligation and contribution could be visible in the common work of learning.

In "Black or Multicultural Curriculum" Weber expands these ideas by observing that, in countries she has visited that are governed by blacks, a sense of participation in defining the country creates space for individual self-definition and clearer thought about issues among its black citizens, an idea she took up again in "Inquiry" (Part I). She acknowledges the limitations of school as a place to address the devaluing in American schools. Indeed, she sees such acknowledgment by educators as a prerequisite for being mobilized and clear in seeking remedies. Her plan for retirement was to study modes of "following after" and "joining with" learning in Kenya and elsewhere here and abroad as means of exploring the situation of school limitation and devaluing, a plan cut short by a hit-and-run accident and subsequent ill health.

The selection of papers in this section, dealing with value for human beings and assumptions of alikeness around intelligence, culminate inevitably in "Black or Multicultural Curriculum." Weber was deeply committed to improvement of education for minority children. This motivated much of her work in the public schools. It permeates her writing. It was a feature of her overseas experiences and part of the pull that the Workshop Center exercised on visitors at home and abroad. At the same time, the minority experience was not usually her primary subject; in this re-spect "Black or Multicultural Curriculum" stands out in her writings, along with her essay "Adapting Classrooms for ALL the Children" (1979a), about mainstreaming.

Typically, Weber approached the minority experience as an aspect of inclu-siveness—what it means and what it takes to be inclusive of everyone, not just of a majority. She sought first the underlying commonality of humaness and human experience; difference within that commonality was far from difference latched onto as the primary and defining characteristic of a person or group. Often the greatest challenge to inclusiveness is presented by the experience of those who do not define the mainstream. It is in just this vein that "Black or Multicultural Curriculum" begins by describing the situation of black youth and goes on to suggest that all youth, and more, are at stake. Toward the end, she says that the lack of valuing of personal capacity and contribution for a large portion of the population is a trend worldwide.

The stance of inclusiveness was a starting point for analysis, a reference point for accomplishment, but it was not meant to spotlight the minority in an isolating, intrusive way. Instead, it opened up and unified many of the issues in education for all children, for all people, that were important to Weber. In an unpublished bio-graphical statement she wrote for City College use in December 1991, writing about herself in the third person, she identified these succinctly:

> Her current major interests, whether in science, language, or political stances, all have a coherence around advocacy of inclusion. . . . She speaks about com-mon phenomena, common experiences, and the power to understand and make sense of these experiences. She speaks about intelligence and teacher decision making and against teacher-proof materials. She speaks about di-versity and the strengths resulting from this diversity as these issues relate to schools and curricula. Of course, she also speaks against testing programs as being reductionist, narrow, and limited.

# CHAPTER 8

# *Education for Young Children in the 80s: An Excerpt*

*1980*

The basis for change in society, for learning from past experience, for teacher education, for adult growth, for parent education, is reversibility, not irreversibility—the possibility for assessment and reformulation. An issue for the 1980s is to remember and to reaffirm this human complexity, to not think that, because testing technology has proliferated, we're now in a position to say, "You tell us everything that is in the human." This is not possible.

## ACCEPTING DIVERSITY IN THE 80s

I work in the middle of Harlem. I work with a largely minority student body. This often is talked about as a *big problem:* Standards are going down! If you work at Hampton Institute you've been working with that kind of majority all the time, so *you* can't relate to it that way and *I* can't relate to it that way. The students I work with are survivors. They may be in their 30s and with a teenage child. They are, however, honor students, honorable by virtue of their survival but honorable, too, by virtue of the tremendous insights, wisdom, hard work, and dedication to being good teachers that they have. When people on airplanes have the nerve to ask me, "You teach at City College? Do they read there?" it is an incredible insult to the students. Students at City College bring a sophistication and knowledge about human beings and learning comparable to that found anywhere. It certainly hurts to see the growing poverty in New York City, and the meanness, and the garbage. These are problems that we have to fight. But don't for a minute also put the human beings there in the garbage pails.

The problem for today is acceptance of diversity and seeing diversity not as a deficit but as part of the human conditions that have allowed us, given us leeway, to evolve over thousands of years. That plasticity and diversity is precisely what we should treasure.

I am enjoined by lots of people, even by some of my faculty colleagues, who cut me off instantaneously, saying, "You know it's no longer the 60s." I don't think there is any way to go on in the 80s without one's roots, one's continuities, including the 70s and the 60s. Those same issues are indeed clarified by the struggles of the past decades. If you're alive today, the 60s and 70s are in your history and mine and we cannot forget it. If you forget, you're denying the human ability to remember and reassess and reformulate. I urge you: Don't forget!

I gather that other speakers brought out the positive gains of the 70s, but pointed out the coming problems of budget and stringency. More than budget and stringency, there is the issue of what's in our heads. There's so much talk about special characteristics, as though if they didn't exist there would be nothing to talk about. But we're talking about ordinary run-of-the-mill mothers, who are the majority; ordinary run-of-the-mill devoted teachers, that's the majority; and ordinary, run-of-the-mill children. I think we've been very captivated the last couple of years with extremes, and the broad continuum of the norm on which we rest has gotten short shrift—in budgets, support, and the belief in the common school.

John Gliedman (Gliedman & Roth, 1980) has said that the handicapped are partly handicapped by the social view of them. The question is, are they part of this species, with its species-characteristic asset—that all humans learn? You may say, "Oh, adult effort produces learning," but no amount of adult effort would make this table learn. Human grasp makes learning possible. Gliedman was pointing out that the mainstreaming law, which was meant to include the handicapped in the broad umbrella of humanness, to take away the "otherness," has taken an interesting variance, because the funding has imposed mass screening in which you don't look for the human species-characteristic capabilities in the handicapped; you look at all the population for what they *can't* do. You hold up Diogenes' lantern to find more handicaps, instead of using it to find, and to reinclude, all of those who have been excluded.

What I want to reinclude from the 60s and 70s is the consciousness of cultural pluralism and diversity as positive. The danger in the 80s, on all sides, is resegregation—segregation around competency tests and tests of all sorts; a schizoid reaction toward mainstreaming, which denies mainstreaming, denies the borderline that we all are, in the broad continuum of the norm, and the simple formulation that we are all imperfect in the sight of God, philosophically. All educative relationship to us is not to our imperfections but to our striving for our potential.

If you look at the way in which the mainstreaming law has been used in many parts of the country, you find that testing has been used as a resegregative tool rather than as a mainstreaming tool. I want to raise that as a problem for the 80s. There are lots of handicaps, lots of imperfections that we have that will perhaps never disappear, but a human being is so complex that it is not just that handicap that exists. There is a presupposition in testing and screening that you're going to find this "thing," like the child doesn't know a particular sound in a phonics scheme and then you're going to have a course of remediation for that very specific thing.

No one has pinned down yet in research the nature of a learning disability — this unknown, borderline thing that is now thrown into the pot as another segregative feature, as though it must be centered on rather than seen as one aspect of uneven, complex, tremendously diverse human beings who have hundreds of other strong aspects that could be worked on. I find that strange, when we have an enormous number of people in our population who are descendants of those who survived the Middle Passage, who survived the genocide of Indian tribes, who survived the Holocaust. The surround of the strong aspects that help you survive is denied, as though that perceptual difficulty, which is still quite undefined, is going to knock you over. The point of the mainstreaming law is to spread the boundaries of the broad continuum of the norm and to demand a look at every human being, not as a statistic of the broad continuum of the norm, but as that particular, specific human within it.

## ONLY ONE FIGHT—FOR THE HUMAN

In an educative relationship, it is incumbent on us to be aware of two aspects of the human — potentiality and specificity. There are, in my view, two groups within society that have a particular responsibility to that specificity of the child — the parents and the teachers. They are the day-to-day, hour-to-hour interacters, the ones who can say, "He'll take it in better if you do it this way," or "This is what she's interested in," or "He doesn't fall asleep right away. That's the way he is." I don't want to knock college professors, psychologists, evaluators, guidance people, but they are assistors to the primary relationship. Our society now, as we enter the 80s, has produced a situation in which teachers distrust themselves and search for teacher-proof materials or have such materials imposed on them, and to this extent they are abdicating their responsibility for applying the utmost of their intelligence as humans to their professional task. And when teachers distrust parents and act as though parents are a burden, as though there's something wrong with the parents and that's why there's something wrong with the child, they are denying the sense of the relationship.

It's a total denial of the sense of the educative relationship when a bibliography on typical and atypical language development for student teachers lists 38 volumes on atypical situations and 2 on normal language development. Ninety-nine percent of children acquire language informally, without lessons from those "dumb" mothers — and I do not mean for a second only from middle-class mothers. I mean from all mothers, all over the world, in all situations. Children cannot acquire language without the intergenerational setting. Children do acquire language, and without parents having a self-conscious technique about it. It is incumbent on us, as teachers, humbly to study that process, not to put down everything wrong that parents have done. The supreme point is that they've done it right. And they carry the continuity and memory for the child. Without that, nothing you do would count.

We cannot push "otherness" onto a piece of the population. We cannot think we're human, but the children are "those kids." We cannot think we are "it" and the parents are an "otherness." We cannot think this about any other culture or race. To the extent that we turn our children into examples of "otherness," quantified by scores showing deficit performance, we are diminishing ourselves. The children come from us. They are our children. We make ourselves vulnerable to being treated in exactly the same way, with teacher-proof materials, for example.

There is only one unified fight, not for children but for the human. I have discarded the fight for just children because I work with teachers and I see the tremendous battering of teachers from many people, including themselves. There is distrust that teachers are people who can observe, make decisions, make adaptations, take responsibility. I ask a teacher, "How's that child doing?" and she says to me, "How do I know? The tests haven't been given yet." That isn't an accurate view of what the teacher knows. She has dissociated her own judgment and trust of her own intelligence. We cannot do it to children, to parents, or to ourselves as teachers. It is one enterprise, and that is the reassertion of intelligence.

As I think of what happened in the late 70s, the biggest weakening in the fabric of allegiance to the common school and to the broad continuum of the norm was the weakening in belief in the educability of teachers and of the child. We got snowed by the tests, the screening, the "evidence" that money had been wasted. We got apologetic. We were willing to accept short shrift and low budgets, on the theory that the population was going down. If the population were going down and there were an honest view of education, we would have smaller classes. But in New York and other places, the population is said to be going down, yet we have classes of 40 now, instead of the classes of 30 that we had years ago. That's putting responsibility on the teacher and children. They're supposed to be apologetic, while the budgets are cut, not because of a lowering of the population but because of a short view of the child and of our future. Unless we go up in smoke, we are going to have a future and that future has to be protected with our advocacy and with our clear taking a look at what really is behind the short shrift.

Looking at children's development with confidence over time should win our advocacy. This view over time must be reinforced by remembering how we, too, were once children, which should give us an inner ear about research reports and innovations that are proposed and whether they ring true to what we know about human beings. If what's proposed is something we can't imagine at all, it should bring us back to looking again, and not accepting blindly.

Even as we think that in the 80s we're going to have hard times of budget stringency, the world picture is quite different. The countries with the resources are demanding a larger share from the countries that own the technology. It is not conceivable that we can act toward our own diversity as though it is all deficit, in this world picture of interdependent diversity. In the 80s this will be so. I think this schizoid relationship is necessarily a temporary one, if you look at the world picture and, indeed, at our own picture in this country. Our fight, as people on the side of young children, must be to try to ease the schizoid quality and to widen the continuum of the norm.

I have two sons and five young grandsons. As a grandparent, you get bigger about your view of flexibility and education. My grandsons join the going enterprise at home, and they know a whole lot about it. Their family isn't "child-centered," but the point is that the situation isn't totally closed; there are cracks for them. Even the old Victorian rigidity in child care perhaps afforded the children quite a bit of privacy and space, whereas today we go for child-centeredness but, oh, big brother's eyes are always supervising. Must we actually see what a child is doing all the time? There's a certain distrust that he couldn't breathe otherwise. As I think of my own childhood, I know very well that we had secrets from my parents, that we had spaces to hide. My mother had six children. She didn't want them around all the time. You did certain things while you were around her, but the idea was "Go!"

For young children who are in day care, for as long as 10 hours a day in some situations, I think we have to rethink whether we go for the school model, even a supportive and responsive one. We have to ensure that the home model is also in there. Think of the things that the child is missing. The child is missing being part of a situation where he helps its going. When my children were growing up, I had a fight with their school because there was too much homework. I'm not against homework but I felt that, since I was alone and had no help in the household, my sons also needed to be part of *home* work. They had to become responsible members of the cooperative household and help with the shopping and the dishes, not as a complete imposition but as an expectation of generous interaction. We live in households where this is even more the case today, where mothers or fathers are single parents, or both work enormously hard. It's a good thing if the child is included, as well as if he has some space and something to do himself.

My son's children feel part of a household. The meaninglessness of a test on this situation! In California, all the children got a test for "giftedness." My 8-1/2-year-old grandson Teddy tells me, "I'm not bright, Grandma." He says, "The children who are bright are going to have a wonderful school. And I might not have any." He thought he was out of the picture. I asked my daughter-in-law about this and she said, "Well Teddy didn't know his telephone number, the psychologist told me." Now, when Teddy's dog was sick, Teddy called the vet — his mother was in her office — and had it all managed before she ever got home. He's never had to call his phone number, because he lives at home. I think we ought to ask people what they *do* know instead of, in our infinite hubris and supposed wisdom, what we think they *ought* to know. We might get a different picture for ourselves, for parents and children.

We are as a species overendowed, instead of underendowed, to deal with the problems that come before us. People do rise in different ways, but what elicits the rising is the assumption of intelligence and the use of that. Human children learn language partly because they are confirmed in the meaning of the beginning sounds they make. The parent assumes intelligence and purpose and intent, and looks for the child's eye contact, gesture, outreach, and gives a name to that. The parent doesn't say, "Oh, he says 'ga,' so he must have difficulties in articulation and we better have some exercises in saying 'k —' instead of 'ga.'" The parent doesn't even hear that. The parent says, "Oh yes, you'll have a cookie very soon." And most of the child's language stabilizes and asserts itself within that.

The assumption of intelligence is a better basis for working with teachers, too. If teachers respect their own intelligence, and assume they have the capacity to make decisions based on it, then they will realize they know something about the world. How can you, as teachers, make any adaptations of your curriculum provisions if you know very little about what's possible within that provision? Knowledge of content is an obligation of the teacher's role. If a teacher has no knowledge of science, it's extraordinarily difficult to make adaptations on science provision. If the teacher has no knowledge of language (although everyone has some knowledge of language), the teacher's obligation is to search for further knowledge. . . .

Surrounded by threats, we still have children, we still have an inter-generational responsibility. We exist and we contribute, because we know more. We have an obligation to study, to know more, to contribute that expertise, but always with respect for that irreducible phenomenon — the complex human being who inquires, has expression, and communicates as part of his or her membership in the human species.

# CHAPTER 9

## *Moral Issues for Teachers*

*1982*

The moral climate in education emerges from the moral dilemmas that today confront teachers. I will not focus on the children as the agent of moral education but on the morality of the structures of education and the relationships of teachers and children within these structures. It is my belief that without this morality there is no moral education, and so I will center on the moral obligation to children.

### THE "I, TOO" OF COMMON HUMANITY

When I began my work in the public schools in 1967, the problems we found were *all* moral rather than strictly organizational. Indeed, the organizational forms that have been adopted in the Open Corridor only reflect our search to support better the moral attributes we thought central to the educational process. Both our critique and our work emerge from this view of attributes and from our concern with how these are or are not enacted by the schools. Much has been made of our stress on human uniqueness and difference, but it is important to know that we placed even more stress on commonalities, intelligence, inquiry, interaction, and communication as givens. We worked for support of these attributes through honesty of curricular content, respect for persons — teachers and children, the building of community between persons, and the encouragement of reflection on what was done.

Our work is often referred to as *open education*. It is in fact many years since I have even used the term. For one thing, its use was an accident resulting from my saying to teachers, "Why don't you leave your door open so that you can see what I do in the corridor?" What I meant was that we would look at how the environment could be made more accessible, so that, for example, the schools with signs that had said "Parents

May Go No Further" could be open to parents, who certainly had at least as much interest in the children as the teachers. I also meant that teachers who had their doors open might even be able to see what the next teacher was doing.

But the issue for us was not *open, closed, direct, indirect, formal, informal* — language inappropriate to express our meaning. Nor was it even a single mode, separate from the others. We soon realized that there are formal elements in any institution, though we try to maintain continuity with a child's earlier informal learning. Even in the home situation the indirect and informal exists along with direct statements — "Sit down." "Did you say thank you?" — statements all mothers make and that are inherent in their role as mentor. The real issue, we believed, was the denial of the child as an intelligent and active learner, a denial that is reflected in the almost complete dominance of the direct and formal mode in traditional education.

I work at City College, in the middle of Harlem. City College is as poor as the proverbial church mouse. Our "whys," the motivations for our work, come from the bitter realities of life that we see at City College. My framework has been, and remains, the framework of public, compulsory education. What does it mean to teach *all* the children? Can the modes of teaching poor children be allowed to function as denial of human attributes? of intelligence? Even my contact with the parochial schools in New York City has been around that issue. A request for help for teachers from the head of the parochial schools in the Manhattan Diocese was motivated by their engagement with the moral issue of school obligation to *all* the children, each one unique and different but all humanly capable, a moral issue raised by denial of this capability in past practice.

I began my work in the public schools in the midst of discussion that labeled children disadvantaged, particularly in language. It was not only often theorized that disadvantaged language was linked to limitation in thinking, but these discussions (by such education writers as Basil Bernstein and Carl Bereiter) affected the programs developed for schools by Martin Deutsch, Siegfried Engelmann, and others. These programs may have been different in emphasis, but all worked from the basic formulation that *these* children — children who were, of course, predominantly black or Spanish-speaking — had some sort of deficiency.

From my stance of 20 years of work with young children, some of whom had no, or almost no, language, I had to ask: Was it true they didn't think? Were "these" children so different from "those" children that specific prescribed approaches, discontinuous with their own life reality, were needed to initiate new patterns necessary for thinking? The various programs seemed to draw from a bank of propositions that weren't connected with an observed, experienced reality. These propositions also influenced the development of reading programs that called for competence in hundreds of separate skills. What children ever learned that way?

When we reminisced with over a hundred people about how they learned to read, some described their memory of learning with 4 skills, some with 6 skills, some actually remembered 10 skills. Returning over and over again to what we knew about children from our work or our life experiences, we could not help but conclude that the discrepancy was enormous between what we knew and what was practiced in the schools, as well as what was being developed in new programs.

The moral issue came to a head with new information from other places, such as England, about a different practice more supportive of children as we observed and knew them. If it was possible to do something about this discrepancy, then there was a moral imperative. I began to raise questions. How do you confront compulsory education? How do you confront widening access to public education? And above all, how do you do so from the stance of "I, too," of common humanity.

Our starting point had to be a belief in human intelligence. What's the point of being teachers if you don't believe in human intelligence? You'll say that's a nonsensical question, but it is the dilemma that confronts teachers today even more than in 1967. They are asked to teach in a climate where belief in the intelligence of the teacher and the educability of children, poor children particularly, is tremendously weak. We answered the earlier critique of the insufficient tie in teacher education between theoretical formulations and practice in the schools with an attempt to develop practice that matched better the accumulated knowledge and theoretical discussions of how children learn.

The current critique of teacher intelligence is far more virulent. The number of teacher-proof programs that exist today is far greater than in 1967. There are now hundreds and hundreds of programs in which thousands and thousands of dollars are spent on materials that assume teacher incapability in observation, ordinary knowledge, ordinary ability. The idea is promulgated that these teacher-proof materials, used robot-like, will help develop intelligent children. I do not think that is possible.

Our critique centered on the empty content in the formal classrooms. We will continue to point out inadequacies of content. Our commitment has been, and continues to be, for more intelligent content. That is not to say that all our work in open classrooms has been good, but it is what we strive for, what we consider a moral commitment: You interact with children with the best of your intelligence; you believe in your intelligence; and you believe your commitment is to stretch your intelligence.

Our view of teacher education cannot include the sense that teachers' growth can be finished. Inherent in our view of teachers' intelligence is a belief in the continuousness of the teachers' reach toward understanding and that it is a reach that can never be final. We can *think* about our reaches; we can reflect on them. We can point to how far we have gone and we can stretch this further. Since there is an infinite complexity that we can never fathom, there is no end. I find this exciting. Some people say, "Oh, how fatiguing!" I say, "All you have to do is to look into the classrooms where the teachers are using teacher-proof materials and you will find the data for 'burnout,' stress, enervation." How can live human beings be treated as dummies and not become exhausted? I may be exhausted, but I'm exhausted with exhilaration, thinking about this wonderfully complex world of common materials that can be looked at and relooked at and in which, when I do this, I am joining with and learning from scientists, mathematicians, writers, and artists, past and present, who all relook and reformulate.

As an example, the book we are using this summer at the Workshop Center — Peter Stevens's *Patterns in Nature* (1974) — discusses some of the tremendous diversity in the world as well as the tremendous commonalities. It is a book on the physics of everyday phenomena, a book to draw our attention to what we are doing when we handle sand or water, or look at spirals, turbulence in air or water, how space is filled up, and how plain, common materials unevenly pressured fit within space. I include this example because inevitably when you talk about open education, since the content is less prescribed, there is controversy about its content or whether indeed there is *any* worthwhile content.

From early on in our work, we realized that enriching content required more than the addition of materials to the environment. It required a stretch in the teacher's conception of content and of learning. As the teacher prepared for classroom work, her decisions involved judgments on the validity of the content and on the link to the learner. What *was* the process of linking content and learner? Questions about children's interest and concentration, about how interest is sustained, began to be discussed. What constituted a question for inquiry anyway?

We found that even to begin to understand these issues, teachers had to reexperience their own learning. They had to realize, through unpackaging the loopholes in their own understanding, that common materials were inexhaustible as content sources. They had to see content not as neat sequential packages that could be opened for a specific time and then considered finished. They had to see the links and analogies — around persistent questions that were certainly not trivial — between a formulation in one field and one in another field. They had to see this through their own experiences. Such experiencing of their own learning helped them see content more broadly and thematically, helped them more easily recognize the pertinence of the child's question to *broad* questions that recurred again and again and so should not be dismissed as wrong or right but related to with recognition and connection. Such broad questions — about conditions of growth, about perspective, about size and scale — cut across subject areas and grade levels. Teachers could recognize the specificity of the child's interest and could expand and extend it because of their own expanded understanding of connection.

In addition to being dedicated to stretching our understanding and resources in curriculum content generally, our efforts are to understand reading in particular. In the early years of our work we were well aware of great worry about children's reading and we made every effort to stretch our understanding of their reading process. Thus, for the first four years, the staff studied, on a regular basis, material from noted psycholinguists and reading specialists like Kenneth Goodman, Frank Smith, Vera John, Edward Chittenden, Anne Bussis, Marianne Amarel, Courtney Cazden, Amity Buxton, Moira McKenzie, and others. We met with them and discussed the controversies in the field. Sometimes we joined their research on how reading competence is acquired by children in situations where more than one approach was acknowledged as possible (Bussis et al., 1985). That doesn't mean that we know all the answers, or even half of them, but we know more than we did and our commitment is to continue examining.

We continue to engage with experienced teachers in the study of reading process. As a result we are able to discuss reading with principals in such a way that for 3 years now we haven't even been asked, "Don't you care about reading?" They know we care about reading. We can now critique what we see of others' work and what we do in our own work. Of course, we critique a school day in which 90% of the day is spent on 500 phonics skills. In such a classroom there may not even be time for reading. Indeed there are many classrooms where there's almost no time for reading, for discussing the reading, for thinking about or for communicating about the reading. There may be almost no time for the child to internalize a strong belief that written text can be understood and that he or she, too, can understand it. So even our view of reading has been for us a moral issue, one again centered around intelligence because, of course, our view holds that reading cannot be divorced, even in the initial stages of acquisition, from context, meaning, or its function in communication.

Our kind of work, with its stress on intelligence and meaning, has met with only minimal support from educational institutions. It has been tolerated, invited in only part of the time for work with children labeled "disabled" or, interestingly enough, even for work with the gifted! Oh, but for the vast range of the ordinary run-of-the-mill normal children, the official attitudes do not encourage perceptive, adaptive teaching. Here the official attitudes are punitive—a demand for "tough" treatment, more work, discipline, and going "back to basics," often with a further demand for more drill. These demands are often interpreted as being demands for the improvement of the moral climate in schools.

Our view is that toughness and discipline in work are empty terms without the basic interactions being centered around meaning in content, with respect for the child that assumes intelligence and the capability of understanding meaning. Our view is that there is no way to bypass the imperative on the teacher, in relating to *any* child, to make appropriate adaptations of learning materials and plans as children's need for them is observed in their individual use of the materials. Indeed, it is our view that these adaptations, these decisions by the teacher based on observation, *spell out* the role of the teacher. They presume intelligence. So we consider attacks on teacher intelligence and demands for teacher-proof materials that eliminate all need for teacher decision making immoral, a *denial* of moral obligation. In no way can such demands *improve* moral climate.

As I've described, we never left "the basics" ourselves. What we wanted was just to have more intelligence in the content and presentation to children of these basics. We assumed that reading was important and focused our concentration on it. We assumed that writing was important and not only never left it, we joined with and used all the newer programs that encouraged writing in the context of communicative intent and meaning. To help further our understanding and our ability to help teachers stretch their understanding and make their curricular resources more flexible, we sought out mathematicians, scientists, artists. I have not been intimidated by the demand for basics. I have not been intimidated by the critiques that point to imperfection in our efforts. How could our efforts be worse than what was being done in the narrow prescribed programs that made no demands on teacher intelligence?

No, the moral statement is not a statement guaranteeing perfection. The moral statement that releases courage is "I'll try. I'll try." What kind of moral statement is it to look at failure—and I'm talking about the inner-city situation—to look at the very bad things happening, and say, "Well, I too might fail, what I do might also be imperfect, so therefore I won't even try." The point is that you learn in the doing. I don't mean learn in the doing by doing blindly. You learn in the doing, in reflecting on your doing, and making adaptations in your formulations.

And so we developed organizational forms precisely to heal the blindness, organizational forms that made what was done far more visible and thus encouraged a deeper reflection and more pertinent adaptation. Children were not really visible in the traditional classroom or at least what was visible to the teacher was a very narrow range, basically only the child's attention to or response to the teacher's question, often a question prescribed by the curriculum. When the teacher related to children sitting as a whole class, she could *see* very little. You notice that I catch an eye here and an eye there. I can't see everybody and I see very little about anybody. All I can see is whether you're looking or not looking. That is the formal classroom. In our enriched and decentralized classrooms children were doing more things and so they were more visible. We could understand them better. We began to learn. But to be willing to flubdub, to flounder, in the middle of a public situation, knowing that you don't know much about organization or content, takes courage. It was so easy to say, "The classroom is so dirty; they don't even know how to take care of animals."

## IMPLEMENTING THE OBLIGATION TO TRY

There was indeed much we didn't know in 1967. But the organizational arrangements that made our errors more visible were also the basis for flexible solutions. When a parent said very quietly, "Have you thought what to do about the dirt?" we said, "You've been keeping house for quite a while. Why don't you come in and help us?"

Even what we were about became more visible to us and to others. Harlem parents, after observing us, said, "You're not doing so much! You're only keeping their mother wit going. That's all." Such remarks helped us further clarify our thoughts on the role of the teacher. Of course it was not to test the child to see *does* he have mother wit; our role was to *assume* mother wit and to go on from there. That assumption is an a priori judgment, not subject to the kind of analysis and testing that is going on all the time now.

And about that testing: "Does the child have mother wit?" "Does the child inquire?" "Does the child read?" As though we need an external appraiser on each thing the child does! We *may* need an external eye when we are unable ourselves to understand, but I think we are making a big mistake when we put every aspect of our functioning, our humanness, or that of children in the hands of testers. We are in a period when testing is increasing, but its increase cannot be said to result from *teachers'* feeling that they can't relate to the child's need without this guidance. Testing is big business, an easy way to respond to public demand for accountability, imposed in an outright denial of the validity of teachers' observation or of other ways of documenting a child's progress. There are now more teachers and parents, even more evaluators, restive about continuing the mistake of delegating decision making to testers. And, just as the child's capability has become more visible in our changed classrooms, the confidence and capability of the teacher to observe and make decisions based on these observations have grown and added fire to the critique of testing.

There were other things that we ended up thinking about with somewhat different emphasis as a result of being able to see our work and its consequences. As teachers struggled with the notions that they assumed to be at the core of the work—that children are unique individuals and that the goal was to develop continuity with the earlier indirect and informal process—the difficulties of such formulations became evident, and we quickly helped them modify their assumptions. Teachers were bothered by questions about their role in the classroom organized to reflect such notions. Could they provide 30 different activities for 30 separate individuals? Was their intergenerational role entirely to provision the environment for individual uniqueness? What kinds of activities might appropriately be organized around a small group or even the whole group? What general curricular experiences might the teacher be expected to offer as age-appropriate, or even in response to societal expectations? Where did communication, language, or, for that matter, any kind of interconnection fit in?

It was obvious that this interpretation of underlying conception and consequent role was wrong. Rather, the conception was a matter of multiple response to variables—to uniqueness *and* commonality, to the indirect *and* the direct mode of learning, to formal structure *and* structure that allowed for informality in relationship. Of course, each of us is unique, but we are also human men and women, with attributes that define us as human though each one different. Commonalities as well as differences had to be stressed and the building of interactive communities in which teachers and children could live and work well became prime in our work. That indeed was the *reason* for the organizational form called Open Corridor.

Another error of interpretation about our classrooms could easily have been corrected through observation of how they actually functioned, but it is still repeated by many writers. The allegation is that children "do whatever they want." In the first place, we have worked within partial change, within a basically unchanged, highly negative and hostile system. Obviously the children don't do whatever they want. Only a little bit of space has been created. But even if our changes were less partial, has our thinking ever supported the notion of "whatever the child wants" as possible or desirable? The child lives with adults who are in an intergenerational educative relationship of obligation derived from their greater experience of both possibility and consequence. What is added to this relationship for the teacher by societal definitions of educative need is put on the teacher as an obligation, prescriptively or at least as offerings she must make available. Also, children live with other children, who are interested in, interact with, and learn from each other's work. Here again, community, interaction, and respect set the parameters for the question of "want," as they do for the questions of individual and unique.

We related to curriculum as well as to community. We could not discuss the child's "wants" without discussing desirability and what is educative or not educative. We think such judgments are obligatory, inherent in the nature of the adult–child relationship. Thus the teacher, as adult, is presumed to have greater experience and knowledge of the possibilities for further development of the content provided. Though each teacher in *fact* is different in this knowledge of possibilities, as a public servant he or she is obligated at least to reach for the further knowledge that can support these judgments for the individual and for the group.

The question is an integral aspect of John Dewey's discussion of interest in *Interest and Effort in Education* (1913/1970). The Froebel Institute's *The Teaching of Young Children* (Brearley, 1969) discusses it in terms of judgments on the ephemeral or trivial in curricular provision. But what is ephemeral or trivial? The judgment is not so simple, because to a particular child any bit or piece may be of significance in making the connection that for him or her furthers understanding. But, as the teacher develops the classroom environment or plans for curriculum, there is necessarily selection, and it is the teacher's understanding of connection that governs this selection.

At the Workshop Center, our work has centered around broadening the range of the teachers' connections to help their recognition of the validity of the child's bits and pieces and their flexibility to respond to these. We try to change the present climate of insufficient excitement about curriculum. We try to get past the use of limited time units in the treatment of content. Through their work at the Center, teachers begin to see, in great variation of form and complexity, similar recurrent and persistent questions in all contexts and at all grade levels, for example, the question of size and scale in the Grimms' fairy tales of the little tailor and in personal and historical stories of human struggle. They begin to see this question in looking at sand and rock, in examining solutions and concentrates, in examining questions of containment and area.

In our analysis, the questions of children's "wants" and of the teacher's role in response can be discussed *only* in the context of the teacher's obligation to reach for an ever-expanding bank of possible response, of the teacher's understanding of the complexity that is contained in the idea of response. Both teacher and child have to engage with the romance of the complexity in all things—the small miraculous "seeings" acknowledged, and the link to important questions currently engaging scientific thought made. Both content itself and *how* content is connected with by any single child are questions for teachers' work. The tensions between the unique construction of knowledge by each individual that Piaget talks about and the inheritance conveyed by the expertise and knowledge of the adult teacher cannot be avoided. These we see as inescapable realities of the teacher's work, additional to the hard realities of the institutional frame in which they work.

The reality of multiple variables and complexity makes mere provision for, or supportive response to, a child's interests inadequate. The issue is perhaps more accurately formulated as one of the teacher's "interest in" rather than "support for" children's interests. Useful response by a teacher is possible only under conditions of teacher development that *enable* response. Our approach has been, again, less separately individual. We assumed provision for specific and individual interests, but also that what individuals did was "interesting to" each other and that the context of "interesting to" needed support from the teacher's "interest in," an interest that must be genuine, and based on the teacher's genuine perceptions of possible connections. The teacher's interest in draws children to be interested in, and in this process what occurs, as viewpoints are shared, is not only a widening of each person's perspectives about what is interesting, but also respect, regard, a growth of empathy—an extension beyond self to other.

Over and over again the visibility of our work has resulted in greater awareness of the variables I've described and in regrouping these in support of even stronger definition and conceptualization of what was inherent in our work. Thus, our valuing of teacher intelligence has also been valuing of the individual energy released by the teacher's voluntary decision to engage. Our valuing of the individual implies a positive valuing of the interaction of differences and of heterogeneity. In the context of these values, we have helped teachers with the imperatives of their role as spelled out by their adultness and their public responsibility. We helped them reflect more intelligently on the nature of their content offerings, plan more intelligently, and keep records with the purpose of aiding their reflective process. We have helped teachers to awareness of their own growth and, in school relationships, of the growth of those around them.

The greater visibility of social relationships in the Open Corridor schools resulted in new emphases in our work with parents. We made an effort to learn from and with parents, quite different from the previous context of "educating" them. We became more humble in our stance toward parents. Particularly as our focus on language interacted with the new closeness of relationship to parents, what we already knew about the primacy of the parent role in language acquisition began to press on our commitments and decision making with greater urgency. We could not bypass bilingualism or our commitment to support children's connection with their mother tongue. With children more visible, we saw the language assessment for bilingual placement as limited and narrow, and we became even more vigorous in our critique of single-dimension evaluation.

Working with parents in this new closeness, we began to see how much more parents knew about living with difference, about continuity and transitions, about accommodations. With parents and teachers, we began to compare and contrast the long time span of home relationships with the limited time frame of the classroom and to understand how that limited frame impacts on decision making in schools. It is from the stance of the limited time frame of the classroom that educators have dared to say "this child is this way," to categorize, select, label, and place. We have tried to stretch teachers' understanding of the complexity of human growth and extend their view at least a bit beyond the 9 months of the school year. It is not that teachers can take on the unconditional commitment of the parent, but teachers *should* take on their own responsibilities with as much intelligence as possible.

Nor do I present these considerations as imperatives solely for informal teachers. What I've been talking about are children and teachers generally. Even in the mess that is so prevalent around us, even though the hard realities are so difficult, there are hundreds and even thousands of teachers who have accepted the obligation of looking at themselves and at the child from the stance of belief in human capacity and at least trying, even if only in a beginning way. Among these many teachers, all different in what they have accumulated as curricular resources, all different in the flexibility and appropriateness of their adaptations, an amazing number have found that the concrete walls of constraining regulation are not quite as hard as they thought. They find cracks that give room for beginning efforts. They find some principals who are interested and supportive.

The imperatives are there for all teachers to enact, in spite of the tension between the hard realities of institutional constraints and the teachers' efforts to put into practice what they may have come to understand. It may be even harder because institutional constraints are constraints even on the teachers' efforts to understand. Certainly, given this tension, both practice and idea are found in many stages of development, showing differences that result from bending to constraints, as well as from variations in understanding.

Yes, hard realities or not, I simply see no way out of it—we have no choice but to try. There is the learner and there is content. Contempt for the world is contempt for content. Contempt for the learner is contempt for humans. The two things go together. And so we have worked to create classrooms in which an individual was visible and in which regard for and interest in what others are interested in could grow. In such classrooms, content, what the learners are interested in, *and* the learners are central. And so I say that our critique of the match of institutional provision with human capabilities has been a critique of the morality of the institution. And all the things we have done and continue to do have been efforts to develop in the classroom a climate of morality.

The demand on all of us to *use* ourselves intelligently, to consider respect for each and all persons an imperative on our actions, is perhaps *the* moral statement for educators, one we reflect on, consider, and reconsider; one we try and try again to realize.[1]

## NOTE

1. As she often did, Weber concluded her talk with an account of the work by others on the issues she was discussing that she had found stimulating. She mentions Dewey, Piaget, Nathan Isaacs (specifically Isaacs, 1957), as well as Ashton-Warner and Natalie Cole. Closer to home, she also cites Vito Perrone's work in North Dakota schools, the film of Kenneth Haskins's school, "I Ain't Playin' No More" (Leitman, 1977), and Patricia Carini's work on observation and recording, specifically *The Art of Seeing and the Visibility of the Person* (1979).

# CHAPTER 10

# Black or Multicultural Curriculum: Of Course — But What More?

*1990–1993*

I've been concerned by the direction taken by the discussion of problems of black youth in the schools. It seems to have centered on criticism of limitations in the current curriculum. The basic response is to suggest that a black curriculum is needed. More recently there are proposals for all-black — even for all-black *male* — schools. I've been concerned as to the implications of these proposals and to what extent such responses are, even for what is a beginning point in planning, adequate to these problems.

## FIRST COMES VALUING

Before you can talk about or plan for a black context, one has to look at what the lives of these young people in schools add up to. What seems to me to be often the case is that there is *nothing* about the presence of black youth (particularly males) in schools that is valued. That presence is looked upon, fearfully, as a problem, something to be discarded, gotten rid of. Certainly the tone used while referring to black youth is of overwhelming encumbrance and bother, and even worse than bother. These reactions of nonvalue dominate the context of search or of suggestions for amelioration. Therefore, my approach to all proposals for amelioration starts with asking whether what is proposed can relate amelioratively to this overwhelming situation of devaluation or nonvalue. Does the proposal provide value additionally to the participant's existence? Is any good meaning given to the membership of that participant in the school?

To say this — to confront the reality of the situation — is for me of such enormous consequence and is so overwhelming that I have to stop and disregard all discussion of curriculum to go still further into this question. Not only are these persons, black youth, felt to have no value to the school, but they are felt to have no value to the whole of society.

This judgment of persons really goes past *black* youth to the even larger grouping of young people "at risk." In fact young people all over the country are at risk of not *ever* becoming adults who are considered capable of contributing to the society. For those young people — and the largest proportion is counted among the black youth, for whom there is no conception at all that they are going to be contributing to the society — I have to ask what *is* the role of the school and even *is* there any? Defining the role of the school as preparer for college participation as it currently exists certainly is not related to realistic possibilities for the largest number of these young people, and the school has assumed no other role, or done so so minimally that it is unnoticeable. And so what dominates is the sense of nonmembership, of nonvalue.

Looking at how this group fits into the larger society, the prospect is of no jobs, and since jobs and self-identity are closely linked, the denial is overwhelming. The assumption is constantly made that the situation of no jobs is a result of this group's lack of capacity. This is the major explanation offered for their lack of full and motivated participation in the school — an assumption in itself increasingly questionable. The lack of provision of jobs, of a means through which the young people can contribute to the society, is so pervasive and so overwhelmingly the case that one can't hold this fact against the youth or see it as resulting solely from their actions. One can't put the blame for the no-jobs on those who have no jobs and say, "Well, see, they dropped out or they weren't motivated. If they had not dropped out and if they had been motivated, there would have been jobs." *That* is what is *very* questionable. It is increasingly questionable right now, when the projection is of a couple of million persons who *have* jobs, and who are adults and *do* contribute to the society, looking forward to losing their jobs. And so how can the situation even be discussed in that fashion and in terms of youth failure?

Additionally, many of the black youth in this group live without provision for decent housing, spaces for interaction with each other in any useful way, or provision that allows for any engagement with the larger society or for remaking this nonfunctional environment, even in a volunteer way. In the early 1970s, when I suggested that schoolchildren could be involved in improving the outdoor space of schools — the playgrounds and the corridors — and could do some of the maintenance to improve *their* context, *their* environment, so that it would be more useable, immediately there was an outcry: Such involvement would be an interference with existing jobs; the unions would certainly object; the engagement of children in remedying the environment would be an attack on the jobs of the adults.

I certainly don't reject many of the suggestions that come up in the discussion of black curriculum. Many are worthy, and attempt to remedy the inadequacies that have long existed in the provision of historical description and historical knowledge, not only for those whose history has been ignored but also for anybody who attends the schools. The proposals urge that the historical figures, the heroes of the black population, be present in the schools, that their contribution to what has happened in the United States as well as the world be present. Of course, there should be no question on that. One hears it and says, "Absolutely, this is certainly something that should be for everybody. It might reduce the racism, recognized or unrecognized, of the white kids, who are totally without knowledge of these black heroes who have been part of exactly what has happened in their country, even to them, the white youth." Certainly it is a deprivation to the black young people not to have these past heroes present and alive as referent points for their thought and action.

But in what way does that needed presence of past heroes contribute as remedy to the present situation of black young people—a situation in which their presence in schools seems to be meaningless and surrounded at all points by lack of positive effects? What purposes or goals can be defined in the midst of such meaninglessness? Indeed, is or can anything about the presence of the black youth be seen to be of value? Their presence is certainly not appreciated as valuable by the many authorities whose decisions shape the school arrangements. For such pervasive judgments of valuelessness the proposed solutions are too minimal, too small a remedy, even though needed. They are fine; they should have been done ages ago. One can say they are of benefit. But they will not sufficiently impact on this other situation of abyss in the relationships of valuing.

I do not particularly join the criticisms of the proposals for all-black male schools. Certainly the criticism of such proposals as a renewal of segregation arrangements are specious in the presence of the de facto reality that all, or almost all, black schools are the result of housing patterns and also of fixed economic realities. Perhaps, in an all-black male school, the organization of the school and the appreciative values can be freer to recognize the realities of the population of the school and to carry out better the educational obligation of support for development of capacity.

I have taken on the obligation to weigh and to explore these proposed remedies since I participate in groups that criticize themselves for this pervasive school atmosphere of failure and rejection and seek to make things better. These professional groups, largely white, reflecting the dominance of the white population in this country, acknowledge that failure in so substantial a part of school population cannot be ignored and represents for them a failure in their own performance of obligation to each and to the whole. In this context I join the discussion, but with concern and critique of a certain weightlessness, a triviality, in what is put forward in it.

The fact is that the *society is* white-dominated. The choices, the statement of the problems, the characteristics of every aspect of the society that frames the life of everyone within it, reflect the dominance of the white group. And this overriding frame of white dominance sets the context even for the fairly sizable portion of the black population who are said to have "made good." What a tribute to their endurance, their ability to survive, their basically enormous intelligence, which has had to function under such handicaps of derogation! One says that if a young black man makes good as a lawyer or the like he probably had to be, in a large, measurable dimension, better than the white kid who made good, because the success has been in spite of enormous handicaps. And yet the pride of success is certainly not of the recognition and acceptance of one's *own* definition but of success in the joining of the white society—*its* definitions, its shape, its values. Again, there is devaluation of self, of roots, even in the midst of success. That doesn't mean that a piece of definition—personal definition—isn't retained both within the family and in small groups, that awareness doesn't exist that success is the result of tremendous strength of personal character and intellect and that this awareness isn't also a pride in race. Nevertheless, the broad statement can be made that the expectation is that those who "make good" must join the society defined in the way of the dominating society. It is under these conditions that if they are "good," and if there are *lots* of surplus jobs around, then they probably can "make good."

The difference in quality of personal valuing became apparent to me after only a half-hour in an African airport. I saw clearly a whole realm of difference in this society where the dominance was not of the whites. This was a *society* of blacks, the black society participating and shaping and defining. This difference was obvious even though within the black society the economic structure may in fact be dominated by the major white world society. The difference was obvious even within the fact of hierarchical classifications of blacks. Certain definitions were shared in a way that is almost never true in our black–white society without imposition and devaluing. The space for self-definitions and decision making—politically, economically—for stating of problems and issues was apparent, it was there. It became evident to me that this burden of taking on another framework than your own as the price of membership was *not* there, or certainly *less* there. What seemed clear to me was that without this burden of being nonparticipant in decision making or of having a very secondary role in decision making, whether primary or secondary decision making, and without the burden of exclusion from formulation of the problems and issues, thinking was and could be clearer, less impeded, less encumbered.

Understanding how this framework of determination by "another" acts to burden existence, and I believe very deeply that it does impact in this way, is essential to any and all solutions. In this context, I see the whole role of the school as secondary solution. Indeed, within this white-dominated society, which is the locus of our solution making, I don't think the school can really solve this problem in a complete fashion.

Nevertheless, since I am committed by my profession to work to make things better, to enable the flowering of capacity, I *must* seek for solutions, even if they are partial. Those efforts I would want to apply to confronting the issues of valuing, because I think that perhaps through this confrontation one can create a space for *some* valuing, a chance for *some* contribution. Anything short of that, of at least "some," is not adequate. If the talk is of black curriculum without confronting the question of valuing and contribution, then it is only a skin, a surface, without roots and unattached to the real cancer. When I think about these problems, I think I would want to offer — for all young people, but certainly for young people who have not had a chance to feel their own value and their own contribution — an approach that confronts the existence of value — even if my approach is said to be visionary. Let it at least *be* visionary.

I think we limit ourselves if we say, "Well that's how the school is," and then work out little frameworks of adjustment that will only make the situation a *little* bit better. We have to do that anyway, of course, because we're pledged to help *this* person in *this* period of time at *this* moment of history and so we can't say, "That's not the whole of my vision." So yes, we do the best we can. But we have to also have a vision of where it *should* be, of where we can go forward, of where it *might* go, because maybe some of that, difficult as it is to make actual and limited as it is, in my way of thinking, because of the impact of political and economic dominance by "another," still might reframe enough so that the burden of what is rejecting would be less.

## VALUING BUILT ON OPPORTUNITIES FOR CONTRIBUTION

For these young people, or for any young people of high school age, the schooling that is offered cannot be just preparation for a future. The school has to offer ways of *current* contribution, ways of being a partner.

And it has to offer risk. There has to be a real life of worth. The only experiences of loyalty and of "following-after" cannot be just through membership in street gangs. There has to be a feeling that without you this school wouldn't work, without you this classroom wouldn't work, without you the lunchroom wouldn't work, without you . . . , without you . . . , without you. . . . And it has to be *true* — the real thing. And, of course, such loyal participation and identification do not flower in a context that offers only the compulsions and mentoring involved in the imposed necessity and anticipation of taking a test. That can be *part* of the context but, for many, taking the test will not produce the identification and membership of a willing "following-after."

In order to revive the inner estimate of self-worth in a group that has been looked at like garbage, something else must be present. There must be a sizable number of adults in the school, in the neighborhood, in the society, who feel that the presence of the youth is a necessary part of *their own* existence, their own identification as an adult. They must feel it is obligatory as part of their *jobs* to be mentor, to be including, to be educator, to share the ownership of knowledge, to embrace and value the apprentice as contribution to their own adult identification. The adults may act on this only one-tenth of the time, but they *have* to accept that a major implication of being born in an intergenerational world is that they have to take on apprentices, as they themselves were taken on when they were growing up. This activity does not have to be the whole life of the young person or the whole life of the adult, but an interdependent relationship must be there.

I am proposing that if every young person had even one month a year that was real in this fashion, a time when he or she was valued because of the context of contribution in which he or she was functioning, some real change might occur in the relationships of valuing. I am proposing that the functioning of the young person had best be in a real job that is both respected and paid for — so that the participation in doing this, and doing it well, would be recognized. Of course, what must be simultaneously recognized is that a part of the mentor's pay is in recognition that expertise is being transmitted to someone else.

Recognition of the worth of such participation, the power and energy of such an experience, would allow for a period of preparation for the job: "Let's see what's needed for the job you say you'd like to help with. These are the things you have to know and this is how to do them. If you're going to be my assistant cashier or my assistant bank teller or my assistant whatever, you're going to have to know these things. So let's have a quick review. Then, after you've finished your work stint, you're going to have to help the next group of assistants get started; you're going to have to tell them about it and prepare some of the material to tell them about it, because I will have to pick up some other piece of work." I see the work as multifaceted, no matter what it is — involving a choice, preparation, work, and assistance to the next group of choosers.

Now let us look at the things that could be done and that need doing. John Kenneth Galbraith (1958/1976) once suggested that all the things we use in society need an enormous amount of citizen input that cannot be figured entirely on the market economy: parks need this, hospitals, schools, bridges. What is now called the "infrastructure" — about which people say "See, it's crumbling" — ought to have the input of young people who are going to live in this society and who do live in this society and can contribute and should be paid for their input and contribution. A different view of mentor or teacher is needed. Let's say that part of any day of a construction worker — say 2 hours of his 8-hour day — is set aside for taking on, seriously, two assistants from whom he demands good work. And that expectation is an expectation from all adult workers.

This is a very different vision from one of only past heroes. To rely only on past heroes to make up for the vacancy of no jobs is impossible. That proposition is really so lethal that it has been suggested that to kill off these disenfranchised, jobless youth immediately would be kinder. The alternative is to accept and ensure that they are participants in our society. As participants in our society they have to be valued and therefore I think that you have to say, "The subway beds need to be cleaned up, a very risky job. Two people can go with the worker. They're old enough to take that risk if they choose it voluntarily." Think of the risks they take walking on the edge of roofs, killing themselves no less. Some may be injured doing risky work, but at least they will have felt that they contributed something and they will be honored for this as the heroes of the present day. The Guardian Angels, the Hispanic group who were protecting subway passengers from crime, offered something of this, with all its troubling possibilities of vigilantism. It wasn't shooting at another kid who already was down because he's garbage. No, it was they who live in the community undertaking partly the job of protecting the community.

And so I say take the subway tracks and the whole host of things that the society needs but doesn't pay for (not just doesn't pay unionists for, doesn't hire anybody for). Gradually, as everything falls to pieces, give the jobless youth the dignity of labor, of labor as contribution, and labor that has to be done well. And say, "There are things to find out about before you start. There will be things to sum up and to reflect on before handing on the responsibilities." Onto that kind of success add the black curriculum as suggested, plus preparation for a future of contributing as a black doctor or lawyer in a black neighborhood, and soon it begins to become a reality. It can have no reality whatever while it verges on the conception that "You're all garbage."

I say this harshly because I think it is the only way. Anything else is that you're offering an interesting curriculum to middle-class blacks or whites who will find it quite interesting, like an anthropology course. That's nice. I think such a course should be offered. But it cannot possibly be a sufficient solution to emptiness. Nothing I'm offering is a *real* solution. But it is at least more.

The social services — the hospitals and community centers — offer involvement of another kind. They don't have enough volunteers by miles, and they need exactly the kind of assistance I have described. These jobs are not so risky, but perhaps the group of young people who seek them are a little bit younger, 12- to 13-year-olds, in contrast with the 14- to 16-year-olds who very especially need to be heroes and to assume risk. Then I think that you have the things that are in a neighborhood, where the contribution is that you attend tenants' meetings and contribute where you can in what the discussion brings up. When I was in China, I remember, the children from 10 up assisted the farmers, in the couple of weeks of the summer term or the spring term. I remember a movie about Kenya or Tanzania in which the children are asked by the community to help with something: with building, with the setup for clean water filtration, and so forth. They help with what we would call community jobs.

The real risk jobs around maintaining the infrastructure and the community social service jobs add up to a sizable number of jobs, where young people can certainly begin to have some sense of contribution. Ed Farrell, in his book *Hanging In and Dropping Out* (1990), discusses how important it is that the work kids do be something that is seen to have value and *is* a real contribution. If it isn't, it's nonsense. It is out of such real contribution that you can build community loyalty, valuing, and identification.

All this assumes that all the kids *have* instincts for loyalty and bravery and not being "chicken" and can share, through such work, a definition of being human, a man or a woman. The issue is whether we give the expressions of group loyalty and contribution meanings where they have real value. If we can't, then what? Do you build more prisons? The choice must be that clear. I am presenting the idea of a hero as something that needs to be rethought in these terms. It's not just the risky jobs that I've talked about that could be available for some of the older kids who are adventurous and want to do that, but the idea of doing jobs that need that kind of commitment and the idea of ordinary people doing ordinary jobs as being heroes. That is the thing that you really want to emphasize.

The older kids still in school, the ones in middle school, should be able to take on the maintenance of the school as assistants. I think that in giving young people and then still younger children this experience of being assistants from whom good work is demanded, you will be giving them both value and a chance for contribution and therefore an experience of being valued.

Around this you build other things that are needed. You say, "Well the person who minds the electricity in this place needs to know this and this. And, if you're assistant to the cook, then this is what's needed. If you're asked to divide the pie into six, you have to know how to do that and what that means." This is not a drill for knowing something with no attachment to use or meaning. It is quick work with the expectation of getting it done because something else has to be done, like a father in a home who says, "Hurry up. I have to get this done, because I need to do that as well," or "I'm painting the garage — you can't dawdle around there. You have to come and help me quickly." That isn't an all-day thing at home, and it wouldn't be an all-day thing as I'm projecting it. It doesn't push out the need for the young people to be making, in play fashion, projections with their own graphs or recounting how something works. But it gives a piece that takes him or her out of the framework of being an encumbrance and an intrusion into the institution that you have them in. If black youth are regarded solely as an encumbrance and an intrusion, then to keep them in the situation is on the level of cruel and unusual punishment. To keep them in the situation at all, we have to figure entirely differently. So I'm asking for an approach that is not within the usual school system, but neither does it imply that you're taking the whole thing away. You're taking part of it away and giving a chance for regard by the building of additional meanings.

Within this approach, the adults and the older young people who are participating *must — must —* have very clear the notion of citizenship, of membership in a neighborhood. And therefore their contribution has to be also to their community. An empty lot full of garbage can be used by the young people in the school as an additional outdoor space and also as a contribution to others who may want it for chess or checker playing or a mural site, or a vegetable or flower garden. The empty lot is there, it exists, and does not vanish, because no budget has been allotted for it. The reality does not allow us *not* to contribute, while the budgetary problems remain. The existence of these things is not excused by saying, "Well the budget doesn't allow us to hire more union workers." You have a whole society that is allowed *not* to contribute while you don't budget for these things.

Participation in the remedying of a community and contribution to a community must go on regardless of whether you budgeted for it or

not. And the campaigners for a better budget must be the young participants who live in the community, so that they can be active citizens and
not simply be testing their bravery in some absurd way like shooting into
the air, which sometimes even gets babies killed, without intent but as
fooling around in the absence of any real contributing role. The invitation
to daring is difficult, but risky jobs are and must be inherent in life itself
because that's the challenge and how it is. The participation in risk jobs
must end up as contribution, not as crime.

There are additional aspects of preparation for the job that must be
included: the history of the work, how it used to be done; the story of
inventions, of ways of past apprenticeship and training, of the significance
and hurtfulness to meaning of conveyor belt organization, of the minuti-
zation of labor tasks, of the struggle of labor and unions for the retention
of at least some ownership of work, of jobs. All these are obligations of
adults to hand on along with expertise.

## OTHER MODELS OF VALUING AND SELF-VALUING

I have some more suggestions. Given the overwhelming situation that
faces everybody, it is useful to hear about all struggling efforts to make
things better. A friend is working with AIDS children in a largely black
neighborhood; certainly we want to hear that story. Another friend works
within independent schools to break the totally dominant-group presentation that exists, even where they seek for minority teachers. Yes, we want
to hear that. We want to hear how it operates and of any processes in
breaking down such dominance classifications. We want to hear all these
small stories, but with the humility to know that they are not even close
to complete solutions. Nevertheless, every little bit counts.

We have to see the situation in bigger terms so that we always know
that a bigger thing must be involved, in our own participation and in what
we present. Wilson (1990) writes in the *Journal of Black Studies* on black
orientation — basic for environmental planning and designing in the black
community — and makes an interesting point on the use of outside
space — the street, the alley — now given only to those who are dodging
around in connection with drugs or something like that, instead of being
possessed by the community as living space. This kind of living space, I
would say, is needed for everybody, but if one wants to say that it's part
of black culture to use the outside space — great! Let's take the outside
space and make it *good* space, good space where people can sit and talk
and so on.

Whatever it takes to do these things is needed because it is not pos-

sible to throw away 50% of our youths. And I say generally — youths, but
youths with no prospects whatever of a useful job and contribution just
because they didn't go to college, like there is nothing else. That is a disaster for everybody; it just can't be lived with. When they say that one in
every four black youths has already been part of or is under control of the
correctional system — one in every four! — think what they are saying! Can
we have a black curriculum around the news of the past? These young
people have to be news in their own right. They have to be necessary to
society. I think it is possible to have at least minor solutions, minor stabs
at solutions, while we work for a bigger thing.

On a fancy level, if one wants to use psychological terms, the thing
I'm projecting is what Barbara Rogoff (Rogoff & Lave, 1984) has called
"guided participation." Only I would say: Have it in the midst of life, not
as a laboratory projection at all but as something I think is implicit in
what I have raised as "joining-with" and "following-after." That requires a
willingness to absolutely take apart the structure of the school system so
that you have something that can support a vision of decency and of contribution. We have to *not* build a culture in which not only the plastic and
glass but also the humans are thrown away. If we plan in this way, perhaps
we can escape trivialization. We would then reinvite and reconsider the
smaller criticisms made by Lisa Delpit (1986, 1988) and would be lifted
to larger criticisms and the possibilities of larger contributions. Perhaps
what I am projecting is another form of James Comer's (1975) view that
the basic necessity is respect and social decency and it is only on these that
you build.

School, reflecting society and inseparable from society, can offer only
partial trials of solutions — partial in all aspects, because we are trying to
find for everybody an identification as contributors within a framework
that does not in fact include everybody. Yet school itself is not an absolute
or the same in all aspects in every place. People bend this or that, find
cracks that allow a trial, and so — here and there — a vision can be tried
and can impact enough for the memory of it to hold for yet another trial,
maybe with a society no longer so completely oppressive in its control of
part by other dominant parts.

I think that the existence of strong societies that *are* finding the road
to self-determination will help in itself, because their presence in the world
will help all of us get off of a narrow definition. The existence of the solutions that are being found in South Africa, Tanzania, and other places will
set firmly into the story of possible contexts that this exclusionary way
isn't the only way to define a society, to pose the problem. So I think it is
possible to have hope for the future.

I want to say very clearly that I'm well aware that I'm not defining a single format, *my* way. These are things that I have found and have learned from in the writings of those who struggle for self-definition in societies where it is possible for them to frame self-definition around being the dominant group in that society. I'm talking within things that have set me thinking about this, things I have both heard and read from Nelson Mandela (Benson, 1986), Julius Nyerere (1978), and others — not in order to educate me (but it has in fact educated me) that show that there are other ways to define a problem and so one has to look at how we have done it and know that present definitions are far too limited.

What shocks me, you see, isn't only the situation of the black youth. It is that the notions of success in the society have totally devalued physical work and participation and contribution in the fashion of blue-collar workers. It has not only happened this way in our capitalist society, where you have a 50% dropout rate. The whole discussion prior to the changes in Eastern Europe was in a way that devalued work, even in a socialist society, and the events in China indicate that the work I described is also devalued there. That, it seems to me, is a very serious disease that has affected our societies. If that's the case, then you have to rethink what has happened in terms of the devaluation of work. The Swedes have worked on this problem a certain amount, trying to reinstate value by reinstating contribution to the definition of what is done. What they suggest is that unless you're part of the definition, part of the shaping of the task, it's easy to devalue it. But even in Sweden, there has been much misgiving over the separation in value and in reimbursement from the very basic quality of all the things that are shaped and made. Even when one is not part of the excluded, there are disturbances stemming from this question of how you participate. Certainly for those who are already eliminated, the impact of a narrowed definition of contributory work is enormous. So what has to be said has to be said in very clear and harsh terms. Without valued work, seen to be contribution, a large portion of people are condemned to what is tantamount to death. Are you going to make that decision — for death, or to put them all in jail? Or are you going to work toward something where people can live?

I can list many writings by African leaders and African teachers that add to our understanding of the significance of engaging and being participant in the political process, in decision making on what the society in which one claims membership is. Even in a society where dominance by others is so fixed that full participation seems hopeless, engaging in the political process is certainly of the essence. The people we're talking about, who have the right to engage in the political process at age 18, but who have no power, are the ones who are ignored, who are thrown away. Those ignored, a sizable part of the population, should be in preparation for such engagement all through their adolescent years, even before their adolescent years, certainly from age 16. Their contribution to their community, the community where they live as well as to the larger community, their function, has to be interpreted, or ways have to be found for contribution, so that their participation is not a negative one in which the only desire of all the other participants is to isolate them, to cloister them in some way — if not to totally erase their existence in the society. What we must engage in is finding ways of contribution.

As we go through the communities that cloister the ignored, questions are raised about reclaiming instead of torching boarded-up housing, about reclaiming empty lots being used at present as garbage dumps but badly needed for the engagement of people in outdoor activity, reclaiming sidewalk use for games, for people interaction kinds of things. Albert Shanker (1990) suggests the engagement of dropouts as paraprofessionals and in preparation for being paraprofessionals and of transmitting this engagement afterward, very much as I have suggested for other jobs. If we put our minds to it, we can find the paths of contribution. And only when we find such paths, when we have addressed issues of valuing and of return value, can we discuss performance. Unfortunately, such job policy is *not* on the current political agenda. There are those who will do some of the work I have described in order to survive, even though reimbursed in ways that indicate devaluation. That the unvalued work is what makes *possible* the valued and highly reimbursed work of others is unsaid. The political power and dominance remain fixed and unreconsidered.

# PART IV

# The Status of the Vision

In retirement, Weber looked back and thought forward. It had always been her practice and method to review what she had done as a means of gaining insight into what still needed doing. The two papers in this section lay out her vision particularly clearly and broadly, while detailing the achievements and limitations of change to date and analyzing bluntly the continuing impediments to it, which she saw as both imposed from without and resulting from contradictions internal to the school and the teacher's role.

Differences between the two papers result in part from differences in their dates and circumstances of production. "The Status of the Vision of a Democratic Community in Education Today" was a talk given October 18, 1986, at the conference "Progressive Education: A Reassessment." The conference was sponsored by the libraries of Bank Street College and Teachers College and took place at Bank Street. The text that remains appears to be an edited transcript and contains some additional editing and notations in Weber's hand about points to be added or expanded on. In spite of its sweeping topic, the paper seems at first to deal only with Open Corridor work, which was fresh in her mind from a series of visits to the schools she had set up as part of her transition to retirement.

"Reexaminations: What Is the Teacher and What Is Teaching" was her last paper, dictated at home in November 1993. She was anticipating yet another major surgery and the moment was weighted with the increasing risks of age and deteriorating health. Prompted by an invitation from William Ayers to contribute to his book (1995), "Reexaminations" looked ahead to the book of her own work that Weber was planning. She meant the title literally: She introduced each new topic in the essay by referring to earlier papers on the same topic and then proceeded to discuss how her thinking had changed or become refined in the interim (the references to earlier papers have been deleted in editing). The essay is a reexamination on three levels: of the Open Corridor and the Workshop Center and the issues of practice and theory that these programs uncovered for her; of the underlying commitments, understandings, and ideas themselves and of her approach to them; and of her own progress in understanding.

Relationships were central in Weber's vision. In this sense, her vision did not demand a specific format of implementation but, rather, involved an open-ended exploration of possibilities, to be "revised and delineated more clearly in the *course of implementation*," as she puts it in "The Status of the Vision of a Democratic Community." Her analysis of school structures and adult roles was directed toward facilitating relationships of the kind that would maximize children's possibilities for growth and learning. "Community" and "democratic community" are terms she used to describe these relationships.

In her usage, community refers to interactivity and integration of the group within classroom and school—contrasting with the more typical isolation from each other of teachers, children, and parents. It means inclusiveness and heterogeneity—in contrast with the too familiar patterns of selecting some, judging others, and isolating all. It means sharing among teachers and children, with children, for instance, being able to move in and out of classrooms according to interest. Democratic community invites participation and decision making by all participants and stands in contrast to the traditional, passive absorption of "teachings" by children and teachers. Democratic community means teachers' taking account of children's deep interests and adapting the institution and the curriculum to further them. Realizing these relationships meant urging public education forward to its true meaning.

These features of vision remained fundamentally unchanged but continually reworked from beginning to end of Weber's work. Each implementation based on the vision, and each change within the field of education or in public policy on education, prompted her to renewed consideration of one or another aspect of the vision. An accrual of thought, reference, vocabulary, and ultimately of idea resulted, so that, unwavering, the vision also became richer, denser. Such a process is visible in the juxtaposition of "Status" and "Reexaminations." Although there is much continuity and overlap between them, there are noticeable additions and expansions in "Reexaminations," which can be traced through intervening papers in this collection. For example, "Reexaminations" includes review of her work on the modes and context of learning represented by the papers in Part I.

Revisiting the schools and reexamining the work and the ideas, what did Weber find to be the status of the vision? There has been, she says, "a retreat from the first vision without loss of the whole" ("Status"). She notes with approval where there was a richer curricular context with possibilities for children's choice. She reports feeling friendliness and ease in the schools and a freedom of movement that suggested participants' sense of belonging to the school and of confidence in children. But other aspects of the vision had not been realized, either because of external limitations and obstacles or because of inherent contradictions in the teacher's role and in the school as an institution.

Weber relates that public policies and education trends over the years—notably on testing and tracking but also on employment, child care, health care, and the like—often created external limitations on realizing the vision. Weber's attitude to these external limitations was that they had to be fought, most effectively by joining with others. Speaking at Bank Street on another occasion (1987), she exhorted educators to take a position on policies that are not in the interests of children:

> Working so many years with young children I have, of course, been quite aware that children do not grow up by themselves and that the questions that relate to their parents, to women, to homes, are of paramount importance to their very lives, to their survival. Is there a home? Is there a job for their parents? The possibility of preparing for a job? Is health care assured? Can parents implement their own decisions on family size? Is there assurance for the children of life without threat of nuclear annihilation? All these questions—vital for the lives of parents—are also vital for the lives of children and are the context within which educational provisions, which are secondary to these questions, must be discussed.... We should not support programs that further label groups of children as one of the requirements in allocating money ... or an increase in the already enormous burden of paperwork and bureaucratization, an increase of accountability practices in the multiple ways that turn the task of caring for children into the task of fulfilling Federal requirements. We should not support things that take away from local initiative and from the diversity that occurs within it. We should not further distance homes and home/parental responsibility from child care in the name of—in defense of—intense professionalism. The risk of isolation, of loss of a rich social and personal network of interaction, is too great.

Such statements on broad public issues take second place in "Reexaminations," as in much of her concrete work, to grappling with the limitations inherent in schools, especially as they are traditionally structured. She identified these impeding school structures in two periods of sustained analysis, in the mid to late 1960s and again in the early 1990s, in many of the papers in this book, culminating in "Reexaminations." Here Weber says that there has not been enough analysis of the school as an institution. Instead, blame for limitation too often falls on the parents, teachers, and children. She points out that the school's custodial and controlling functions inherently contradict the purposes of teachers and schools. No matter how much teachers intend to relate to children's learning, their first role is to manage children in groups, to control them; this is the school's role, too. But issues of control obscure children, even for educators inclined to a more informal approach, as for instance when principals and even teachers felt that their newly opened corridor needed its own teacher. Another limitation and contradiction around control is that the school, supposed to support every child's learning, engages in gatekeeping, monitoring who can go on and who cannot, often with devastating results to a child's real growth. Yet another manifestation of control, centralized and mandated curriculum, thickens the screen obscuring the teachers' observations of their children's needs and interests, no matter what bit of leeway for interpretation it may give teachers.

The way schools are organized presents further limitations when contrasted with the circumstances that actually foster children's growth. Schools tend not to "remember" children in much, if any, individual detail from year to year, and hence do not support a child's sense of personal continuity, let alone the continuity of his or her interests and experience. Schools are are not very multigenerational, and thus cannot provide children with opportunities for learning by watching and joining, or with a sense of an ongoing enterprise in which they have a role. Indeed, schools typically provide little that engages informal modes of learning.

In addition to these inherent limitations on realization of vision are limitations resulting from unanticipated consequences of the changes in corridor organization and related implementations that Weber had set in motion. One such consequence was the phenomenon of teachers' using their new latitude for their own creativity and self-expression. On the surface this was a desired outcome: The point of giving teachers more autonomy to decide curriculum, classroom organization, and the like was to enable them to respond to the particular children's needs and interests. Instead, teachers sometimes became so enamored of their own interests and inquiries that they neglected the real reference to the children. She noted that often teachers' absorption involved literally closing the door that had been opened precisely to allow children's access to other activities and a larger whole (Alberty & Weber, 1979). In "Reexaminations," she recalls for teachers that the proper role for teachers' interests is as a means to discover and further the children's.

Parental role required a similar reconsideration. In the public struggle for a different vision of school, parents and teachers joined on an equal footing, but parental role in the school was often reduced to helping teachers with the teachers' agenda. In the 1970s, Weber (1977) had seen parental role as an undeveloped possibility. In later works, she not only lamented the marginalization of parents as a terrible limitation on change, but focused increasingly on the informal and formal qualities of educative experience outside schools, for which parents and home provided a prototype.

Toward the end of "Reexaminations," Weber points out how teachers' missing or partial grasp of their first responsibility to the child and the school's sidestepping of real parental contribution both constitute and result from a limited idea of what community is. Among its other adverse effects, this limited definition curtails the school's ability to relate to its surrounding community. In their professional absorptions, teachers and schools, Weber says, can blind themselves to the educative possibilities and thrust of the community. They thereby devalue not only the community but the children who come from it, and they risk undermining their own efforts to support the children. A comprehensive belief in the children, a broadly conceived unconditional acceptance, was essential.

The expanded analysis of limitations on change in "Reexaminations" parallels Weber's broadened consideration of outside-of-school educative contexts in other papers in this volume. Although the focus is on limitations, "Reexaminations" does not present a discouraged view. Limitations are construed as opportunities to understand better and to direct continued effort; they are important, in some ways defining, moments of professionalism. As Weber concludes: "The path of constant reexamination, of grappling-with that assumes no final end or conclusion or perfection in any of the settings, is a feature inherent in being a teacher and in being an educator of teachers."

# CHAPTER 11

## The Status of the Vision of a Democratic Community in Education Today

*1986*

I will relate only briefly and occasionally, in what I say, to past visions. My task here, as I see it, is to recount what I can of *our* visions, certainly of the part in which I was actively involved, and of the refocusing and adaptations of my vision over the past 20 years of implementation—and to describe its present holding power, its relationships to a network of visions, and the current discussions on the sources of possible revitalization.

### AN INITIAL VISION OF CHANGE AND ITS REVISION

We had a vision of democratic community influenced, certainly, by past visions, but not entirely shaped by them. We were not raising the question of the context for citizenship training in a democracy, or of the practice necessary for future function in it. We were relating to the present, to what we saw as inherent to and necessary for the human child's active search to make sense. We were relating to issues of the child's selective focus and interest, related to but not entirely the same as, for example, Dewey's (1913/1970) discussions in *Interest and Effort in Education,* although from such discussions we learned a great deal. We were relating to learning as it occurred informally at home and in the community, which we contrasted with learning in school. We were relating to issues of access. It is in this context that we critiqued the structures of the school as inhibiting not only to the child but to the possibilities for the teacher's intelligent response to the child's search to make sense of the world and so to the teachers' continued search to make sense of and define their role.

It is appropriate, I think, to ask me to talk of the status of the vision of democratic community. In the last 2 years I have considered just that question of where we are in the implementation of our vision for changed structures in schools, structures that would be more supportive of children's development as intelligent and active learners and more supportive of teachers' function as intelligent supporters of children's intelligence, and structures that would include the educative process that goes on at home and in the community. My project in these 2 years has been to go around to schools in which I was actively involved in the beginning period of change 20 years ago to see what is still there at this point of much criticism of schools, with many mixed messages around, which use our words but with different or limited reference. It seemed to me a good enterprise, before I retired, to see whether the directions that we had engaged in collaboratively with teachers and parents had had the power and strength to go on, on their own, even without the support of our presence.[1] Was there evidence of this holding power even without active support from external advisors? How much had teachers and principals taken hold? This, it seemed to me, would be useful in evaluating the status and sense of the vision, because what had been attempted had two aspects: one, critique of what existed and, two, proposals for change.[2]

The critique we made of what existed was around the lack of both community and democratic community. I separate these two situations because they are not necessarily synonymous. Our critique was of passivity in the learning situation on the part of teachers and children and, more than passivity, of an expectation of *following* patterns — the teacher being expected to follow instructional and hierarchical patterns without making her own contribution, and the children being expected similarly to "take in," to follow patterns laid down externally to their own searches. The critique was of lack of participation in decision making relative to the functions of both teacher and learner. It was of lack of democracy. In addition, and perhaps even before this critique of decision making, our critique was of the isolation of teacher from teacher, class from class, children from each other. It was of the ethos of individual effort, which ran counter to our own vision of an ethos of expectation of help from each other, with joinings of efforts toward common ends. In this sense the class was certainly not a community, the school was not a community, and I will not even speak of isolation from the broader community; that was so, too.

The word *vision* also merits a comment. For us it indicated a trial of possibility and a direction of change, *not* an expectation that upon initiation there could already be a full and complete vision that could fully determine planning. We understood that our vision would be revised and delineated more clearly in the *course* of implementation. Indeed, what it meant and what the implementation was could not be defined except in the *course* of implementation and reflection on implementation. That aspect of our efforts became clearer even early on and differentiated us from efforts that tried to institute a complete format dependent on prior understanding and agreement on all aspects of what was to be undertaken, whether within a public or private school frame. Our vision was a reshaping, a re-vision, of the already existent public school structure and related to all children and even to all teachers. It was dependent on voluntarism, not on judgments of capacity and therefore on selection. Further direction was in relationship to the directions already undertaken and was based on evaluation of small changes in that direction.

The things we were talking about in terms of democracy, the structures we were setting up, were not just about decision making but were about interaction. What interaction actually meant as a learning force became clearer as we worked. We increasingly shaped our context around interaction as meant by the psycholinguists who discussed it as the propelling motor in language development. It was their words we used, and they in turn used our situations, where language use was visible and the possibilities for evoking language were rich, for developing their words.

Considering our vision as a vision of meaning in compulsory education drew us into the additional meaning of respect for and inclusion of individuals within a context of responsibility and respect for each other. The isolation and passivity we had remarked earlier included that the school was organized around custodial care of children, without necessary obligation to serve children's differing needs of growth. In our context of obligation to as well as inclusion of all in the definition of compulsory education, bilingualism and pluralism became part of the discussion of community. The discussion centered around the rich contribution of diversity and interaction, heterogeneity in grouping, promotion policy, and curriculum — what was "same" in curriculum?

It is obvious that our changes were partial, even where a community of volunteering teachers and parents, wanting change and in agreement on at least some beginning steps, existed. The changes were framed by the rules of the larger school community that followed existent structures. They were impacted on by the rules of a still larger community that had begun to define the existent structures in tighter, more technological terms. Thus, along with our attempts to change school structures and the practice of teaching, teachers faced the growing technology of testing and curriculum development in support of testing. Along with our efforts to establish as a principle of group organization a heterogeneity that described *all,* there was, by 1974–1975, a new pressure to categorize a quite large segment of the population as Special Education, and to define promotion policy in different ways than we had envisaged.

These were all definitions and rules developed externally to the discussions of the small body of parents, teachers, and principals who sought to develop structures internal to the classroom that would be responsive to children's interest. But they had authority over these small voluntary groups and pressured them to conform. What influenced our first recasting of definitions were not the external pressures but the struggles of the teachers to achieve better understanding, interaction, and curriculum.[3] It is these struggles around the teacher's decision making in the classroom that I will first discuss.

In that initial period of change, we were acknowledging difference and unevenness in children's growth patterns, interest, and selective focus, and the importance of active engagement around interest. We did not yet take into account the relationships of the broad bands of curriculum as defined by the board of education to curriculum as defined and developed by the teacher in the classroom. Teachers often did not identify what they offered in the classroom with these broad bands of focus. The prescribed specificities and sequence were so despised that it was thought possible to reject the area itself. Thus, expert, adult-formed curriculum was not linked to input from the child around the search to make sense. What was recognized was that the child's choice, own question, was important. But choice around what? The legitimacy of questions on space, time, and relationships that define for us history or geography, science or math, as aspects of the child's search to make sense was not yet clear. Persisting intellectual interests as distinct from ephemeral and bypassing interests were hardly discussed. Questions of connection, continuity, and interest, as Dewey had discussed these, and the widened consciousness that resulted from community interaction of many different perspectives, were hardly discussed. All of these issues surfaced later as important things to consider.

The first focus was on developing communities that were able to respond to the child's interest at all, that included in developing respect the importance of an example from the teacher of interest in another's interest. They surfaced as discussion focus *after* the first provision of a variety of entry points making sense was established, *after* the creation of sufficient visibility to allow for the surfacing of new questions. What were especially not clear in this beginning period were the differences and relationships between teacher interest and children's interest and how interest and respect for each other can help these different interests contribute to each other.

## HOW HAVE OUR EFFORTS FARED?

Given all the conceptualizations and efforts around the democracy and community of the classroom — all intended to foster respect for each other's interest, space, and goals and to encourage the interaction that can foster learning, all in the midst of the reality of prescribed curriculum — how have our efforts fared since the first period of change? How the broad bands of search to make sense relate to choice is still being unpacked. To help in this process, in understanding the dynamic of grappling with understanding in contrast with receiving *answers*, teachers' experiences of their own learning patterns are still being developed at the Workshop Center and at other such centers. But amazingly, given the existing reality, what I see is that the goals — around support for children's making sense and developing personal knowledge, and around developing a genuine life in the classroom with an ethos of responsibility to each other — *do* exist and are actualized in many situations. They exist especially in those situations established with principals' and parents' support. They exist, supported by the teacher, side-by-side with a relationship of the teacher to the children that is contradictory. They exist in the midst of an imposition of external decisions on the teacher's actions and the children's function that is totally contradictory — supportive of the passive/obedient model as much as before, pressured to become even more so.

What I want to remark on is that only part of these contradictions comes from the impact of testing pressures, prescribed curriculum, and the ethos of work and even more work, homework and even more homework, all valued merely as "work" and unrelated to the child's search to make sense. Even at the early period in the search for democratic community, 1967–1977, there were difficulties over the place of the child. Slogans were being bandied about — for example, children were to be considered responsible for their own learning — with little understanding that a child could grow only slowly toward responsibility and sometimes needed help in making choices.

Only part of the trouble came from a distrust that children *do* seek to learn and *are* responsive to a stimulating context from which they can draw questions that carry them further into understanding. The other part came from the teachers' response, in the situations they had set going, to the chance to define themselves creatively and professionally as teachers. The chance for teachers to develop their own curriculum, to give play to their own interests, to shape their classrooms, was intoxicating. Many of them worked hard, in creative ways. They researched material and taught, and indeed overtaught, anxious to answer deprecatory remarks about their curriculum with demonstration of children's high performance. I am not describing whole-class teaching, as might be presumed. I am describing a reaction by teachers who were part of the changes, both defensively and outreachingly, to their prior oppression and to the current assumption, which was in continuity with the prior oppression, of teacher ineptness and ineducability.

This reaction of teachers to their new, active role in curriculum selection did not necessarily include the vision of democratic community with children or acceptance of unevenness and difference in children's development. The inclusion of children's interest remains weak; the inclusion and acceptance of their development and the growing point of their development is still weak. Perhaps, too, as teachers accepted the chance to "refer" children with difficulties, to label children as having deficits, it became easier to bypass the obligation — within the skills expected of teachers and the development of interactive, adaptive, and responsive practices — of the vision of mainstreaming *all* children put forth in 1967.

Let me say that even in incompletely realized form, the contrast with previous formal classrooms and relationships, the improvement in the richness of the context for choice, in the energy of the children and teachers around curricular activities, and in the atmosphere of respect for and interest in others, is evident to me and to most visitors. I am looking here not only at long-established classroom communities where teachers have consciously grappled with these issues, but at the smaller evidences of change in these directions that can be seen in single classrooms where teachers have attempted to depart from the frame of passivity inherited from the past. They *have* a vision. They think it is possible to try.

Another aspect of our vision was related to the school as community, not only to the classroom. Our vision was of breaking through the isolation of each teacher and the isolation and discontinuity of the progression of classrooms. It was in challenging the inherited format of one teacher alone with 30-odd children that the corridor as an active element of school structure was proposed. Again, the seduction of personal creativity asserted its power. Teachers turned to the chance to develop *their* creativity, *their* classroom. Their uncertainty of conviction about children's own search to make sense, to learn, got in the way of children's success or choice in less directly supervised contexts. Since no accepted mode of cross-classroom access or use of the whole school existed, their doubts were reinforced.

Yet, even without clear definition of this as being a break with prior patterns, in schools that have worked toward such goals it is evident that children do *use* the school, they walk as individuals and not only as controlled groups, they are interested in the work of other classrooms or children from other classrooms. In some of these schools teachers meet together to discuss children and placement; to have a voice in teacher training, teacher hiring, choosing of curriculum themes; to share with each other what they have developed in their own classrooms; to assist teachers new to the school or new teachers. They are open to each other and are a community of teachers developing an ethos of their school. Again the situation is one of incompleteness, of perhaps limited vision of what a community of teachers can be.

Retreat from first vision without loss of the whole is plain also in relationship to parents. Parents were supporters and even shapers of the first statements of goals and of possible development. But in the context of teachers' uncertainties during the period of first shaping, teachers asked to be *assisted*, if at all, with *their* efforts, with what at that point in their own development they felt able to do. Parents were to some extent pushed back as equal collaborators in change. This situation changed, at least in theory, as the contribution of parents to language development was acknowledged and pushed toward study of the parental mode. An additional aspect of parental mode worth study for possible implication for classroom modes of learning, the joining-with that characterizes child-parent interaction, has since been pinpointed. Even as recognition of this mode of interaction opens up new possibilities for a more inclusive parent/teacher/child community, the reality is that the economics of family life currently create less possibility for parent-classroom interaction.

## THE BROADER SCENE

And now, a final point in this brief schematization of elements that define the present status: It must be obvious that the political climate of today, stressing obedience and supposedly more efficient structures, constitutes in itself a major hindrance to further development of democratic community. It invites defensive statements instead of vision. It is itself unclear, existing in the midst of many statements that sound like contradictions: Advocacy of teacher decision making, of "space to teach" rather than prescription, is pressed by many. But questions on children's learning, questions on the shape and structures of the school, are few. A depressed view of possibilities even to ask these questions is certainly widespread. A community-supported view of schooling as an active process, fostering strength in shaping and contributing that will redound to community strength, is certainly not widespread. But perhaps particularly on the high school level where, as response to exclusion from decision making, hostility threatens the very existence of the institution, such questions *must* be asked. In third-world countries, where reference to *all* is an essential quantity in the shaping of educational vision, such questions *are* asked and visions of what is necessary are projected. These must be studied for relevance to our task. For us, the incompleteness remains a challenge, but the questions remain — not to be dismissed.

I may have seemed to be focused only on the status of my own efforts, but I am part of a worldwide network of educators who search for the democratic framework that they feel is necessary for their efforts. I do read reports about the status of efforts elsewhere for a democratic community and also participate in discussions to further define the goals of such efforts. I have focused here on my own efforts because I think that, with all their incompleteness, they do still carry significance for further efforts. Definition of efforts around mainstreaming, around *all,* have significance.

In specific preparation for this presentation, I have spent much time over the past few months reading current discussions and rereading familiar classics on the issues of personal knowledge and the interaction and collaboration that root this knowledge (in addition to the obvious role of interaction with the physical reality of the outer world), and thinking about what learners draw from the community and contribute back to the community. I have reread Dewey's *Democracy and Education* (1916), *Experience and Education* (1939), and *Interest and Effort in Education* (1913/1970). I have reread the sections on interaction in Katherine Mayhew's *The Dewey School* (1966) and in Elsie Clapp's *The Use of Resources in Education* (1952) and Clapp's brilliant discussion of work with and for the community. I have reread many of James Macdonald's (et al., 1973, 1975a, b) essays defining and redefining progressive education; discussions by Julius Nyerere (1978) and others in third-world journals of community relevance to educational planning in various African countries (Kenya, Tanzania, and also about work in the Caribbean, South American countries, and China). I am of course always reading material on the relevance of educational structures to the struggle for democracy sent to me from England, Australia, Berlin. I have also read the recent statements on educational policy from Aronowitz & Giroux (1985), and other Marxist critics.[4]

What's difficult for me is to relate to these issues quite so linearly, so "historically" that they seem ahistorical. The issue for me is how to support the developing strength of individuals, their utmost "humanness," and to build the societal context that will allow that development. The very possibility of building that society and its schools necessitates the presumption of the possibility of that individual development. Societies that want all their people to join their struggle for liberation also speak with confidence about *all.* That building has to be based on public education. How schools can be structured to support such development is still to be envisaged.

Because images of a liberating education are more likely to be found among groups struggling for societal liberation, the search for these images must include such sources. I was sure of that when I said to my students from Spanish-language backgrounds that they could offer substitute readings from José Martí (1953, 1979). I suggested then that among the writings of anyone struggling for a democratic society there would be writings on wider inclusion, on a liberating education. That was true and I still make that suggestion for search.

## NOTES

1. The Open Corridor Advisory work tapered off in the mid-1970s because of funding declines and Weber's shifting emphasis toward working with teachers at the Workshop Center, which she refers to in "Language Development and Observation," in Part I. Advisory work was halted by the fiscal crisis of New York City schools in 1975–1976, in which many of the corridor communities were broken up by the transfer of teachers by seniority and the firing of many. Individual teachers, advisors, and principals were able to adapt and retain elements of the corridor work in their new situations, using the Workshop Center as support.

2. At this point in the manuscript Weber made a marginal note, which generally indicated a point for further development. "Possibility. *Can* children learn without *direct* teaching? How, how much?"

3. Another of Weber's marginal notes: "Teachers had to prove themselves / Quality of their curriculum."

4. Again in the margin, Weber jotted the names of other authors and movements whose work she characterized as "instances of confidence in wide capacity, Democratic Vision": Lois Barclay Murphy, "the 8 year study," Charlotte Winsor, Barbara Biber, Claudia Lewis, Natalie Cole, and German progressive education. Slightly apart are the words "play, tests, Sp. Ed."

# CHAPTER 12

## *Reexaminations: What Is the Teacher and What Is Teaching?*

*1993*

As I look over the accumulated mass of statements I have made since 1967 about the changes we've made in the schools, I find that I have concentrated most on constant reexamination of issues of teaching and teachers, questioning their pertinence to what I have come to see in more expanded fashion as the reality of the child's learning. In my first formulations about school change in the late 1960s, I concentrated on creating a context in schools of relationships of teacher to child and child to teacher that would facilitate the child's use of context and enhance the child's possibilities for building, for questioning, for rearranging in new forms. My comments were a critique of the barrenness and sterility of context in schools. I was full of wonder at what I had seen of children's learning, for example, in English infant schools and in the first Open Corridor schools, from a rich surround of environment and from easy relationships that joined them in what was focusing their attention and that responded to their attention with recognition of the importance of this focus for them.

Teachers interested in creating new contexts supportive of children's growth and development were certainly interested in these newer kinds of relationships, stressing observation and appreciation of children's functioning. But the teaching was always in a school, and soon after our initial school changes, teachers began to express the need to cope with the institution, to confront institutional obstacles to newer relationships and context. My writing on teaching became descriptions of successful arrangements and suggestions for what might ease context and relationship arrangements. Teachers, too, have written about their struggles to recreate context and relationships and about the discoveries they have made about what worked or did not work in their practice.

But as time went on it seemed to me that the emphasis on teaching became an overloaded one. The teachers' focus was so strongly on *their* own struggles to unblock the institution and to free themselves; one reads again and again about teachers' struggles to share in decision making, for example, to participate in curriculum building. What teachers had built, had found it possible to change, was important to their development of self, and to their sense of empowerment.

Meanwhile, however, many things that had been important in the first efforts to change—for example, the building of community with other teachers, parents, and the community around the school—while not lost as worthy goals, were certainly muted. The observation of children, although remaining important, was given importance to some extent in terms of how the teacher could manage to have *this* child focus on the goals the teacher felt were necessary for the classroom, for the control of so many different children, and for certain curricular goals.

The teachers' struggle for self definition has taken place increasingly in a context of severe criticism of the schools, often focused on the old schools, not on the modified schools that had become more exemplary of teachers' decision making. In such an atmosphere of criticism, parents worried and organizations were founded that concentrated their criticism on teachers and teaching, and criticized very little the emptiness of context in schools and of relationships within the school of child to child, child to teacher, teacher to teacher, parents to parents, and so on.

The teacher education institutions have been analyzed and reanalyzed as cause and source of teacher and school deficiency. The word that seems to express what is found wanting (and what many think should be a central focus) has been *professionalism*. This led to the proposition that the universities ought to offer material that would bring out and focus teacher education on strengthening the teacher as professional. University focus settled on teachers' formal knowledge of their content field and of research that would indicate the best mode of teaching. The focus of this critique, and on a "best" mode of teaching, was narrow rather than broad. Neither the child as learner nor the school as institution was being examined under this magnifying glass. The questions about professionalism seemed shallow, and bypassed what it is that defines the teacher. This then became important to me.

The analysis of the school as an institution that *blocked* the teacher from functioning in ways that I thought related to this definition and to the teacher's commitment raised the need for "rethinking," "deconstructing," "deschooling," and "deteachering" in order for those first goals to emerge again with some strength and clarity. It was important to turn the discussion of limitations away from limits in children's capacities to learn and toward the pervasive limits all around us—the structures that both facilitate and limit our family and social life. How much and what in a school can be "deschooled"? How much can we move away from the existing view of the teacher as mechanic carrying out already set plans? How much of this view can be revised toward a new view of the teacher as creative constructor? What could allow some refocusing on the commitment of teachers, on the definition of teachers' role, on the teacher as supporting the child's learning rather than as *teaching*?

The preparation of candidates for teaching follows from the analyses we make clarifying the definition of teacher and teaching. The teacher's commitment must include the context supportive of learning and of the child's further development or education. Thus, for every aspect of teaching that has been discussed as professionalism, in my view the definition of what the teacher is and what the teacher's commitments are must take precedence. These are the questions I've explored for the past 5 or 6 years, and hope to pull apart in the following remarks.

## SCHOOLS AND THE CONDITIONS OF GROWTH

I take from the planning document for the 1993 meeting of the North Dakota Study Group on Evaluation the oft-reiterated phrase "the schools at their best" as my starting point. What is the "best"? I think of the best as the *conditions* that I see as necessary accompaniments to human growth and development. These conditions accompanying human growth and development are not limited to school context but are present in many contexts.

One constant accompaniment to human growth is the presence of people of many generations, creating an unevenness in both the child's human and material surround. Human growth always occurs in the presence of people, some of whom are further along in growth and others of whom have not even approached this growth. Thus, whatever is happening is multifaceted from the first moment of growth, and the numerous facets of growth are increased as we live. We can increase the impact of one condition over the other in a conscious kind of way, but only rarely and questionably do we do this in a planned fashion. Human growth doesn't seem to take place in a laboratory kind of way. Thus, the study of that *context,* in all its specificity, where human growth does take place, is obligatory if we are to impact supportively on the child's growth.

What is the context within the school? We have to examine whether the context is complex enough, is multifaceted enough. Certainly in the past, the context has been a single strand, one whose conscious purpose was to sequence one lesson after the other and to have everything else either removed or at least controlled — controlled meaning quiet, for example, and with all attention on the teacher's presentation. But school "at its best" would take some of the multifaceted context of the world that exists outside of school and have it within the school. In such a context, the stimulus of past experiences, the memory of them, can still impinge and weave its way around again for a focus that may be individually determined or group determined.

Another constant accompaniment to human growth is continuity of context, which can help weave the sense of personal continuity. Continuity is far from existing evenly in all the various contexts in which human growth takes place. There can be great unevenness and interruption in continuity of the child's, the human's, history, at the most intimate level of one's remembrances. But these discontinuities in growth and relationship do not obviate the simultaneous continuities, the importance of which becomes evident when they are lost. The continuity represented by our own remembrances of who we are and of our surround is supported by the continuities in the surround of others. The family from whom we emerge has a major function in carrying the memory of who we are. Before we could remember and when we can't remember, the family reminiscences keep us whole. Among new people, a group memory exists. New people estimate how old we are and where we came from, and acquaintances carry at least a generalized memory. Without these different memories that give us continuity with ourselves we would be seriously handicapped.

Schools, even at their best, are impediments to this continuous memory. They have perhaps the longest contact with a child outside the family, but in most schools, 9 months is the maximum time of continuous memory carried in any adult's mind. Say that it is even 2 years, or even a little more. It is still without the genuine continuity that exists elsewhere. In school, continuity is mediated through organization of progression and records. It is focused around a selective memory of performance and engagement with current tasks. Assistance to children who do not fit this narrow kind of memory requires the revival of a broader memory and an assertion of who they are in a more whole fashion than school accommodates. Thus we come to an even larger condition that supports human growth and development. This is, simply, the acceptance of the child's own identity, the acceptance of who the child is as a person. And that is not bargained for in most schools. It is not weighed as important. I am not talking about acceptance if the child does certain things the school requires. I am talking about the unconditional acceptance of the child's "isness."

All humans are born into a multigenerational context. They are born to somebody, a somebody who is within a network of other relationships. Thus, immediately, the child is born as part of all of these relationships that exist in a set of mores and culture and historical moment. The child absorbs the particularities of relationships one way or another, but the fact of his or her belonging and relatedness is without question. Obviously, such unconditional acceptance is not part of schools, even at their best. On the contrary, discussion of assessment, of equality, of excellence, of standards, bears with it the condition of performance as the price of a child's acceptance.

The question is *can* schools accept the child unconditionally? If we talk about schools "at their best," would they at least be moving determinedly toward unconditionality? And what could this mean for schools, not only with respect to assessment and performance, but also with respect to race, ethnicity, difference, amd the right of children not to divest themselves on school entrance of their culture and language?

On this question I have to go to "What exactly is the teacher's commitment?" Obviously, this is extremely complex. If the teacher is defined by a commitment to every child within the group, if every child is accepted as part of the teacher's commitment to further growth and development, then there is an unconditionality. But mostly what we have is unconditionality *in absentia* or very much qualified with, "Well, I certainly do the best that I can, but after all he has to perform a certain kind of way." I realize the hedging and the problems around unconditionality, but I think it is central to our discussion of schools at their best to face what follows from the commitment of the teacher and to decide that yes, the commitment does indicate necessary revisions of school context that can stretch existent modes into the utmost unconditionality possible.

The importance of the conditions accompanying human growth and development that I have outlined above became clearer in the course of my rethinking. The renewed question is, "What is it possible to demand of the school?"

## FIRST CHANGES AND REASSESSMENTS

Another point of rethinking, prompted by a number of writers in the past few years in counterbalance to a search for professionalism relying on university research, has been the question of the meanings attached to the teacher's commitment to the profession (Buchmann, 1990; Little, 1990). What is the professional and what is central to it? This question highlights a difference between those concentrating on professionalism in a limited way and those relating to it in terms of human caring and human compassion.

When I first looked for aspects of school context that could be modified, I did not have this list of the conditions necessary in any learning context to assist my analysis. My focus was first on the life of the classroom and the quality of life in the classroom. I looked at the classroom and at the child, and at the possibilities of meshing with where the child was, and how I, an enabler, would help the child go forward. What I saw in England in 1965 reinforced the feelings I had previously developed in working with small children and focused my observation in the schools when I returned (Weber, 1971). I thought of the teacher as being engaged with where the child was going anyway, as enabling the child to get there, to fulfill what was already existent and pushing forward in the child.

The question of difference and unevenness in children's growth was interesting and enormously important to me. The teacher had to understand that what was set up to foster the child's development had to be responsive to this difference and unevenness without predictive conclusions. The need to take a long view of the growth of a child was important to me. It could not be assumed that the unevenness was a stable thing and meant differential development within the child for good. That is, if the child was not yet speaking, it could not be predicted that the child would never speak. Making an educational situation supportive of the child's further education and development meant taking a "let's wait and see" stance, and creating an enabling environment in which whatever you were *not* seeing in the child was encouraged to emerge. The setting could not be one in which an existent state of the child or any observation of that moment would lead to conclusions about the permanence of what was seen.

I considered the possibilities for change of institutional structures. How could these structures be at least partially bent to become less intrusive, less interruptive of any efforts to change? The administrative structures were so detailed, the judgments were so external to the particular children. They were not in relationship with where the child was and where he or she was going. One had to look and see where there were cracks or entry points where one could make at least some trial efforts at bringing the school structures into another relationship, or where one could interlace with them and so turn their operation away from blocking development.

In this early period of my thinking on change in the public schools, there was no template for how the teacher should act. Rather there was an idea that what was true about the child was the capacity for growth and interest in the world and that ways had to be found to bring at least some of the child's earlier interactions with the world into the school.

There was not really a questioning of the fact that school existed and was compulsory, that children had to go, or of the idea that school was valued for many different reasons by parents, perhaps even eventually by the child, or that this was the teacher's work and that training had gone into the teacher functioning in the school.

Initially, my question was how to evade the structure of the school and thereby release some of the interaction and reinitiate some of the things that had supported the child's learning and education *before* the child got into the school. That was what was called, in England, "informal education." I sought for what would free the teacher to be supportive of the child at a more fundamental and general level, supportive in a context of awareness that outside of school children do not learn in an empty set or with constant focus on the adult. Instead, they reach out tremendously from the first day of birth, making use of whatever they can in the environment that they need to continue their growth. The child is not an empty container being filled by the teacher.

Opening the corridor created a context where people could see and interact with one another and where there was a broader diversity of children (in age, for example) and of activities that could be chosen, where engagement would be in and out so there would be relaxed control and diversity in modes of teaching. In the corridor, a teacher might be reading a story, a child might be drawing a character of his or her choice, and so on. The open corridor presumed that the teacher had created a context, was moving around to catch the thread of the child's engagement with the context, and was adding to the context. The open corridor also presumed that the child was adding to the context and that the group would sometimes draw together to share their perspectives and be stimulated to additional possibilities, to new thrusts. The role of the English headmistress as engaged in assisting the teacher to relate to the child, to make use of whatever pliability of context was possible, interested me. Therefore, I came up with a notion of the "advisor" and of how teachers could help each other by being visible to and thereby stimulating solutions in each other. A teacher would have an idea for getting through some of the institutional blocking points and then another teacher, seeing the implementation, could say, "That's good. Let's try that." The whole enterprise would then gain in flexibility.

The advisor was somebody who would help the teacher with what followed from this awareness. The advisor could observe what was going on, see what the teacher was trying to do, and share what he or she had observed of other teachers' efforts. The advisor could point out and assist the teacher in finding some of the flexibilities and stretch within what seemed like a granite structure that had no entrance points. I focused on what was necessary from advisors who would carry forward in their role some of the things I had seen in England as supporting the teacher's use, for the benefit of the child, of the context and structure the English headmistress had set up. In England, the headmistress embodied the institutional forces. In the United States, the advisor had to have a role that would be allowed in the school but would foster the strength of the teacher in finding flexibilities for growth. The point was that the advisor role should not be grafted onto the old supervisory role, making judgments and evaluations of the teacher's performance in relation to mandated standards. The advisor had to be helpful to the teacher, recognizing in the teacher the same differences and unevenness that I hoped the teachers would recognize in the children's development. Therefore, there could be no template for what had to be, but a responsiveness, an appreciativeness of some aspect of an individual teacher's strength and a courage to try to explore the possible. In our continuous evaluation of the advisor role we fine-tuned the various ways the advisor could relate to the structures of the school to give teachers more space for their own emergence as creators in the classroom. Did the context the advisor had helped the teacher create further the child's own stretch in reaching out toward making sense of the world? Was the modified context supportive? And—was the advisor essential to the development of this context?

It became clear that we did not totally control the advisor's function. In evaluating the advisory function we had to take into account what the institution did with the advisor. The institution allowed the advisory, but often also reinforced its own imposition, limitation, and control on what could be done by claiming that the advisor was essential. Without the advisor, it was said, teachers could not develop new ways of working, through their own reflection, conviction, and fascination with children's growth, and through sharing with each other and estimating "Where are we now?" and "What has happened with the children's growth?" Trust in teachers' capacities was not something many administrators had.

By saying that advisors were essential, administrators put blockades in the way of teachers' individually and personally assuming responsibility for searching out the ways and paths of their own development. They said that if schools did not have advisors or education of teachers in this way, the teachers could not do it. Mandated paths for teacher performance had to be followed unless someone graced by further training guaranteed that no terrible disaster would occur. The fact that the educational system did not provide structurally or in salaries for advisors, that the role required special funding, led to questioning about how an advisory *could* work and limited the advisory role and the spread of change.

It was my conviction that what I believed was true for children—that learning occurs in context and through interaction—was also imperative for teachers. That is what gave meaning to the teacher's role. But I did not believe that this *required* a prior preparation of teachers by advisors. After all, as attempted actualizations and descriptions of practice in the modified settings grew in numbers, more and more teachers—experienced, beginning, or students—felt hope in possibility and reinforced in the meaning of their commitment. Thus, I did not believe that an advisor was such an essential piece of support that one could not function *without* the advisor. I felt that one had to think of moving in the direction of teacher autonomy in making decisions and of respect for the teacher's own observations, believing that teachers *could* learn and reflect, and that this was also an essential piece of their belief in the children.

Nevertheless, it was the children who came first in my mind. In talking about the teachers' joining a group that wanted to begin a process of change and to work with me or the advisors in looking at context, interaction, and primarily at children, I felt that the teachers' belief that it was possible to do so, and their unhappiness with being cogs in a mandated situation that did not respect their role in interaction, was more important than anything else. The frame that I set up as necessary for the growth of change was that the teacher *wanted* to change and sought out supports for the process. Change could not be a designate from the principal, as if teachers were interchangeable cogs—"You can have any two teachers for your project." Those two teachers had to be *interested* in and *critical* of what the current situation was. Did they fully understand this? None of us did. Did they fully understand how to go forward? None of us understood that. But that they felt that it was *possible* to go forward—that was essential. That kind of prior condition was to me the sole condition. Not intelligence. Not talent. At least sufficiently, those were assumed.

For me, the complexity of a projected direction is possible to understand only as the direction is pursued in a complex *lived* situation, wherever it is located and with many people participating. My idea to maximize what could be learned from trials was to release the teacher from the bondage of isolation in the classroom, to find ways to break the barrier of the closed doors. Then teachers could see the trials, the small efforts, of their colleagues, and could also see the children in a larger setting than just in response to what that teacher had prepared. This would give them new material to think about. The idea was also to open the classroom to visits by and interaction with parents who, like the teachers, had made a voluntary choice to explore the modification of the institution to which they had entrusted their children.

The deprivations to the teacher's autonomy in the administrative structures of the school had been so marked that even small releases — for example, being able to make small decisions about what to put into the classroom to build up a denser and richer setting for exploration and inter-action — were intoxicating to the teachers. The settings we created, which allowed social interaction with other teachers and widened the classroom environment to include at least two or three or four other classrooms where changes were also being tried, were experienced as pleasant by many teachers. But complexities about identification, ownership, and do-mains emerged.

A strong push from the teachers became apparent — not just as an imposition from the administrator — to reassert teacher territoriality. This was *their* classroom, where even the advisor was present on sufferance. The *teacher* was making the major decisions in the classroom. That door was important, and was open only a little bit, although even that little bit was a big change from the previous total closure. Even though the teachers wanted something different from the past, their vision of com-munity was weak (Weber, 1973a, 1975a, b). The structure of the school was much stronger, and the teacher's only domain, reliably hers or his, was that classroom, even though in a freer way.

How did this reassertion of the teacher's authority in the classroom operate with respect to the original focus on children? That focus re-mained, but the teacher's dominance in the creation of context became an expression of the teacher's creativity that was terribly important to the teacher, and understandably so. Still, a question was left floating in the air. Was this context various enough, dense enough, to be responsive to and supportive of all the particular children and groups of children? Was there a sufficient mesh with the child's interests? Were the child's contributions to context encouraged? Were the child's interests even understood? Ques-tions of children's interests were not really discussed at length until we had been doing this kind of work for quite a while. The teacher as a person had become the enormously important focus, for the teacher and for what was developed, at that point anyway. The sense of teacher as continuing to control and direct the children's focus, even as the teacher supplied more possibilities for children's independent focus, came to the fore in the notion of the need for a corridor teacher. There was a sense that the chil-dren needed to have the control and supervision of a teacher at all times. A loose piece, not clearly preenvisaged by a teacher in its use, was found to be uncomfortable in any of the modifications first tried.

(Of course, advisors also felt possessive about their work. It was clear that they had a strong need to be needed as well. To some extent the advisors supported the administrators' tendency to believe that they were essential to teachers' development, that the conformance of teachers' actions with their increasing understandings could not proceed without the advisor.)

Conflicts in the understanding of community within the school and of supportive interaction between children, classrooms, and teachers became apparent as the Open Corridor program continued in the early and mid-1970s. The effort toward community took second place to the teachers' sense of territoriality and control of their classrooms as they experienced a positive growth in their sense of themselves as persons, with interests, fresh experiences of their own learning, creativity, and possibilities for further development. In schools where a process of change was initiated it was usual to feel an atmosphere of friendliness in all the connecting structures of the school: in the office, on the playground, in the corridor. The children could walk to the office without being challenged as to why they had left the classroom. There was an assumption that they were part of the whole. The children *did* benefit from the increased richness of the teacher's presentation. But yes, it was a question of degree, and retreat from the community was real, and the Open Corridor development itself as supporting community and place certainly receded. Of course, the retreat was not total. Use of the whole school, of the corridor not just as passage but as an additional place to explore and to develop communication and collaboration between children and classrooms, and of course the small alternative school development, represented instances of continuation of the efforts to build community.

The further development of the teacher's own resources, experiences, and awareness of the role of context and interest in learning facilitated the teacher's growth in ability to work in a modified way. It was reflected in greater support for children, in greater conviction about children's capacities, and in greater awareness of these forces in the child. It was visible in the greater richness and density of environmental context. Founded in 1972, the Workshop Center as educative force supporting these developments in teachers became a major factor in our analysis of appropriate teacher preparation. Investigation at the Workshop Center made teachers more aware of their own learning process and what supported *their* continuation of investigations.

The issue was that teachers, with confidence in children's capacity for growth, could seek to develop a situation that was more supportive of children's growth. They sought to examine the context that would further the children's focus and reaching-out to understand the world, one another, and themselves. What was an educative context? What were the contexts that would be supportive? Was school such a context? What would it take to make school more so? For this child, or that one? Raising these and related questions began to shape what made sense in teacher education because in raising them, you were expecting the teachers to look at what would be supportive. Your responsibility was to enable them to go further in assisting the child to go further.

Expanding the view of the educative context that supports learning and development in teachers was one factor in an increasing emphasis on observation of how children use context. What in the context of home and home relationships had fostered growth and unfolding in power to understand and to use? What in the street? In the neighborhood? In the stores? In the community? In the world? Also raised was how other people seeking to understand the interdependent roles of teaching and learning had considered these questions. Journals became tools of reflection. A reflective attitude that encouraged self-observation, observation of one's own doings and the doings of others, became a way of developing sensitivity to the impact of even small changes in setting and interaction on their scene of action. Reminiscences about what had been educative to the teachers when they were children became strong in the analysis of their own learning.

All these aspects of change, at least in awareness, began to appear in discussion of teacher preparation, but it was also clear that the already existing and mandatory modes were strong as countervailing forces, and that what we were pointing toward had been really actualized only minimally. We did not have sufficient examples of other ways.

A way that had moved me to much thought was the requirement in Norway's early childhood teacher preparation programs for prospective teachers to spend a year living in a family to experience the variety and complexity of children's reactions and the relationships in a home. In our U.S. teacher education context, where this was not a requirement, reminiscence about one's own growth, reevocation of one's own childhood, and descriptions of childhood in literature could help but not obviate the need for study of this major educative setting for the child. Home observation was certainly an absent aspect of teacher preparation. Another missing element was exploration and thought about the community where the child lived as educative context. The school had to think of the community as full of things that had contributed to the child's understanding of how things work, as full of relationships of positive complexity.

Throughout the 1970s and 1980s, in the context of continuing and widespread failure in the accomplishment of mandated goals, just about all aspects of schooling were criticized as inadequate: The parents were inadequate; the children were inadequate and ineducable; the teachers were inadequate, ignorant, falling short of any real resources in the content of the mandated curriculum. Not only were teachers seen as inadequate in their understanding of the content as subject, as discipline, but inadequate also in their understanding of how children took content in and understood it and of the progression in the child's natural growth and understanding of these things as the child made sense of what surrounded him in the world.

In the midst of all the criticism, where and how could change begin? Such overwhelming and all-inclusive critique invited a more narrow look at what seemed more manipulable. It was difficult to critique the parents because at least to some extent they held political power over the school. It was difficult to totally critique the children, though they certainly could be ignored and devalued. After all, if they *were* ineducable, then what was the point of the teacher's efforts? Criticism was more easily narrowed to focus on the teachers, who were wage earners within the school system and dependent on salaries and therefore also on approval and acceptance. And so, by default and by accessibility to critique, it seemed possible to center all criticism on the teacher. What was critiqued was the supposed ignorance of the teacher; the trouble with teachers was that they were subject-ignorant. But the teacher who was critiqued was not the teacher we saw in the Open Corridor schools, the enormously hard-working teacher thrilled with new possibilities, new responsibilities, and creativity. She was the teacher in the context of the old sterility, without significant indictment of the institution as source of deficiency. Displacement, it seems to me, had occurred in clarity of vision, and in focus about change.

The university school of education was also faulted, accused of pandering to subject ignorance with a thin gruel of methodology. It was not fostering in the teacher a knowledge of the research in the field of teaching and certainly not, as we urged, raising the teacher's thinking capacity to enable a multifaceted kind of response and support for the child. The Holmes Group efforts (1990), intended to improve teacher education and preparation, magnified the role of university subject expertise in teacher preparation and the importance of the teacher's knowledge of "research." The research was seldom judged on whether it was based on careful observation of the impact of small changes to the environment, or the impact of what the teacher modified or adapted in an effort to mesh with where this or that child was. There has been some progress in reestablishing this priority and encouragement of what are called professional development schools, where the school context can be controlled enough to guarantee teacher education students such new experiences. But I have not yet seen persistent, clear questioning of the institution itself—its retrograde mode of lockstep influence; its continuing power to restate and shift priorities about change; or its impact on the teacher's commitment to the primacy of the child's possibilities and to the support of the child's development of such possibilities. That kind of questioning, in my opinion, has lost — it constantly loses — focus and must be constantly revived.

## FURTHER REEXAMINATIONS: CONTINUING OBSTACLES TO CHANGE

The *facts* of the institution — that the class is a *group,* that the teacher is presented with a *group,* its group-ness including predetermination of age, of likeness or unlikeness — make it difficult to concentrate on how individual children develop. This results in enormous institutional determination, definition, and focus, and modes of carrying through focus. The *fact* of children in numbers and of a space that has inherent limits, and the fact that the teacher is responsible for these numbers in this space, means that there is immediately some definition of the teacher as responsible for this group and therefore required to be in control. In this description of teaching, the teacher is defined first by the school's being a holding institution for groups, not by her role as an agent of the child's further development and stretch into the world. What is happening in the growth of any child and how the teacher can support and enrich the child's path are not the first questions that the teacher has to contend with. On the first day, she has to contend with the fact — "Here they are." There is *this group.* The importance of the group in the child's learning is secondary to the simple fact of a group. It takes the teacher quite a bit of learning about her relationship to the group before she can feel confident and relaxed about individual as well as common use of the terrain known as the classroom. The critique of the school that I started with remains incomplete because this major definition of the school's function largely remains as it was at the time of my first formulation. The allocation to the teacher of responsibility first for the group is still there. Even as teachers critique the school as institution in its most controlling forms and in its control of what they are doing about understanding the children, they must still adapt to the facts of limited and specific space and to the numbers of children for whom they are responsible.

The possibility of separation between what happens educatively and what happens because of what seem to be the institutional necessities requires the constant confrontation of issues of responsibility and accountability, stretching to relationships and curricular material that children are expected to take in. There is little analysis of the origin in real life of what children take in and how to make the school a place that can hold the experience so that, for instance, rainwater is not just something the child passes through quickly, holding onto mother's hand, running through it so one does not get wet, but something that can be held in the classroom for examination in a more detailed fashion, relating to the various perspectives of different children.

It is possible to think of the kind of accountability reflected in tests based on a determined lesson format as resulting in learning experiences not too different from the quick passage through rain, a momentary drenching. The sequential curriculum of the old patterns set a more restrictive tone: "Now it's finished, now we go onto the next thing." But its shrinking of the experience of the environmental surround to a quick passing-through nevertheless still allowed thoughts about and return to the experience, if the classroom retained any traces of it, however inadvertently. Such returning, allowed "on the side," may indeed enrich greatly. Of course, an actively negative stance toward the classroom surround as a place of experience can even further restrictively equate with the barrenness of surround we all know.

If the teacher were looking at "How do I function with response to the child in this institution that I am in?" the critique of the institution would involve a break in the sequential, lockstep curriculum. It would involve the building of a surround that could be available to the children, where things could be a focus one time and a passing-by, peripheral observation at another. This would enable the stirring of memories of how it was: "Oh, it's a little different than it was yesterday," or "Last week this wasn't there." Acceptance by the teacher of responsibility in critiquing the existing institution and of creating a different kind of context would involve reviving the teacher's own self-awareness as learner. The teacher would have to reconfront many experiences and get excited about the world again.

In examining the teachers' situation, often a double strand was clear. A context had been created that was sometimes rich and intensely used, but the primacy was, and is still, around what the institution mandates for curriculum and progression. This mandate may be modified by teachers enriching the curriculum with their own understanding and interest. Perhaps a few additional perspectives are added in, but still "we have to move on." But the central, mandated focus is retained. In this situation, the centrality of the teacher continues, without the teacher assuming the additional roles that come from seeing the child's centrality as definitive. These additional roles involve sharing with children the teacher's lifetime of interests, joining with children's interests, and then weaving the thread openly and obviously and at a pace that doesn't cut out and leave stranded those interests. The new perspective is not only a brief nod of acknowledgment at the child's different focus and perspective, but also is at least an attempt to make the joining of the teacher with the child's perspective and the child with the teacher's perspective a true one. Within the new frame there may be a need for direct presentation of things unknown to the child, that the school as institution may demand and the parents may worry about ("When will they learn about this?"). What results is a mixed situation with various degrees of presence of one mode over another.

I think it's important to unpackage the complexity of these stances because, in our changed situations, teachers' entrancement with their own creativity is so great — inevitably and understandably, considering that such response has been suppressed for ages — that one must step back and get reentranced with this or that child's way of entering this world. One must do that as part of one's commitment as a teacher, not as something lesser but as something wonderful. "Isn't it amazing that the kid saw that? I remember something I once saw — ages ago."

In the building of context and relationships that are stimulating and responsive to the child's thrusts toward understanding, observation that notes the impact of small change, the direction of interchange, and how the child latched onto something that the child finds of value and interest is enormously important. Without that, and without the teacher's entrancement with her own commitment, the job becomes intolerable. It is clear that there is no education without the child's having latched onto something that helps the child endure, live through, and continue growing in spite of all the errors of control and interruption that are inevitable as numerous people — parents, teachers, others — interpret and come in and out of the mandated structure that surrounds the child's living in school. The teacher's identification with the commitment to build an educative context that supports the child's efforts to understand is or can be the engine forcing change.

I saw the importance of the Workshop Center where teachers engaged with their own learning, and how totally they enjoyed the chance they had there to shape the focus and path of their explorations. I saw also how the difficulties of direct translation to the classroom were a constant overwhelming reality for them. I remember one instance where a few of the teachers were looking at plants that had tubelike structures carrying fluids to the far reaches of the plant, and of course comparisons with aqueducts and pipes came up. One of the teachers had worked out a system of tubes carrying fluids quite a distance around the Center and then worked out how to do this in the classroom. None of his concerns dealt with the need for connection with the interests of the children. His report on the project illustrated the difficulty. "You know," he said, "I spent all day Saturday working this out at the Workshop Center, but when I tried it with the kids, they were bored stiff, the little bastards." Well, it's amusing. Who hasn't seen that? One's choice of a story falls flat and accommodations are made along the way. But it's important to pull this phenomenon out and look at it. It may well be a necessary first step for teachers to accept certain boundaries and demands of the institution, but certainly they must work toward a situation where they will determine the specificities of the work *in relationship to their commitment to the children.*

Sometimes teachers' fascination with what's been happening in their own heads, and the examination of the content more abstractly, leads to a change in their profession. The analysis of the process becomes all-fulfilling. The engagement with the trials of understanding and close interaction with *this* child become of less interest. The daily interaction with the wonders of the ordinary for this or that child — in which there's an element of interest in how you yourself have understood or modified your understanding as well as in what it is you're understanding in that child — wanes in interest. It has certainly happened that teachers have become researchers, let's say, or professional students of the interaction of teachers. But I think it's important to restate the presumptions of the beginning period of change, to see where the process has led and to ask if that's really where you wanted to go or whether there's something that has been lost, which you need to be reminded of.

My reexamination also unpackaged the intense desire of the early period of change to deal with the teacher's isolation, the fact of being alone with the children and all that that implies of helplessness and need to control and overcontrol. There was an intense desire to open up — for that one teacher alone in the closed-door arrangement of a group in limited space and with a limited definition of difference — as the first overture to change. This was at the root of the concept of the Open Corridor program. The corridor could be a mechanism for each teacher to see what other teachers were doing and to converse with them as adults. The children could see some of the teacher's planning, hear conversations about the whole, and thus see the teacher in this working enterprise, not entirely focused on them, but focused on trying to create an atmosphere in which they — the children, too — had a stake and could cooperate in defining and shaping this whole. The children could see a wider range of other children's interactions — "Look, there are some older kids doing something we may be able to join now, or see what it's about before we take over next year" — and not just have it reported to them.

In an interesting way, the wider interactions actualized by opening the corridor had complications of their own that affected the development or nondevelopment of children and teachers. As teachers saw the possibilities of creative engagement each with her own shaping of curriculum, with some interaction with children's interests, the limitation that the classroom, defined as the *teacher's* space, presented became clear. This limitation really took precedence for many teachers over the struggle against isolation and over the idea of community.

The parallel development of what I consider positive directions in the modification of the school and inertness about modification is what currently focuses my thought. I am looking at the limitations of the changes that have been made, not because I think it's the end; I think of all modifications as being incomplete. But there must be clarity about whether one wants change to go in that direction and there must be continuity in edging around these desired directions. Several other aspects of development in Open Corridor situations illustrate this. Sometimes it was difficult for teachers to have confidence that children could learn by direct engagement, that each thing didn't need to be controlled for its possible outcome. Some teachers found the open door to the corridor threatening, formulating this in the question, "Who is in control?" The open-corridor structure demanded their ease in joining, with appreciation, the inquiry that a child had made that perhaps had not even been planned by the teacher. Teachers did not necessarily appreciate this or that activity in the corridor or in their classrooms was now visible. The open corridor worked remarkably well for several years without any disruptive incidents; the children engaged with the possibilities the corridor offered, and few problems of control existed. But as the teachers' own richness and range of possibilities grew and became more visible to the teachers, there seemed to be a growth in desire for ownership, for acknowledgment, for resumption of control. Children were often called back from the corridor. For all these reasons, some teachers, and usually the principal, saw the corridor as needing its own *special* teacher.

An obvious limitation in reorganizing a school is that the budget isn't open-ended. At the outset, it seemed to me that if you wanted change to be espoused by teachers who wanted to try but who were not in direct relationship with an advisor, you had to focus on the minimum of personnel or special arrangements with which change could be initiated and continued. But once the idea took hold that you couldn't have a program in the corridor without a special teacher assigned to it, the in-and-outness and interaction between what was happening in the classroom and in the corridor at least partially ended.

Rereading what I wrote about the corridor development in the 1970s, and the questions that arose about the corridor needing its own teacher and observations of how the privacy of the classroom came to be reestablished, I am confirmed in my thinking that these factors in decline of community must again be confronted. Although there remains a friendliness in schools where a number of teachers are working openly and responsively in interaction with children, a friendliness not often seen before the period of change, the definition is still "class" and "classroom," with control and accountability also so defined, even though in ways different from the past way of punitive control and much to be applauded.

Another occasion for reexamination was my essay on the multifaceted nature of teaching ("Inquiry," Part I), where my analysis indicated that "telling" was only one aspect of teaching. This essay was a consolidation of various threads of consideration about the limited nature of fundamental change in the teacher's role, and the limited nature of understanding of commitment and of how the child learns. As I focused on the residual effects of the teacher's retention of control and on the persistence of "telling" as the source of knowledge, I reconsidered the many forms of intake that in fact exist, additional to the child's own independently propelled question-asking. I see important roles for the adult *beyond* "telling" and even beyond support for the child's independent learning. Teaching is also present in the *context* that allows or fosters noticing, following-after, and joining-with, as well as providing support for the child's independent inquiries. The adult carries the context of life into the classroom or into the school, thus making important contributions to the functioning of the whole educative context. The adult functioning in this way can include the cooperation of the child. The teacher is not *just* assisting the child. The teacher is present as adult and adds to the educative context of the school by that presence. The work of the teacher has to be visible so that — very much as children consider everything they observe about adults at home or about adults working in the world — children are able to consider what it is the teacher does.

In the traditional school and sometimes — too many times — in the school as revised to be more responsive, adult functioning is difficult for the child to see. The process of building context, of collegial sharing and discussion — little of that is observable by the child. Many teachers, propelled by their commitment to the child, want very much not to take anything away from the time children have to do their own thing or from the path of their own grappling for understanding. The inclusion of children in the adultness of the classroom or the school — something one takes for granted in the home, where children are included in at least some of the adultness — is left out, as if that isn't also part of what children want and need to make sense of.

Questions about grouping and assessment, and judgments about whether the child can go on or not, remain big issues in schools. Ideas of capacity and unconditionality are certainly not the ruling convictions. The judgments the school makes as gatekeeper are still central to administering the school, even though modified a certain amount. The way in which the child is held back may be modified by mixed-age grouping, for example, but it still exists.

Changes in school proceeded, but in limited kinds of ways, not as a big sweep that could then have support from the larger social setting. They were insufficient to really impact on the critique of the schools (others would say of education) as carriers of failures because of the way in which they were set up, as gatekeepers. It is assumed by this setup that there *will* be failure. It seemed easiest and obvious to lay the cause of failure on teachers.

I cannot say strongly enough that the focus of the widespread societal critique is not what I've been critiquing. Everyone was unhappy with the old, empty, lockstep teaching, with sterility of context. We focused differently on causes. I have been critiquing the limitations of change, the loss of focus on institutional change and on community.

## THE IMPERATIVES OF CONTINUING ACTION AND REFLECTION

The questions I've been asking, in the presence of both old critiques and formulations and more recent ones, are questions about the changes we were trying to make. How much has been actualized? How much of the old is residual in current efforts? What are the limitations and possibilities today? Each reexamination summed up what accomplishments had been found serviceable in practice, but also pinpointed their limited relationship to what had been aimed for. The restatement of goals was clarifying, gave sharpened focus to our efforts, but also raised questions about limitations. The questions raised stemmed from what I think was a deeper and broader understanding of what the goals implied, a view not accessible before the modifications made more visible the possibilities and the difficulties.

The current critique of the schools seems to me still largely related to the unmodified school, not even attempting to build critique in a way that took account of any changes attempted in the last 2½ decades. My own efforts are to take account of the impact of these attempted changes. What I have written here is all reevocation of what it was we were trying to do to start with and a reassessment of where we were at any given point and whether what we had done was consistent with our first commitment.

In "Moral Issues" (Part III), I said that doing what is moral is the first commitment. If you're supporting the child's development and capacity and you know that the testing structure in no way does this, you may decide that — since no option exists that allows you not to administer the mandatory tests — you have to go along obediently. But if so, then your "going along" is not one of your moral acts. You know it's wrong and it's hurting the child. You may not be able to help it, or you may make a judgment that "at least I can continue working and working against this." The moral effort for teachers always has to go back to the search for what is better and to support what is possible for that child, in that situation. Then there is the question of why one struggles anyway, given that here is the institution. In spite of clear insight about limitations, the struggle is carried on because the goal is too important to dismiss and a way must be found. The conclusion arrived at is that even small accomplishments were worthwhile because they created some easement and space for the child's development.

Thus, movement toward *continuity* of experience and connection with past experience continued, even though it was plain that accomplishments were limited. Some schools created a better experience for children than others, and this phenomenon was examined for the factors of continuity that had produced differential success. But here, too, a barrier to fuller accomplishment was evident. My understanding of settings where the context of educative support was not so limited became deeper through reexamination of what didn't happen within the school setting, as well as what did happen. Other settings besides school—certainly the home, and also the neighborhood and the community, with sustained occupation of the site by the same people—might offer more continuity of experience and more simultaneity of multifaceted experience. The obligation to learn from these nonschool settings and take into the school whatever could be taken from them, even though it would be limited by the nature of the school, became clearer and clearer.

The simple fact of the numbers of children and of different groups within the institution created its own imperatives. The attempt to modify and ease the impact of the numbers and groups had partially succeeded, but very partially. The imperatives of the fact of the group meant a responsibility for the teacher that partially equated with custodial functions, with control rather than with seeking how to rethink and redefine the institution. Yet, on examination, multiplicity of learning drives present in any group and even in any person could also be considered positive aspects of the group: What does a group *give* to a child in his or her learning efforts? What does the child draw from that presence and interaction with a group that doesn't equate with control and all doing the same thing? What is the nature of cooperative learning? The accountability to parents who demanded specificity and individual focus, which for teachers meant that at some point there had to be a story of where *that* child was, certainly tended to continue the isolation, competitiveness, and stratification of the school setting.

The changes in modes of teaching that we attempted—from more direct to more indirect support and stimulation of the child's interest, through the setting and then facilitation of what it was that the child wanted to do with the setting—was simply not as complete an account of modes of teaching as we had first thought. Many reexaminations over a long period of practice time directed our attention to additional forms of learning that were not contradictory to active learning. At no point is the human being inert like a chair or a stool or a pot. But saying "active learning" deals insufficiently with the differences in relationship of learning to setting and teacher. *How* do human beings take in from the neighborhood, the street, the home, the community? In each educative setting, what are the modes of learning?

The major mode of learning in all the outside-school settings is noticing. Certainly noticing is an active process. But the mere fact of noticing, and of course of cogitating about what is noticed, is important to underline as a mode and to underline also in thinking about what the teacher's role is. How did the teacher support this mode? How did the setting impact in a facilitating manner? Such questions stressed the teacher's responsibility for the setting and for modifications of the setting in light of how children used it.

Observations of other settings pointed to the obvious: The child at home followed after the adults and even other children. Studying that mode could lead to some greater insight on the attraction, the glue, within *any* group development. The patterns of leading and following-after, not simply of obedience and following directions, are again more apparent in home settings. The adult carries on the adult work, not in a closet removed from the children but openly, in front of the children. There is either a conscious invitation for the child to "join with" or it happens anyway, even when joining-with is rejected. I remember my son putting up a heavy outer door, over 200 pounds, and his not-quite 3-year-old running after him saying, "I help you, Daddy!" and my son roars, "Out of my way!" because of the danger. Nevertheless, the fact of the danger, the fact of being pushed aside, is part of joining-with, of seeing what is dangerous and what isn't. This happens in the kitchen and everywhere in the home.

What I came to see was that at least some insight into the teacher as adult person grappling in continuous ways for understanding, for how to shape, was important for the child. The teacher, as an adult carrying out an adult occupation, is absolutely nowhere near as evident to the child in school as parent activity is at home. What the child sees in school is the teacher's focus on observation of the child, on facilitating the child's work, on controlling the child. But the teacher's adult prior-to-class work of preparing the context is not evident. The thought of the adult in collaboration with other adults in this thing called a school, the reporting and thinking further and developing, is not evident. So if a child is to play out what it is to be a teacher, the child enacts the stereotypes of control — "Sit down!" — even if, in that school or classroom, control may not be a major mode of teaching or a definition of what the teacher does and the child has thus had different experiences. The play shows no sense of under-standing the complexity and multiple-strandedness of the teacher's work and very little joining-with such work of the teacher. Though the teacher may join with the child in the child's efforts, joining-with the *teacher* in her work is virtually nonexistent. But perhaps at least bits of this *can* come into the boxed modes of teacher function — "Oh, I mustn't waste a minute of the teaching time" — and can ease the image of ideal teacher perfor-mance in the minds of parents, administrators, and teachers themselves. It seems to me that this limited and closed view must be opened up to at least a little wider view of teacher function. The child's effort to uncover the path to the adult world requires that perception.

Joining-with is partly dependent on an expansion of the view of own-ership. What is understood at home — "This is your home and it can't function without your participation" — is not really understood about school. The school cannot function if it is a place solely for the child or even groups of children to produce to adult mandate or expectation. What enables the school to function is participation. A sense of identification and ownership of the place, an openness — "Well, we can't get *this* done without getting some of *this* done" — must be built into the daily function-ing of the participants in the life of that place.

In another reexamination, "Black or Multicultural Curriculum" (Part III), I discussed the question of ownership and contribution of work, and of valuing and being valued. Discussing the relationship to school this way gives body to the ideas of the school as community and of join-ing the community. The idea is community feeling not only in the sense of, for example, a cooperative group production ("Here's what the third graders could do to help") but rather in the sense of contribution to the whole school. That is where teachers' possessiveness about classrooms and their closing off from the school as a whole, protectively for themselves and, as they think of it, for the children, becomes a question. Work for, contribution to, value for *our* place has some resonance in the classroom, but it has larger resonance as there is identification with the larger context of the whole school.

"Community" on the part of the school's inhabitants could include the sense of responsibility for the school, of identification with the school, but it was certainly something wider than the classroom. The sense of the school as a community could help a school function in a way that recog-nized its relationship to the context of home, neighborhood, stores. But this local world is in fact far less recognized as important to school defini-tion. Only a very little bit is the school seen as a positive force in the local community and the local community as a positive force in the development of school. There are all too many schools that regard themselves as saviors of the children, as a bulwark or barricade against the community. But this is where the children live and where the positive forces exist that can regenerate this community and contribute to the development of the possibilities. The school has not yet really emerged as a force in this regard, even within its own confines, or even in the relationships within the school, where the *classroom* still defines the teacher.

Unfortunately, many teachers and administrators turn away from the community around the school as harmful to the children. Even in this conception, however, an eased sense about work and contribution would help, even with the supposedly savior aspects of the school. I am proposing that there is no way to relate to children as though they must be protected from their homes and community context. There may be enormous negative factors in the community, but the elements that can rebuild the community are also situated within that community.

With all its limitations, there is the school. We have it. Without being the savior or the bulwark against the community, school exists as a place that children inhabit for a long time, and it exists in a way that, in the past and today, poisons children's feelings and causes teachers feelings of despair and disappointment because it is not working as they imagine it might. Seeing this, we continued to make efforts by learning about other settings and being more observant about the complexity of the process and more respectful of the complexity of each bundle of capacities that is the child. The school exists and so one continues the effort to make it better. The first principle of making it better must be to do no harm. This is an operant imperative within all the caring professions. First, do no harm. Second, continue your efforts to understand the thing enough to make it possible to continue trying to better the impact of one's efforts and to release the efforts of the child.

The path of constant reexamination, of grappling-with that assumes no final end or conclusion or perfection in any of the settings, is a feature inherent in being a teacher and in being an educator of teachers. It is a process that can help sharpen our focus on any setting, since we are teachers, and on the school in particular as an educative context. The process includes examination of what isn't there and what is there. It includes how whatever we've tried to do, whatever small changes we've made, has impacted on the child's learning. It includes the effect of certain processes that we didn't even notice before but that now emerge, perhaps because of something released by a small change, and how we can take advantage of it. And so on. This kind of reexamination is what I have tried to do, giving the history of what and how things became visible for me in many,

many reexaminations and what they meant to me in terms of how children's learning process was affected by the teacher's commitment and clarity of commitment and the teaching process that resulted from that.

Teacher education and preparation, it seems to me, comes down to an intensified examination and reexamination of this type, to learning about the various educative contexts, to learning about what is inherent in a teacher's commitment, and to recognizing that what teachers do — teaching — cannot be defined as only direct "telling." On the contrary, that is only a bit of the adult function. The ways of carrying out the teacher's commitment are various and complex. They expand and grow as we practice our profession and reflect on it.[1]

## NOTE

1. At the end of the tape, Weber dictated an additional short text about her recent reading and how it had impacted the thinking in the paper. Among the authors she mentions, sometimes referring to specific articles and sometimes to their work generally, are Buchmann (1990); Little (1990); Seymour Sarason (1985); Patricia F. Carini (1979, 1982, 1987); Donald Schön (1990); Elizabeth Newson; Uri Bronfenbrenner (1979); and Susan Isaacs. Most of her commentary responds to Buchmann's discussion of teacher professionalism and the contradictory consequences of teacher "self-actualization," and Little's discussion of privacy and the teacher's domain; Weber found both articles sympathetic and stimulating.

# A Brief Biography of Lillian Weber

Lillian Weber was born on February 7, 1917, in the East New York section of Brooklyn; she was the third child of Samuel and Celia Levine Dropkin, both of whom were immigrants from White Russia (now Belarus). Her father, who had been an activist in the anti-Czarist underground, started life in America as an organizer for the fledgling Amalgamated Clothing Workers Union; her mother, who had originally written poetry in Russian, in this country emerged as a major poet in Yiddish. For the five children in the family, the father's evolution from union organizer to manufacturing entrepreneur brought many changes of place: Lillian attended elementary schools in several neighborhoods of Brooklyn, and various high schools in Bluefield, Virginia; Bluefield, West Virginia; and Fall River, Massachusetts. She began higher education at Hunter College, but upon her marriage to Frederick Palmer Weber in 1935 transferred to the University of Virginia, where she completed her undergraduate degree in 1938 and continued for two years of graduate study in sociology and philosophy. There followed a move to Washington, D.C., where her two sons, William Palmer and John Pitman, were born. In 1944 they returned to New York and settled in the Riverdale section of the Bronx; in 1945 she was divorced.

It was a local parent-cooperative nursery school to which she sent her children that pulled Lillian Weber onto the track of teaching. She began as a volunteer at Spuyten Duyvil Infantry in 1944, took a summer institute in childhood education at Vassar in 1945, and started as an assistant teacher in 1946, subsequently becoming a full teacher and then director of the Infantry. All told, she spent some two decades there, during which time she acquired a master's degree in early childhood education from Bank Street College in 1959; her thesis and its accompanying film, *First Steps* (with Hannah Williams), were on separation and the process of change in a nursery school. A few years later, at a summer conference of British nursery school educators at Vassar College, the reports she listened to on the English system inspired her to take a leave of absence, go to England, and study the ways their preschool, nursery, and early grades were operating in the public sector. Out of her observations of inner-city schools during a year and a half stay in England came her study for which she received an associate's degree from the University of London in 1966. At the same time, she wrote and produced a film, *Infants School* (1966). A version of the study became her book, *The English Infant School and Informal Education* (1971). The book was widely read, influencing teachers and parents all over the United States.

In 1967 Weber joined the City College faculty and began working with student teachers in the local Harlem public schools. To help her students implement her ideas of teaching based on how children learn, she invented the Open Corridor program, in which a cluster of classrooms with their doors open to the corridor created a common living space that not only abolished the isolation of the traditional classroom but enhanced the individual teachers' resources through shared materials and arrangements. In 1970, with a Ford Foundation grant, she set up the City College Advisory Service (1973a), a training program for selected teachers who fanned out into the schools to assist in reorganizing classrooms along informal, or open, lines. In 1971 she initiated a three-week summer institute, still held annually, during which teachers, provided with a rich assortment of materials and experiences, could engage in an intense experience of their own learning, including a sustained personal inquiry. The success of these programs led to a strong increase in funding from local schools and districts, federal sources (National Institute of Education, the Office of Education, the Far West Laboratory), as well as private and corporate foundations (Rockefeller Brothers, Jesse Smith Noyes), so that in 1972 Weber could establish the Workshop Center for Open Education, incorporating the Advisory Service, classes for undergraduates who would be future teachers, activities — lectures, seminars — for parents and other community people, and a publications program that disseminated quarterly and special bulletins relating to the theory and practice of open education. The Workshop Center offered a year-round schedule that became a magnet for educators from all over the world who were concerned with school change. In 1975 Weber organized a national conference on the roots of open education in America at City College.

Weber was a founding member of the North Dakota Study Group on Evaluation, a national organization devoted to discussion and research of change in schools. She served also on the boards of the National Consortium on Testing and the Prospect Archives and Center for Education and Research. In 1973 she delivered the annual John Dewey Society Lecture in Chicago, the first woman ever invited to do so. She was part of a government mission to China in 1977 (1979b), and led seminars on her work in Australia, Israel, Norway, Germany, Kenya, and Tanzania. She was awarded an honorary doctorate from Bank Street College in 1987. After her retirement that year, she planned a new phase of her work that involved returning to Africa for more protracted study related to her increasing dissatisfaction with the limitations of schools. Her plans were unfortunately interrupted by an accident that led to multiple surgeries and aggravated chronic health problems. Nevertheless, she continued to write and, when possible, to speak, until her death on February 22, 1994.

*— Ruth Dropkin*

# References

Alberty, B., & Weber, L. (1979). *Continuity and connection: Curriculum in five open class-rooms.* New York: City College Workshop Center.

Alberty, B., Weber, L., & Neujahr, J. (1981). *Use and setting: Development in a teachers' center.* Grand Forks, ND: University of North Dakota Press.

Aronowitz, S., & Giroux, H. A. (1985). *Education under siege: The conservative, liberal, and radical debate over schooling.* South Hadley, MA: Bergin & Garvey.

Ayers, W. (Ed.). (1995). *To become a teacher: Making a difference in children's lives.* New York: Teachers College Press.

Bank Street College of Education. (1985). *The voyage of the Mimi* [Film]. New York: Holt, Rinehart & Winston.

Benson, M. (1986). *Nelson Mandela: The man and the movement.* 1st ed. New York: W. W. Norton.

Bereiter, C., & Engelmann, S. (1966). *Teaching disadvantaged children in the pre-School.* Englewood Cliffs, NJ: Prentice Hall.

Bernstein, B. (1970). A critique of the concept of "compensatory education." In D. Rubinstein, & C. Stoneman (Eds.), *Education for democracy.* London: Penguin Books, Ltd.

Bernstein, B. (1972). A socio-linguistic approach to socialization: With some reference to educability. In J. J. Gumperz & D. Hymes (Eds.), *Directions in socio-linguistics: The ethnography of communication* (pp. 465–497). New York: Holt, Rinehart & Winston.

Bettelheim, B. (1979). Individual and mass behavior in extreme situations. In *Surviving and other essays* (pp. 48–83). New York: Alfred A. Knopf. (Original work published 1943)

Brearley, M. (Ed.). (1969). *Fundamentals in the first school.* Oxford: Basil Blackwell. [Published in the U.S. (1970), as *The teaching of young children: Some applications of Piaget's learning theory.* New York: Schocken Books]

Bronfenbrenner, U. (1979). Beyond the deficit model in child and family policy. *Teachers College Record, 81*(1), 95–104.

Buchmann, M. (1990). Beyond the lonely, choosing will: Professional development in teacher thinking. *Teachers College Record, 91*(4), 481–508.

Bussis, A. M., Chittenden, E. A., Amarel, M., & Klausner, E. (1985). *Inquiry into meaning, An investigation of learning to read.* Hillsdale, NJ: Lawrence Erlbaum Associates.

Carini, P. F. (1979, September). *The art of seeing and the visibility of the person.* Grand Forks, ND: University of North Dakota.

Carini, P. F. (1982). *The school lives of seven children: A five year study.* Grand Forks, ND: University of North Dakota.

Carini, P. F. (1987). *On value in education.* New York: The City College Workshop Center.

Cazden, C. (1968). Some implications of research on language development for preschool education. In R. D. Hess & R. M. Bear (Eds.), *Early education: Current theory, research and action* (pp. 131–142). Chicago: Aldine.

Cazden, C. (1976). How knowledge about language helps the classroom teacher — or does it: A personal account. *The Urban Review, 9*(2), 74–90.

Clapp, E. R. (1952). *The use of resources in education.* New York: Harper.

Comer, J. B. (1975). Black education: A holistic view. *The Urban Review, 8*(3), 162–169.

Delpit, L. D. (1986). Skills and other dilemmas of a progressive black educator. *Harvard Educational Review, 56*(4), 379–385.

Delpit, L. D. (1988). The silenced dialogue: Power and pedagogy in educating other people's children. *Harvard Educational Review, 58*(3), 280–298.

Dewey, J. (1970). *Interest and effort in education.* New York: Augustus M. Kelley. (Original work published 1913)

Dewey, J. (1916). *Democracy and education.* New York: The Macmillan Co.

Dewey, J. (1939). *Experience and education.* New York: The Macmillan Co.

Dickerson, M. G., Davis, M. D., & Rose, G. P. (Eds.). (1980 ). *Young Children: Issues for the '80s.* Little Rock, Ark.: Southern Association on Children Under Six.

Dropkin, R., & Tobier, A. (Eds.). (1976). *Roots of open education in America.* New York: City College Workshop Center for Open Education.

Duckworth, E. (1972). The having of wonderful ideas. *Harvard Education Journal, 42*(2), 217–231.

Duckworth, E. (1979). *Learning with breadth and depth.* New York: City College Workshop Center for Open Education.

Duckworth, E. (1987). *The having of wonderful ideas and other essays on teaching and learning.* New York: Teachers College Press.

Duckworth, E., et al. (1990). *Science education: A mind's on approach for the elementary years.* Hillsdale, NJ: Lawrence Erlbaum Associates.

Education Development Center. (1970). *Man: A course of study.* Washington, DC: Curriculum Development Associates, Inc.

Erickson, F. (1974, February). *Politics of speaking.* Paper presented at the Bilingual Leadership Training Institute, California State University, Los Angeles.

Farrell, E. W. (1990). *Hanging in and dropping out: Voices of at-risk high school students.* New York: Teachers College Press.

Galbraith, J. K. (1976). *The affluent society* (3d ed.). Boston: Houghton Mifflin. (Original work published 1958)

Gliedman, J., & Roth, W. (1980). *The unexpected minority: Handicapped children in America.* New York: Harcourt Brace Jovanovich.

Holmes Group. (1990). *Tomorrow's schools: Principles for the design of professional development schools: A report of the Holmes Group.* East Lansing, MI: Author.

Howell, R. R. (1968). *Everything changes.* New York: Atheneum.

Isaacs, N. (1957, December). What is required of the nursery-infant teacher in this country today? (OMEP lecture). *National Froebel Foundation Bulletin.*

John-Steiner, V., & Osterreich, H. (1975, August). *Learning styles among Pueblo children.* Report to the National Institute of Education, University of New Mexico, Albuquerque.

Kamii, C., & DeVries, R. (1993). *Physical knowledge in preschool education: Implications of Piaget's theory.* New York: Teachers College Press. (Original work published 1978 by Prentice Hall)

Leitman, A. (Director). (1977). *I ain't playin' no more* [Film]. Parts 1 and 2. Newton, MA: Education Development Center.

Little, J. W. (1990). The persistence of privacy: Autonomy and initiative in teachers' professional relations. *Teachers College Record, 91*(4), 509–536.

Macdonald, J. (1975a). Moral problems of teaching. *The Urban Review, 8*(1), 18–27.

Macdonald, J. (1975b). The person in the curriculum. *The Urban Review, 8*(3), 191–201.

Macdonald, J. B., Wolfson, B. J., & Zaret, E. (1973). *Reschooling society: A conceptual model.* Washington, DC: Association for Supervision and Curriculum Development.

Margulis, L. (1985). *Sharing with children: New ideas on the evolution of life.* New York: City College Workshop Center.

Martí, J. (1953). *Our America. The America of José Martí: Selected Writings of José Martí.* Juan de Onis (Trans.), Federico de Onis (Intro.). New York: The Noonday Press, pp. 138–151. (Essay written 1893)

Martí, J. (1979). *On education: Articles on educational theory and pedogogy and writings for children from the age of gold.* Philip S. Foner (Ed.). Elinor Randall (Trans.). New York: Monthly Review Press.

Mayhew, K. C. (1966). *The Dewey school.* New York: Atherton Press.

Morrison, P. (1970). The curricular triangle and its style: Experimenters in the classroom. In *The ESS reader.* Newton, MA: Elementary Science Study of Education Development Center. (Original article published 1965 in *ESI Quarterly*)

Morrison, P. (1971). *The full and open classroom.* Boston, MA: The Educational Research Center, MIT.

Morrison, P., & Morrison, P. (1984). *Primary science: Symbol or substance?* New York: City College Workshop Center.

Newson, E. (1978). Unreasonable care: The establishment of selfhood. In G. N. A. Vesey (Ed.), *Human values* (pp. 1–26). Atlantic Highlands, NJ: Humanities Press.

Nyerere, J. (1978). *Crusade for liberation.* New York: Oxford University Press.

Perrone, V. (1989). *Working papers: Reflections on teachers, schools, and communities.* New York: Teachers College Press.

Rogoff, B., & Lave, J. (Eds.). (1984). *Everyday cognition: Its development in social context.* Cambridge, MA: Harvard University Press.

Rosen, C., & Rosen, H. (1973). *The language of primary school children.* Harmondsworth, England: Penguin Education for the Schools Council.

Sarason, S. B. (1985). *Caring and compassion in clinical practice.* San Francisco: Jossey-Bass.

Schön, D. (1990). *Educating the reflective practitioner.* San Francisco: Jossey-Bass.

Shanker, A. (1990, September 16). Where we stand: Notes from the annals of competitiveness: The American's last wish. *New York Times.* Advertisement.

Smith, F. (1971). *Understanding reading: A psycholinguistic analysis of reading and learning to read.* New York: Holt, Rinehart & Winston.

Stevens, P. S. (1974). *Patterns in nature.* Boston: Little, Brown and Company.

Tizard, B., & Hughes, M. (1984). *Young children learning.* Cambridge, MA: Harvard University Press.

Tough, J. (1976). *Listening to children talking: A guide to the appraisal of children's use of language.* London: Ward Lock, Drake Educational Associates.

Weber, L. (1949). *Study on Maureen.* Unpublished manuscript.

Weber, L. (1959). *Study of development of adjustment practices at Spuyten-Duyvil Infantry, Cooperative Nursery.* Unpublished master's thesis, Bank Street College of Education, New York.

Weber, L., with Howell, R., & Ventriglia, L. (1960). It is winter. *Elementary School Science Bulletin* (57).

Weber, L. (Director). (1966). Peter Theobald (Photographer). *Infants School* [Film]. Newton, MA.: Education Development Center.

Weber, L.(1968). *Comments from teachers on all the small things that contributed to the function or dysfunction of the corridor and whether they feel that in so far as it functions, it was a success.* Unpublished manuscript.

Weber, L. (1971). *The English infant school and informal education.* Englewood Cliffs, NJ: Prentice-Hall.

Weber, L. (1973a). *City College Advisory Service 1970–1973.* Unpublished report to the Ford Foundation. New York: Workshop Center for Open Education.

Weber, L. (1973b). *Toward the finer specificity. Evaluation reconsidered.* New York: Workshop Center for Open Education.

Weber, L. (1973c, November). *But is it science? Science in the open classroom* (pp. 3–10). New York: Workshop Center for Open Education.

Weber, L. (1973d, December). Letter from the director. *Notes from Workshop Center for Open Education,* 1–8. [Revised and republished in *Notes,* Winter 1977]

Weber, L. (1974). Education for ALL the children. *Notes from Workshop Center for Open Education,* Summer, 2–20.

Weber, L. (1975a). *City College Advisory Service and Workshop Center for Open Education 1973–1975.* Unpublished report to the Ford Foundation. New York: Workshop Center for Open Education.

Weber, L. (1975b). *Report on City College Advisory Service and Workshop Center 1974–1975.* Unpublished report to the Rockefeller Brothers Fund. New York: Workshop Center for Open Education.

Weber, L. (1976a). *The school's purpose.* Unpublished article for *The Amsterdam News.*

Weber, L. (1976b). Introduction. In R. Dropkin & A. Tobier, (Eds.). *The roots of open education in America.* New York: City College Workshop Center.

Weber, L. (1977, Winter). Issues in parent participation. *Notes from Workshop Center for Open Education.* (pp. 2–8) New York: City College Workshop Center.

Weber, L. (1979a). Adapting classrooms for ALL the children. In S. J. Meisels (Ed.), *Special education and development.* Baltimore, MD: University Park Press.

Weber, L. (1979b). Children — Streets and Schools in China. Unpublished paper. (An abridged version appears as: Early childhood education. In R. N. Montaperto & J. Henderson (Eds.), *China's Schools in Flux: Report by the State Education Leaders Delegation and National Committee on US-China Relations* (pp. 124–134). White Plains, NY: M. E. Sharpe, Inc.)

Weber, L. (1985). *On relationship with schools (teacher education).* Unpublished manuscript.

Weber, L. (1987a). *Remarks on the occasion of receiving an honorary doctorate from Bank Street College.* Unpublished manuscript.

Weber, L. (1987b). Untitled journal of a trip to Africa. Unpublished manuscript.

Weber, L. (1994). *Reflections.* New York: City College Workshop Center.

Weber, L., & Dropkin, R. (1972). Development in Open Corridor organization: Intent and reality. *National Elementary Principal, LII*(3), 58–67.

Weber, L., & Williams, H. (Directors & Producers). (1959). *First steps* [Film]. [Script and supplementary documentation of the film is contained in Weber (1959)]

Wilson, B. N. (1990). The black orientation: A basic for environmental planning and designing in the black community. *Journal of Black Studies, 21*(1), 23–39.

# Index

## About the Editor

Beth Alberty is Director of Collections at the Brooklyn Children's Museum. She worked at the City College Workshop Center from 1976–1981, and intermittently with Lillian Weber from 1968 until Weber's death in 1994. This work centered, for the most part, on Weber's writing and included research projects that resulted in joint publications. Alberty has been an assistant curator at the Metropolitan Museum of Art and a research assistant at Bank Street College of Education. She has been an active participant in programs of the Prospect Archives and Center for Education and Research, and a member of its board since 1979.